Praise for

JAPAN
RESTORED

Thirty years ago, the name Clyde Prestowitz stood for the top Japan-basher who was warning the US to get its act together. But the true Prestowitz also had deep respect for Japanese values, was proficient in Japanese, and adopted a Japanese boy as his son. Now, in his latest book, he is advising the Japanese how to get its act together based on his own experience advising the US. It is a worthy read.

—Richard C. Koo, Chief Economist, Nomura Research Institute

Can Japan reverse decline? We all have a stake in this. Japan, after all, might be a model for other advanced post-industrial societies. There has probably not been a prescription for revival as radical, as pertinent, and as challenging as the one that Clyde Prestowitz lays down. Yet as I read it I found myself hoping that Japan will adopt his advice and continue to make its contribution to world civilization.

—Bob Carr, former Foreign Minister of Australia

"Ever since Japan successfully challenged American industrial dominance in the 1980s, Clyde Prestowitz has been a leading voice in urging us to think differently about this remarkable and still-misunderstood nation. His newest book builds on his rich career in trade and economic policy to probe more deeply into both Japan's persisting problems and its still-enormous potential to remain a creative force in the global economy."

—Martin Fackler, New York Times Bureau Chief, Tokyo

Fascinating story of how a country could reinvent itself, in a world where the focus is on China and Japan is yesterday's lunch. Clyde Prestowitz does a terrific job of creating a fictional blueprint of how Japan can become a world power and the impact it will have on our children and grandchildren. It's hard to put down.

—Daniel M. Slane, Commissioner, Congressional US-China Economic and Security Review Commission, Washington, DC

JAPAN
RESTORED

HOW JAPAN CAN REINVENT ITSELF
AND WHY THIS IS IMPORTANT
FOR AMERICA AND THE WORLD

NEW YORK TIMES BESTSELLING AUTHOR
CLYDE PRESTOWITZ

with Hiromi Murakami and William Finan

TUTTLE Publishing
Tokyo | Rutland, Vermont | Singapore

Published by Tuttle Publishing, an imprint of Periplus Editions (HK) Ltd.

www.tuttlepublishing.com

Library of Congress Cataloging-in-Publication Data is in process

ISBN 978-4-8053-1346-6

Distributed by

North America, Latin America & Europe
Tuttle Publishing
364 Innovation Drive
North Clarendon
VT 05759-9436 USA.
Tel: 1 (802) 773-8930
Fax: 1 (802) 773-6993
info@tuttlepublishing.com
www.tuttlepublishing.com

Asia Pacific
Berkeley Books Pte. Ltd.
61 Tai Seng Avenue #02-12
Singapore 534167
Tel: (65) 6280-1330
Fax: (65) 6280-6290
inquiries@periplus.com.sg
www.periplus.com

Japan
Tuttle Publishing
Yaekari Building, 3rd Floor
5-4-12 Osaki, Shinagawa-ku
Tokyo 141 0032
Tel: (81) 3 5437-0171
Fax: (81) 3 5437-0755
sales@tuttle.co.jp
www.tuttle.co.jp

First edition
18 17 16 15   10 9 8 7 6 5 4 3 2 1   1507CP

Printed in Singapore

Contents

Bookends

first saw Japan on the cold, gray morning of February 5, 1965, as SS *President Cleveland* steamed into Tokyo Bay toward Yokohama after a storm-tossed six-day voyage from Honolulu. Accompanied by my American-Chinese wife Carol, our four-month-old daughter Anne-Noelani, and my wife's Chinese uncle, who ran the ship's laundry, I looked down from an upper deck at the totally unfamiliar scene below as the tugs nudged our great vessel into its berth.

As we marched down the gangway carrying luggage and baby, and passed through passport and customs control, I quickly realized that the year of Japanese language study I had just completed at the East-West Center in Honolulu was not going to get me very far. The passport and customs officers seemed determined to speak with the cadence and speed of machine gun fire, and I could read only a very few of the Japanese words on the signs and instruction posters around us. Carol's uncle helped us get a cab to Yokohama's Sakuragicho station, where we boarded the train to Tokyo. Our car was full of women, many of them wearing colorful kimonos; and of men, some of whom were wearing boots or shoes with a separate section for the big toe—like a mitten, but for feet rather than hands. I remember thinking, "Well, you wanted something different. Looks like this is it."

This trip had originated two years previously as I was trying to figure out my expected graduation from Swarthmore College in June, 1963. I had been an exchange student to Switzerland in high school and had been bitten by the travel bug. I wanted to see the world upon graduation from college, but I had a small problem: money; or rather, the lack thereof. So I looked for grants, and while doing so, stumbled upon the East-West Center, at the University of Hawaii. It was offering a super deal—a two-year grant with tuition, room, board, books, and travel all paid, along with two hundred dollars a month for spending money. Grantees were required to spend a year studying any subject they desired at the university. They were also required to study an Asian language; the second year of the two-year grant period would be spent studying or working in the country of the language that had been chosen. It all sounded like a good deal to me. I applied, was fortunate enough to receive a grant, and set out for a year under the waving palms of Honolulu. Hey, somebody had to do it.

I had initially thought I would study Chinese, but my father was a chemist and metallurgist who worked in the welding and steel industry. Now remember, this was 1963, and China—then under Mao—was one of the poorest countries in the world, while Japan's economic miracle of postwar recovery was about to be announced in the January 1964 cover story of the *Economist*. My dad said, "Look, son, why do you want to study Chinese? They don't make anything. You should study Japanese. They make stuff." So that's how I came to register for Japanese when I first enrolled at the East-West Center and the University of Hawaii in September of 1963.

Although the *Economist* had hailed Japan's rapid economic development, to a twenty-three-year-old American kid the country didn't seem all that developed. Most people rode bicycles and buses or walked to their destinations. There were few traffic jams in Tokyo, because there was little auto traffic. I remember marveling at the delivery boys on bicycles who balanced bowls of steaming noodle soup without spilling a drop as they ferried them to customers' homes. While our Japanese friends described it as a luxury dwelling, the apartment my wife and I managed to find had no hot running water, no bath (remember that our daughter was four months old), no stove, no central heat, no dishwasher, no washer or dryer for clothing, and only two electric bulbs. (We did, however, have a Western toilet.) These were the days before disposable diapers, so we had to boil diaper-washing water every day, and there was no such thing as washing your hands and face with warm water.

We cooked over two small gas devices that looked like the Bunsen burners in my high school chemistry class. We had one four-tatami-mat room in which we lived and slept, and one two-tatami room where we kept the baby's crib. We heated the rooms with a kerosene stove that had to be turned off at night because of the ever-present danger of earthquakes tipping the stove over in the middle of the night and burning the whole neighborhood down. We bathed at the *sento*, the public bath where the dividing wall between the women's and men's baths was shorter than the average American. After undressing, the men handed their baskets of clothing to young female attendants, who returned them when the men had finished their soak in the public pool. In the streets on winter nights, one could always recognize those who had just been to the bath because they would be enveloped in the white cloud precipitated by the action of the cold air on their moist, warm skin and clothing. Upon returning home from the *sento*, we went to bed on futons rolled out on our tatami floor and dropped off to sleep as the exhalation of our warm breath formed clouds in the cold of the unheated room.

Luxury it was not. Yet we did not feel deprived by the experience. Rather, we felt greatly enriched by it and privileged to have had it. This was a last glimpse of a less Westernized, less modernized Japan that has vanished forever. That magical time was the first bookend of my ensuing life and career, and nostalgia for that era has been part of the impetus for this book.

I left Japan in late 1965 and entered the US Foreign Service, first as vice-consul at the US Consulate General in Rotterdam and then as third secretary of the US Embassy in the Hague. Later I became a business executive with the Scott Paper Company in Philadelphia and Brussels. But I returned to Japan in 1976 as vice president of the Swiss consulting company Egon Zehnder International. I discovered that in the decade that I had been away, Japan had become a rich, developed country. The bicycles had not only yielded to automobiles, but the automobiles were causing endless traffic jams. Indeed, *jutai* (traffic jam) became one of my wife's favorite Japanese words. And the *sento* were mostly gone also, having been replaced by the *o-furo* (hot tub) now routinely included as part of the Japanese home or apartment. Of course, this modernization also had its downside. The air quality of Tokyo had become so poor that face masks were routinely worn by a large number of Japanese.

This was the heyday of Japan, Inc., the market-based but government-guided system of capitalism that had accomplished the postwar economic miracle and that now, in the late 1970s, was conquering the world's markets in steel, textiles, and consumer electronics. It might have been called capitalism with Japanese characteristics. Those special characteristics included lifetime employment for a cadre of "regular" employees; extreme company loyalty on the part of employees who considered themselves part of a corporate family and who would almost never consider changing employers; enterprise unions rather than industry-wide unions; and protection of the domestic market from imports by a variety of means. Japanese businesses also featured a corporate structure dominated by quasi-cartels of interlocking firms known as *keiretsu*; just-in-time delivery; *kaizen* (continuous improvement); six-sigma quality control; government targeting of and subsidies for the development of so-called strategic industries (machinery, semiconductors, computers, steel, etc.); and a policy of keeping the yen undervalued versus the dollar as a way of indirectly subsidizing exports and imposing a tariff on imports.

First as a consultant primarily to foreign companies trying to crack the Japanese market, and then as the CEO of the Japan branch of a US medical equipment manufacturer, I learned how the system worked through tough experience in the school of hard knocks, but also through the patient explanations of a few friendly Japanese and American tutors. In the late 1970s, the Japan, Inc. system appeared to be unbeatable: Japan's automakers were using it to begin attacking the Detroit automakers, while its semiconductor producers started aiming at Silicon Valley. By 1980, both the US semiconductor companies in the Valley and the US auto makers in Detroit had joined representatives from the steel, textile, machine tool, consumer electronics, and other industries in a pilgrimage to Washington, DC to demand that the US government take some action against Japan's "unfair" trade practices.

Of course, it was in 1980 that Ronald Reagan was elected president, which meant that a whole new set of senior officials would be taking the reins of the US government. In September, 1981 I was appointed to the US Department of Commerce, first as deputy assistant secretary of commerce, then becoming acting assistant secretary, and finally counselor to the secretary. In these positions, one of my main responsibilities was to help lead what had become an endless series of trade negotiations with Japan.

Indeed, it seemed that there were negotiations in virtually every sector of the economy. Semiconductors, television sets, autos, almonds, rice, tobacco, telecommunications equipment and services, insurance—you name the industry, and we had a negotiation going either to open the Japanese market or to stop predatory Japanese practices in the US market. It all looked very complex, and if you tried to absorb all the details, it was. But in essence it boiled down to two competing claims. US industry and the US government negotiators continually complained that Japan was "cheating" by not playing by the rules of free trade and free-market capitalism. They said its industry was being subsidized, and was dumping (selling below cost or below the price in the home market) products into the US market while its home markets were protected like the impregnable castles of feudal Yamato by a variety of means. Japanese industry and Japan's negotiators responded by essentially saying, "What are you talking about? Our markets are more open than yours. We have fewer and lower tariffs than you do. The problem is that you don't try hard enough. In fact, you hardly try at all. Your quality is atrocious, your labor relations are adversarial, your delivery is always late, your service is non-existent, and you put the steering wheel on the wrong side of the car [Japan is right-hand drive, like Britain]. You should stop whining and mau-mauing us and pull your socks up with that legendary American 'can do' spirit you're always talking about."

Between 1980 and 1985, the US trade deficit with Japan grew from US$10 billion to US$50 billion, which could be translated into about 500,000–800,000 lost jobs during a period of recession.

My mission was to stop this sudden flooding away of American production, jobs, and technology in a manner that would also maintain free-trade rules and US competitiveness. In particular, my task was to open the Japanese market to American and other foreign imports and investment.

As noted above, the debate was kind of a standoff, with the US side arguing that Japan was acting unfairly, and Japan saying the problem was simply a matter of incompetence by US business and its US government champions (namely me). In fact, there was truth in the Japanese argument. For instance, it was often the case that US companies had fallen down on quality. In the auto industry, independent quality analysts like Consumers Union consistently found the reliability and quality of Japanese autos to be superior to that of the cars made by the "Big Three" Detroit-based US producers. Similarly, Hewlett Packard unleashed a firestorm in the early 1980s when it released a quality comparison study showing that Japanese semiconductors were of better quality, on average, than semiconductors made by US producers.

But this was far from the complete truth. For it was also the case that the Japanese economic miracle system that I had come to know so well had been specifically designed to keep foreigners out, and to promote production in and exports from Japan. While it was true that Japan had tariffs that were generally lower than US tariffs, it had huge tariff spikes on products like rice for whose production it was not competitive. Even more importantly, it kept the yen undervalued versus the dollar and maintained an intricate web of non-tariff procedural, regulatory, and structural barriers to market access. The *keiretsu* structure of interlocking shareholdings and directorships among companies itself had been constructed to prevent takeovers of Japanese corporations by foreign companies.

Distribution chains presented another formidable barrier. For example, in the United States, auto dealers are by law established as independent businesses whose sales cannot be controlled by the auto producers. Thus, a dealer can sell Fords, Hondas, Volkswagens, and any other brand that appears attractive. This structure meant that when the Japanese auto companies entered the US market, they did not have to build their own dealership networks from scratch. They just piggybacked on the existing Ford, GM, and Chrysler networks. Not so, however, in Japan; there Toyota dealers sell only Toyotas, and woe to the renegade dealer who tries to break suit. This structural difference in the two markets made it much more difficult to enter the Japanese auto market than to sell into the US market.

I could go on, but I'm sure you get the idea. The task of opening the Japanese market, which the White House had assigned to its trade negotiators like me, essentially meant restructuring the economic system that had produced the miracle and that seemed to be conquering all before it. Trying to change what all Japanese were convinced was a winning system was not our only handicap; many in Japan were certain that their economic system was a product of their culture and thus uniquely Japanese, and my colleagues and I were therefore perceived by many as attacking and trying to change that culture. Our final handicap was that many American economists and commentators didn't understand the nature and structure of the Japanese economy and assumed that because it had low tariffs, and because Japanese officials insisted that theirs was a capitalist-market economy just like that of the United States, that it indeed was just like the US economy—with, to be sure, a few quirky Japanese elements.

As a result, many Japanese and American commentators criticized us for unduly trying to open a market that was already open. As lead negotiator, I, in particular, was branded as a "Japan-basher" by Hobart Rowen of the *Washington Post*, and that moniker stuck for a long time in both the Japanese and American press. It was a very troubling term for me because it implicitly tagged me as a racist. Consider for a moment that Rowen could have called me a critic of Japan. But criticism is intellectually and morally legitimate. "Bashing," on the other hand, is emotional and irrational, full of hate, and with intent to harm for no good reason. Because it was a handy bit of shorthand, journalists thoughtlessly bandied the term about and it gained great currency, but it was deeply and fundamentally dishonest and misleading. It was intended to—and did—deflect the discussion of US-Japan trade from legitimate complaints about Japan to personal defamation.

This was a painful period for me both professionally and personally. Professionally, while I managed, along with other US negotiators, to drive a few deals like the US-Japan Semiconductor Agreement and the Telecommunications Agreement, which did actually open a couple of Japanese markets at least to some extent, most of our effort seemed to be in vain. On a personal level, it was extremely unpleasant to be personally subjected—and to have my family (especially my adopted Japanese son) subjected—to a constant stream of media stories calling me anti-Japanese or even anti-Asian. Some good friends in Japan attempted to rebut this line by writing letters to the editors of leading Japanese newspapers, but their passion was not sufficient to counter the bad image of me being fostered by media commentary.

I left the Reagan administration in 1986 and wrote the book *Trading Places: How America Is Giving Its Future to Japan*, in which I tried to explain the major insight I had gained from my years of working in and negotiating with Japan. It was that Japan wasn't cheating and the United States wasn't falling down on the job. Rather, the two sides were simply playing different games. The US was playing baseball while Japan was playing football. Japan wasn't cheating or playing bad football, and the US was playing good baseball. The difficulty was that the Americans kept acting as if and insisting that both sides were playing baseball. Because they weren't, and because the Americans (for reasons both of economic orthodoxy and geopolitical convenience) refused to admit that, and because football is a rougher game than baseball, the Americans were taking a beating.

Upon completion of *Trading Places*, I moved on to writing about other issues such as the creation of the World Trade Organization and the North American Free Trade Agreement, and became more and more detached from Japan. Indeed, the term "Japan passing" came to be used in the 1990s to describe the phenomenon of people passing by Japan on their way to China, Korea, and Southeast Asia, overlooking the Japanese market in favor of greener pastures elsewhere. I became one of the passers.

Ironically, despite appearances to the contrary, Japan would have been wise to have listened to the small band of "revisionists" (in addition to myself, these included Jim Fallows of the *Atlantic*, Chalmers Johnson of the University of California at Berkeley, and Karel van Wolferen of the Dutch newspaper *NRC Handelsblad*) who were calling for reform and opening in Japan. As things turned out, Japan's waves of exports and huge trade surpluses were not so much signs of success as of trouble. The Japan, Inc. catch-up formula for achieving the "miracle" had worked. But it is sometimes possible to have too much of a good thing. The miracle had been based on high savings, high investment in manufacturing, relatively low domestic consumption, and ever-rising trade surpluses of manufactured goods. By the early 1980s, constant repetition of this formula was already creating overinvestment in excess production capacity in Japan.

The economy was becoming seriously unbalanced. Japanese consumers were falling further behind their peers in the United States and Europe as the country continued to expand its huge, modern manufacturing sector while neglecting its increasingly inefficient and outdated services and new business development capabilities.

The big trade surpluses were creating pressure on Japan to strengthen the yen versus the dollar, and eventually it did so in 1985. This should have resulted in a restructuring and rebalancing of the economy. But the Japanese government and industry pulled out all the stops to keep the old miracle machine going. The central bank flooded the markets with cheap money, and investment became easier than it had ever been. Indeed, for major companies like Toyota in 1989–1991, the cost of capital became negative. That's right—the markets paid Toyota to take the money. Of course, that made it easy for the manufacturers to add yet more capacity. On top of that, the easy money aimed at keeping Japanese manufacturers competitive despite the rising yen also created a huge real estate and stock market bubble. It was the bursting of that bubble in 1992 that set the stage for the ensuing two "lost decades" that have left Japan in its present crisis.

In 2011, I became engaged in a project comparing some key Korean industries to their Japanese competitors. While doing this project, I realized more and more that Korea was eating Japan's lunch. At first, I couldn't believe it. Hyundai was taking market share from Toyota in the US and European markets? Samsung was treating Sony like a ninety-pound weakling? And looking beyond Korea, Apple was acting as we used to expect Sony to act. Samsung and Apple were battling it out in the smartphone market, but there were no serious Japanese contenders. Sony had only a single-digit market share. What was going on, I asked myself.

To answer my own question, I began spending more time in Japan talking to old friends and new acquaintances in business, government, academia, labor, and the media. What I found was disturbing. The old cooperation and communication between government and business seemed to be mostly dead. Despite lots of talk and some efforts, the economy had not taken many steps toward becoming rebalanced. There was also a kind of "nothing can be done" mood in place of what I remembered as the old Japanese spirit of optimism and perseverance summed up in the much-used rallying cry of *"Gambatte!"* Particularly among young people, pessimism was rampant. I found myself worried for their future, for the future of the children of my Japanese friends, and for the future of the country that had so much been a major part of my life. I was also approaching my seventy-second birthday, and was increasingly conscious of the passage of time and the fact that I had been watching and working in or on Japan for fifty years. What could I do to warn the country and help it reverse course?

I decided to write this book—in some ways a second bookend to my long involvement with Japan—in the hope that my experience might produce some insights and suggestions that Japan could use to restore its former vitality. The story opens in the year 2050, when Japan has, in fact, been fully restored. It is the world's leading country in a wide variety of technologies and arts, as well as in business, innovation, and clean energy. Students around the world no longer want to go to Harvard or Stanford; rather, they want to study at Tokyo University or Kyoto University. Patients around the world no longer flock to the Mayo Clinic; rather, they go to the Meguro Clinic in Tokyo. This is very different from the way things looked in 2015. Of course, the question is: What happened?

The rest of the book tells the story of "what happened." But first it emphasizes the point that "what happened" is potentially possible and fully believable. After all, Japan has reinvented itself twice in the past century and a half—once in the Meiji Restoration of 1868, when Japan opened itself to Western influences after centuries of isolation, and again after World War II. So we know that Japan is capable of revolutionary change. Japan can do it. The question now is only how to do it again.

The previous reinventions took place after moments of great crisis. So it is logical to conclude that the third reinvention will also require one or more crises. As it happens, Japan is already facing several severe crises, which are outlined in chapter 2. Most important in the short run is the threatening collapse of the economy in the wake of the failure of Abenomics. In addition, chapter 2 also introduces some conjectured crises, such as an Israeli attack on Iran and the withdrawal of the US Seventh Fleet from Japan, which are easily possible to imagine. These and other crises result in a national emergency and the creation of an Extraordinary National Revitalization Commission representing all sectors of the society, and which is charged with the task of once again reinventing the country.

Chapter 3 turns to the question of Japan and the international scene. For many years Japan has become accustomed to being sheltered under the American security wing, and many Japanese cannot imagine that this situation would change. But the fact is that it will. So it is important to understand that Japan's major problems will have to be faced in the context of a world in which the US security assurance will be more limited than it has been since 1945. In this chapter, America adopts a policy of withdrawing its military forces from Japan to the second island chain, and Japan is forced to become a much more substantial geopolitical and diplomatic power, although the US does not entirely disappear from the scene.

Chapter 4 begins to deal with Japan's key problems as I see them. The first is not the economy. That, of course, is a major issue and the most immediately palpable, but the truly existential issue facing Japan is its demographics. The country is dying; I cannot even add the qualifying adverb slowly, because the rate of population aging and shrinkage is rather rapid. Today's 124 million Japanese could become as few as 88 million in the thirty-five years it will take to reach 2050. It is not too late to turn this around. Other countries like Sweden and France have done it. But in just a few years it will be too late. So Japan must very quickly take the steps that other countries have already shown can work. Mainly this will require a dramatic change in the role of women and the attitudes of men, as well as in immigration policies.

Chapter 5 deals with Japan becoming a bilingual nation with English-speaking ability similar to that of countries like Finland, Poland, and Germany. At first glance this may not seem to be a high-priority issue like demographics, but it has a huge bearing on demographics, which in turn has a huge influence on other issues facing Japan. If Japan could speak English well, the country would attract highly talented people from abroad as long-term residents and even, perhaps, as citizens. It could easily stay up-to-date on the latest developments in science, technology, business, finance, and everything else. Thus it is essential that Japan become highly capable in English.

Chapter 6 attacks the need for Japan to promote and become a global leader in innovation by reducing the high risk attached to entrepreneurial activity in Japan. Chapter 7 looks at how Japan could become energy-independent by means of developing its many potentially inexpensive domestic energy sources. Chapter 8 suggests how Japan might modernize its corporate structures and systems with particular emphasis on equal status and treatment for all employees, and Chapter 9 reinvents the structure of the Japanese economy to get rid of the monopolies, barriers to competition, regulatory roadblocks, and powerful interest groups like the farm cooperatives and the medical association. Finally, chapter 10 foresees a fundamentally decentralized and democratized Japan organized along federal lines like Germany and the United States.

It is my hope that future Japanese will remember me as a friend who offered some small but useful suggestions.

In closing, I should emphasize that this book was completed in April, 2015. All events described until that date are real and actually occurred. After that time, all events mentioned are entirely my own forecasts and conjecture based on my experience and understanding of history and of global trends.

CHAPTER 1
Tokyo, 2050

It's spring 2050, and you're embarking on a business trip to Tokyo, a city you haven't visited for thirty-five years. You board your All Nippon Airlines flight in Washington, DC, and after a smooth ride of about two and a half hours find your Mitsubishi 808 supersonic jetliner circling Haneda Airport in preparation for landing.

Though it is not the world's first supersonic jetliner, the 808 is almost twice as fast as the Anglo-French Concorde of the 1970s, carries more than three times the Concorde's passenger load, and has almost three times the Concorde's range. Made of carbon nanofiber and the most advanced electronics, the plane and all its components were entirely developed in Japan after Mitsubishi Heavy Industries acquired Boeing in 2020. This occurred as a result of Boeing's bankruptcy in the wake of the continuing fires and groundings of its 787 Dreamliner, which many analysts had waggishly come to label the "Nightmare Liner." Now all of the world's major airlines depend on the 808 for their long-range flights. Exports of this plane, which is made only in Japan, have helped drive the Japanese trade surplus back to levels last seen in the 1980s.

As the flight settles into its landing pattern, you see spread out below one of the world's most advanced and convenient airfields. Haneda long ago replaced Narita Airport as Tokyo's main gateway, and visitors immediately fall in love with it because of its user-friendly systems and the fact that it lies within only thirty minutes of downtown. There is no need for passport or customs control because your travel documents have already been scanned on the plane and reviewed electronically during your flight. After deplaning, you are met by luggage-carrying robots programmed to recognize you as the owner of the suitcases; they accompany you to the train or intelligent vehicle terminals you have preselected.

Here is where you truly make first contact with modern Japan. There are no limousine buses and no taxis with drivers from the airport to downtown Tokyo and other destinations. Rather, there are only robot-driven high-speed trains and driverless vehicles to transport each passenger or group of passengers. No one drives in Japan any longer; the vehicles are all smart, as are the roadways and buildings. A passenger simply steps into a vehicle and tells it the desired destination. The vehicle then automatically moves the passenger to the destination via the fastest route at that particular time. Thanks to these innovations, there are virtually no transportation-related accidents and thus no transportation-related injuries or deaths in Japan anymore.

Smart transport is safe, but also inexpensive, because Japan has developed a variety of low-cost wind, photovoltaic, ocean current, and methane hydrate energy sources and energy-storing devices, linking them all together in a country-wide smart electrical distribution grid. This has reduced the cost of electric-power generation to almost nothing, far below the cost of Japan's former outdated mix of nuclear and fossil-fuel power plants.

As the vehicle quietly enters the outskirts of Tokyo, you are surprised at the height of the buildings. Because of the instability of much of the land of Japan due to the prevalence of earthquakes, Tokyo had always been a relatively low-rise city. Of course, advances in earthquake-resistant construction had enabled the construction of skyscrapers there beginning in the 1970s. But Tokyo did not then go on to develop a skyline like those of New York and Hong Kong. Now that has changed. Always the leader in earthquake-proof building designs, Japan has pushed its metallurgical and structural technology for dealing with earthquakes to even higher levels, so that the risk of earthquake damage to buildings in the Tokyo area is virtually nonexistent. But even more important has been Japan's development of the carbon-fiber-based UltraRope technology. First introduced by Finnish elevator-maker Kone in 2012, and then further advanced by Japan's carbon-fiber and heavy equipment makers, this technology has created cables that are one-seventh the weight of conventional steel cables. Before UltraRope was developed, skyscrapers required riders to change elevators once or twice in going to the top of the building. The extra elevators also made the buildings heavy and thereby limited their height because of pressure on the foundations. The UltraRope cables allow elevators to rise more than a kilometer in a single run, making lighter buildings possible. This has led to the construction in Tokyo of a multitude of office and apartment buildings higher than Dubai's Burj Khalifa, which was the world's tallest building in 2015.

Not only has this allowed for more efficient use of space and more comfortable office and living arrangements, it has also resulted in numerous unexpected economic benefits. Greater urban density, as it turns out, fostered a smart city environment that stimulated entrepreneurial activity, which in turn led to more and faster innovation. Of course, other cities around the world have followed Tokyo in building taller structures, but Japan is the global center of advanced structural design and know-how. Its engineering and construction companies are in great demand worldwide, acting as the leaders for most of the world's major engineering and construction projects.

Upon arrival at the designated hotel, you are greeted in impeccable, unaccented international English by the staff. (This is just a small piece of evidence that Japan has become a fully bilingual country, in which all students must master English as a condition for graduation from high school and for obtaining a job. You also quickly note that many television and Internet broadcasts carry English subtitles, and that many programs are broadcast in English with Japanese subtitles.) You are guided immediately to your room without going through any check-in procedures—those have all been handled electronically from your vehicle while you were en route from the airport.

Indeed, to say everything has been handled electronically may give a false impression. As far as the individual is concerned, it would be more accurate to say that everything is handled verbally. Japanese electronics, telecommunications, and software industries have evolved to the point at which people can simply give verbal commands, statements, or queries to ubiquitous smart devices that perform the necessary and requested operations. People wear watches or other jewelry with embedded electronics and voice-recognition capability. These devices communicate with enormous networks that link vast clouds of databases and hypercomputers. Needless to say, the development of all these capabilities has required the invention of completely new materials, industrial processes, sterile environments, tools, communications technologies, and much more. Of course, Japan is not the only country with such capabilities, but it is where most of them were invented or developed, and where they are the most advanced and the most numerous.

For instance, many visitors come to Japan these days for health reasons. Some have health problems and come for the latest treatments—including stem-cell-based regeneration of severed nerves and malformed limbs—and advanced diagnosis services. Others come to undertake health-related study or to work in Japanese hospitals and institutes. From all perspectives, Japan has become a mecca for people interested in health care, particularly those interested in sustaining their quality of life after age sixty-five. It is easy to understand why. The average life expectation at birth in Japan is now ninety-five, about eight years longer than in any other country. For those who make it to eighty, an age of more than a hundred is virtually certain. Most importantly, the incidence of Alzheimer's disease and dementia has been dramatically reduced, so that most older Japanese are not only alive, but living well.

This is partly due to diet and positive environmental factors such as public hygiene, clean air and clean water, community health programs for elders, and regular exercise. But it is also due to the most advanced medicines and health-care services on earth. Medical tourism has become one of Japan's leading industries, topping even the aircraft industry in the yen value of its exported services. Today, everyone in the world with serious medical problems seeks to have a Japanese doctor assist with any operations via video linkup, and they typically seek second opinions from Japan's best and brightest doctors. The Japanese pharmaceutical industry has become the world leader in mass production of the antibacterial agents that have replaced antibiotics in the fight against infectious diseases, as well as a multitude of drugs and treatments for dealing with dementia, Alzheimer's disease, and other illnesses of old age.

At the same time, Japanese makers of medical instruments such as CAT and MRI scanners, robots for automated surgery, and patient-monitoring equipment have become by far the world's leading producers. In addition, Japan's expertise in life-support systems, chemical medical analysis, and smart artificial limbs, eyes, ears, hearts, hormones, and even partial brains is unmatched. Even more impressive is what the Japanese medical industry has been able to do with stem cells and stem-cell technology. Aged skin can be rejuvenated and replaced. Badly damaged or diseased internal organs such as the liver and pancreas can be mostly removed and recreated. Of course, many genetic disorders can be diagnosed during the fetal period and prevented by use of a combination of targeted gene removal and replacement and stem-cell treatment.

Perhaps the most important and impressive advance has been the evolution of the Japanese medical profession into the unquestioned world leader. Students and interns from all over the world strive for admittance to Japanese medical schools, postdoctoral positions, and internship programs. Japanese doctors, with their advanced medical training, are eagerly sought by foreign hospitals and as speakers and lecturers at leading universities and conferences. At this moment, if you're going to have surgery, you want your doctor to be Japanese. If you are planning to have a partial brain transplant, the doctor has to be Japanese, because no non-Japanese doctor has yet mastered the technique.

As in medicine, so in athletics: anyone aspiring to be a world-class player in almost any sport will need a Japanese coach. This was made very clear by the complete dominance of Japanese athletes in the 2020 Tokyo Olympics. In the twentieth century and even in the first two decades of this century, Japan was not renowned for its world-class athletes—except in the Japanese martial arts, where Japan dominated the list of world champions.

But in the just-completed Timbuktu Olympic Games, Japanese athletes took eighty gold medals, twice as many as the runner-up Americans. In the past, the Japanese had always been handicapped by small stature, largely as a result of inadequate nutrition in childhood years. By the turn of the twenty-first century, however, Japanese nutrition was not only good; it was better, broadly speaking, than that of any other country, as were medical treatment and disease prevention. The competitive drive of Japanese athletes had always been strong. Once they also had competitive size, they wasted no time in becoming the world's most feared opponents. Soon they were producing outstanding coaches and developing entirely new training techniques, and increasingly dominated global sports in the same way they came to dominate global construction and global medicine. It has been years since any non-Japanese made it to the top sumo ranks, while Japanese baseball pitchers now hold virtually all the global pitching, batting, home-run, and other baseball records. It goes without saying that Japanese golfers, soccer stars, and tennis players dominate the world matches, and the old America's Cup sailing race is now called the Yamato Cup.

Not only are Japanese bigger now, but there are also more of them. Japan is one of the few major countries with a growing population and workforce. Women of childbearing age are having an average of 2.3 children per woman, significantly above the population replacement rate of 2.1. In addition, Japan has begun to welcome immigrants, especially those with advanced education and skills. Thus, after a dip in the first decade of the twenty-first century, Japan's population is growing again and will soon surpass the 150 million mark, even as surrounding countries such as China, Korea, and Russia continue to suffer the slow death of population decline. Naturally, the population growth is driving economic growth. As a result of a growing workforce, combined with strong productivity increases and advances in technology, Japan's GDP is now increasing at 4.5 percent annually, far beyond that of any other major country and just under double that of China.

The foreign businessmen who visit the headquarters of Japanese corporations quickly see a key element in this explosion of population and economic growth. Almost half of the executives with whom they meet are women and non-Japanese. Indeed, if the event is a board of directors' meeting, foreign executives sometimes wonder whether their airplane accidentally landed in Oslo or Stockholm instead of in Tokyo. There are so many women on Japanese corporate boards that they actually surpass the Scandinavians in percentage of female board members. This, of course, has revolutionized the policies, mindset, mode of operation, and character of the Japanese corporation. Offices are mostly empty after 5 p.m., as are the bars and fancy watering holes to which Japanese businessmen famously resorted late into the night in the not-so-distant past. Company golf weekends have also become rarer and less lavish, replaced by family-oriented visits to nice resorts and child-friendly attractions. Also a thing of the past is the elaborate system of formal sign-offs (the *ringi* system) on new proposals by every corporate office. This has been replaced by Skype calls and quick approvals. In the wake of these changes, Japanese companies have become admired and feared for their bold, risk-taking attitudes and quick decision making.

Of the leading global companies in the Nikkei 1000 (formerly the Fortune 500), fully a quarter are Japanese. Partly this is because Japan now boasts the world's best business schools. For example, Harvard Business School is now ranked no better than number ten on the global scale, with Japan's Hitotsubashi,

Keio, and Kyoto University business schools considered the top three and the European INSEAD ranked in the fourth spot.

The rise of Japanese business schools, along with the new role of women executives, has sparked dramatic shifts in corporate governance. The concept of necessary and adequate profit has replaced maintenance of employment as the main objective of the Japanese corporation. Beyond this, two shifts in the global economy have tended to favor Japanese management and economic doctrines and practices. Rather than becoming more interdependent, as long predicted, the world economy has tended to become somewhat less integrated and less globalized over the past thirty-five years. It has also developed more along the lines of China's part-state, part-market capitalism, as opposed to America's mainly free-market capitalism.

Contrary to the predictions of most experts in the period around 2015, global finance and production grew more nationally and regionally based, rather than ever more globalized, over the ensuing years. Partly this was due to the impact of several financial crises in the early years of the century. For instance, the 2010–2014 euro crisis actually drove some members of the European Union to impose capital controls, making it clear to investors everywhere that financial integration without political integration was a recipe for disaster. Similarly, the collapse of the US real-estate bubble between 2006 and 2012 led to greatly increased and more nationally oriented regulatory measures. At the same time, China's push to make its renminbi (RMB) a reserve currency competitor to the US dollar tended to splinter financial markets further. The dollar had been as close to a global currency as the world had seen since the gold standard of the late nineteenth century, and the effort to substitute the RMB thus led in the direction of less, rather than more, globalization.

New technology developments such as 3-D printing, in concert with rising global wages, ever-increasing automation, and the imposition of carbon taxes, made the extensive global supply chains of the early twenty-first century more and more obsolete. With 3-D printing came the capacity to build a product like a car or a home, or almost any other device, using essentially the same technology used to print books. An operator simply takes cartridges of different materials (metal powder, ground plastic, etc.) and feeds them into the printer like ink. The printer deposits the materials according to a pre-programmed pattern and eventually produces a three-dimensional object—a lock, a hammer, a fork, or what have you. This process sparked a veritable revolution by reducing the importance of economies of scale while also automating or doing away with the necessity of assembly operations. It thus tended to move production of items as close as possible to the source of demand and away from low labor-cost locations because very little labor was involved.

The imposition of steep carbon taxes to offset the impact of pollution and to encourage development of alternative energy raised the cost of air and sea delivery, which also moved production closer to the source of demand. This all worked in favor of the Japanese, whose managers had always tended to control production directly instead of relying on extended and complicated global supply chains. And, it was, after all, the Japanese who had, in the 1950s, actually invented the government-backed capitalism that today is associated with China. Thus has the world moved Japan's way over the past two generations.

Another important element of the Japanese corporate renaissance has been its extension from manufacturing into the service sectors in which Japan historically lagged. Now Japan's market share in hotels, insurance companies, banks, online retail stores, and other service industries is equivalent to its strength in manufacturing, and Japan's overall productivity leads the world.

Business visitors and tourists to Japan these days are also greatly impressed by the size and elaborate outfitting of Japanese homes, apartments, and condominiums. Large living spaces have given ordinary Japanese families room to have live-in domestic or elder-care helpers. In the 2020s, Japan fully abolished tariffs on imports and farm subsidies in accord with the rules of the Trans-Pacific Partnership free-trade agreement. Around the same time, the laws around land use, land taxes, and the transfer of property in Japan were modernized and made open and transparent, so that a true market in land and real estate came into being. A series of deregulatory measures transferred land used for small farming into residential or commercial farming use.

The Japanese had always argued that, as the country was densely populated with mountainous terrain, there was little land available for housing, and houses therefore had to be small and cramped. In the 1970s, these typical Japanese houses were referred to as "rabbit hutches" by a British trade negotiator—a description that became prevalent. Thus, today's first-time visitors familiar with long-held stereotypes are surprised to find that the combination of advanced smart transportation and the opening of the agricultural land to development has totally transformed the landscape. In place of the "rabbit hutches" are spacious homes surrounded by pleasant gardens. Because Japan has super-high-speed Internet connections throughout the entire country, telecommuting is prevalent, and most homes include fairly extensive office space. These larger homes require more furniture, appliances, and material of all kinds than were needed for the "rabbit hutches." Of course, this demand has also been a big factor in the country's rapid economic expansion.

The major factor in this growth, however, has been cutting-edge technology and the development of whole new industries often started by new immigrants to Japan. Whether in the field of biotech, nanotech, electronics, materials, aviation, chemicals, or software, Japanese researchers and corporations—as in the cases of medical and aircraft technology—are in the lead. Government and private-sector support of R&D now accounts for nearly 6 percent of Japan's GDP. But what has also made a major difference is the fact that this R&D is not random; rather, rigorous review at all stages of funding has made it extremely focused. Moreover, to facilitate and promote technology development, Japan offers bonuses to leading technologists from around the world if they come to work in Japan. Skilled foreigners who move to Japan receive automatic Japanese citizenship, along with grants and assistance in acclimating to the Japanese way of life. This influx of foreign technologists, combined with the entrepreneurial efforts of many new-generation Japanese, has given rise to thousands of new companies and hundreds of entirely new industries centered mostly in Japan.

The increase in Japan's population and the boom in the economy have allowed Japan to avoid the problems of aging and austerity that have come to plague China, Germany, Korea, and most other major countries. As a result of continuous budget surpluses, the national debt has shrunk from 240 percent of GDP to 50 percent, while health-care costs have fallen from about 9 percent of GDP in 2013 to only 6 percent today. Considering Japan's still relatively large population over sixty-five years of age, this decline in health-care spending, accompanied by improved health-care results, has itself been a kind of economic miracle. Japan has become the envy of the rest of the world because no other country can match its record of improved health care with falling costs.

At the same time, Japan's expenditure on defense has grown from 1 percent of GDP to about 3 percent. This expansion began in 2014 when, in the wake of Chinese threats to the Japanese-administered Senkaku Islands, Japan redefined the extent of its defense powers under Article 9 of its constitution, which prohibited Japan from making war. This article had previously been interpreted to mean that Japan could only defend itself against direct invasion; it could not even provide support to an ally who might be under attack while defending Japan. The reinterpretation broadened the self-defense powers to enable cooperation with and support of allies. Later, the article was again redefined to allow Japanese forces to conduct forward defense and to support allies as part of such a defense. Under these reinterpretations, Japan now considers that it effectively has full sovereignty, including the right to go to war when vital national interests are threatened. The military buildup in response to China's buildup has turned Japan into the world's third-ranking military power, with a full nuclear arsenal and advanced cyberweapons, along with a panoply of international ballistic missiles. Its ships patrol the western Pacific, the Straits of Malacca, and the Indian Ocean. The combination of technological leadership, a booming economy, and military strength have made Japan an attractive alliance partner; most of the countries of East, Southeast, and South Asia, as well as the EU and the United States, have full security treaties or other security arrangements with Japan.

Japan's revitalized status in the world has greatly increased the country's already extensive soft power. In the 1990s, even as the Japanese economy was faltering, important parts of Japanese culture were adopted internationally. Sushi became a global food, *kanban* just-in-time delivery became a global management technique, karaoke became a global music form, and reading manga became a leading global pastime. Now, with Japan revitalized and booming, Japanese innovations in design, art, food, engineering, science, and much else are penetrating to the far reaches of the globe. The world's thirst for Japanese performers, professors, chefs, painters, writers, engineers, designers, composers, and scientists—not to mention its political, economic, and social analysts—seems unquenchable. What some hoped would be the Second American Century—and what many predicted would be the Chinese Century—has, in fact, become the Japanese Century.

None of this appeared at all likely just a generation ago. Indeed, in 2014 the prevailing view was that Japan was a national basket case in grave danger of implosion. It was predicted that by 2050 the population would have declined to only about 85 million people, with 40 percent over the age of sixty-five. Some suggested that the last Japanese person might die before 2300. The low birthrate was destroying aspects of Japan that many had always considered fundamental to being Japanese, such as robust families, children as the center of family life, filial piety, respect for and care of elders, and closely knit villages. Men and women delayed or avoided marriage; when they did marry, they had few or no children. The extended Japanese family disappeared as elder care became too burdensome. Thus, from the traditional extended family, Japan progressed to only a nuclear family and often to no family at all. With a shrinking and aging population, the cost of pensions and health care appeared prohibitive in the face of minimal economic growth and a national debt that was a crushing 240 percent of GDP. Japan's high national savings rate had always enabled the country to finance its own debt internally, but with savings falling and debt rising, analysts were predicting that Japan would soon have to sell its bonds to foreign investors. This, it was felt, would drive interest rates up and soon have debt service payments alone eating up three-fourths of the national budget before any other expenses could be covered.

The once-great Japanese corporations of the 1980s had become mere shadows of their former selves, with some near bankruptcy. Sony, formerly dominant in the electronics industry, had been surpassed by Korea's Samsung and America's Apple, suffering loss after loss. In 2012, Japan's third-largest employer, Panasonic, suffered a US$10 billion loss—the biggest ever by a Japanese manufacturer—which led to the layoff of nearly 40,000 workers. Once world leaders, Japanese semiconductor makers Elpida and Renesas essentially went bankrupt in 2012 and had to be rescued. In the auto industry, Honda had become virtually an American company and Nissan had been flying in formation with Renault of France since the mid-1990s. The important innovations of Japanese management, such as *kanban* just-in-time delivery, *kaizen* continuous improvement, and six-sigma quality control, had all become global standards, but new management concepts were slow to emerge. Indeed, many observers noted that Japanese managers seemed slow to adopt the flexibility, hybrid approach, flat organization, and emphasis on innovation of other global managers in Korea, America, Germany, Taiwan, and Singapore. In place of Japanese management techniques, global business schools had begun using case studies of Sony and other Japanese companies to teach how to avoid stagnation, decline, and failure.

Ironically, Japanese business leaders who had been in the habit of criticizing American CEOs for outsourcing and offshoring jobs were now doing the same thing. Similarly, just as the Americans of the 1980s and 1990s had complained that the dollar was too strong, Japanese businesses in the early 2000s were complaining that the yen was too strong. Some analysts wondered whether the whole Japanese economic miracle of the 1960s and the storied virtuosity of Japanese management had been mainly a matter of an undervalued currency and a protected home market. It seemed that Japanese industry was unable to compete on a truly level playing field. In particular, it seemed to be failing at innovation. With a few exceptions, such as Softbank and Rakuten, the hot new ideas and companies of the early years of the twenty-first century like Skype, Google, Huawei, and Samsung came not from Japan but from Europe, the United States, China, and Korea. Smart young people with an eye to learning new things and advancing their careers and ideas flocked to America, China, and even to India, but not to Japan. Meanwhile, young Japanese, instead of traveling or studying abroad or learning English or Mandarin, seemed to stay more at home and to know less about the world than their parents did. It was said that Japan was so comfortable and pleasant there was no need or attraction for Japanese to leave. But clearly this was at best a partial justification, because a large number of young Japanese had become *hikikomori*, people who isolate themselves and stay at home, locking themselves in their rooms, unable to cope with the pressures of living in Japanese society.

The terrible tsunami and subsequent nuclear-reactor radiation release of 2011 had dealt a hard blow to Japan. Not only were entire communities destroyed, along with much farmland, but all of the country's nuclear reactors—accounting for 25 percent of its total electric energy supply—were shut down. While a few were restarted, most were not, and this meant that Japan's dependence on high-priced oil rose dramatically in the years immediately following the catastrophe. With energy so expensive, the prospects were poor for production of anything requiring significant energy inputs.

To add insult to injury, between 2011 and 2012 China moved to humiliate Japan and to drive a wedge between it and the United

States by taking quasi-military and even some overt military action against the Japanese-controlled Senkaku Islands (known in China as the Diaoyu Islands), which the Chinese claimed for themselves. In addition, China later encouraged and provided covert support for the independence movement in Okinawa, the site of most of the US military bases in Japan. Clearly China saw Japan as a state in terminal decline—one that could be pushed around as an example to others who might want to contest Chinese claims and power. The United States was bound by treaty to defend Japan against attack. Yet Washington desperately wished to avoid conflict with China, and tried to please all sides. On the one hand, the United States said that it took no position on the validity of the various historical claims to the islands. On the other, it said that it recognized the fact of Japan's present administration and the importance of not settling the issue by force. President Obama stated publicly in April of 2014 that the islands fell under America's defense umbrella. But many in Japan and in the rest of the world rightly doubted that the United States would actually go to war with China over anything that happened in the Senkaku Islands. And this doubt only further weakened Japan's position.

In sum, the outlook for Japan in 2015 was extremely poor in every way. Certainly no one imagined the reality of Japan's current position in 2050.

What happened? How did Japan change the trajectory of its future?

The purpose of this book is to answer those questions.

CHAPTER 2

2016—Year of Crises

n 2016, new population estimates for Japan painted a sobering picture. The 2010 census had estimated that Japan's population of 128 million would fall to 95 million by the year 2050, with all of Japan's forty-seven prefectures suffering population loss. In the hardest-hit prefectures such as Akita, Aomori, and Kochi, it was estimated that the population would decline by as much as a third. But even Tokyo was warned to expect a decline of nearly 7 percent. The new 2016 projection showed a much more dramatic decline, with the total population dipping below 88 million by 2050. Even worse was the projection for the aging of the population: in 2010 it had been expected that by the year 2040, people older than sixty-five would make up more than 30 percent of the population in each prefecture, with Akita, Aomori, and Kochi prefectures reaching a proportion of over 40 percent. But the new projection was that 40 percent of Japan's population would be over age sixty-five by the year 2050.

The social, economic, and national security implications of these numbers were almost unimaginable. Many Japanese had been comforting themselves with the thought that a smaller population would not be a problem. Indeed, it was often suggested that Japan would be less crowded and thus more comfortable and livable with fewer people. But a cold, hard look at the projections showed a rapidly approaching disaster. Within a very short time, one active Japanese worker would be supporting not only himself, but also one elderly person, as the size of the workforce fell from 87 million in 2010 to only about 52 million in 2050. The implications for pensions were dire. The pension system had been assuming returns of about 4 percent on investment. In fact, the actual returns had for some time been only about 2 percent, and there had already been the possibility that pension reserves would be entirely used up in about twenty years. But by 2016 it looked as if the cost of supporting the elderly would rise sharply. Between 1991 and 2000, social spending rose by about 50 percent. The new projections showed that the increase between 2000 and 2025 would be near 100 percent. With the population shrinking by almost 1 percent annually, productivity gains would have to be in the 3 percent annual range to achieve GDP growth of just 2 percent annually. Yet this level of productivity had not been achieved in the past twenty years. Slow or zero GDP growth could not support the increased government spending that would be necessitated by rising retirement, health care, and elder-care payments.

Beyond the domestic economic consequences, these numbers had huge international and security implications. Could an elderly and frail Japan respond adequately to the challenges posed by a resurgent China? Could it continue to be an adequate ally to the United States or to the ASEAN countries? Could it even maintain its presence among the G7, G8, or G20 countries?

No matter how one looked at the numbers and the trends, they were disheartening. It seemed that Japan would be unable to avoid becoming older, poorer, sicker, and less secure while paying higher and higher taxes for fewer and fewer benefits. Japan appeared to be a dying country.

LIGHTS OUT

In the spring of 2014, the militant Sunni Muslim group known as the Islamic State in Syria and the Levant (ISIS, ISISL, or ISIL) broke out of its base in northeast Syria and quickly overran northwestern Iraq up to the very gates of Baghdad, while also threatening northern Saudi Arabia, Jordan, and parts of Turkey. At the same time, the United States and Iran appeared to be making rapid progress toward an agreement that would allow Iran to continue developing its nuclear-energy capability while still being barred from acquiring sufficient capacity to produce nuclear weapons. The combination of these two developments resulted in an unexpected shift in Middle East alliances. Because of its seminal role in the creation of the Shia Muslim state of Iraq after deposing the dictator Saddam Hussein, the United States felt a strong obligation to prevent the collapse of the new state. It also wished to maintain good relations with Tehran in order to conclude the nuclear deal. But longtime US allies Saudi Arabia, Israel, and Jordan all shared an existential fear of Iran and its surrogate Hezbollah forces in Syria, Lebanon, and northern Saudi Arabia. They deeply believed that Iran was bent on the overthrow and destruction of each of their governments. Consequently, in late 2016, Jordan and Saudi Arabia opened their airspace to Israeli bombers, which launched massive attacks on suspected nuclear facilities all over Iran. Tehran struck back by unleashing Hezbollah rocket attacks on Israel from Lebanon, sinking vessels, and planting mines that closed the Strait of Hormuz to all outbound oil shipments. They also encouraged sabotage by Shia Muslims who, despite being a small minority of Saudi Arabia's mainly Sunni population, held the majority of the kingdom's vast oil fields and refineries along the western edge of the Persian Gulf. Overnight, the price of oil soared to US$300 per barrel, threatening to push Japan into a massive trade deficit and to completely stall the Japanese economy.

Because 80 percent of the oil and half of the liquefied natural gas (LNG) bound for Japan passed through the Strait of Hormuz, the closure of this passage threw Japan into a desperate situation. The government requested help from Russia, but Moscow replied that it had already committed to supplying China and had no additional capacity. Efforts to obtain increased supplies from Indonesia and Malaysia were also unsuccessful, as these countries wanted to ensure that they and their ASEAN colleagues would have a sufficient supply. In desperation, Tokyo turned to the United States in hopes of obtaining emergency imports of shale-gas-based LNG and shale oil. But despite having become energy independent as a result of the development of shale deposits, the United States did not yet have sufficient infrastructure to export substantial quantities of LNG.

To partially offset the loss of oil and LNG-fueled energy, the Japanese government began to accelerate the restart of its nuclear power reactors. These had nearly all been shut down in the wake of the 2011 tsunami-induced partial meltdown of the Tokyo Electric Power Company's (TEPCO) nuclear reactors at Fukushima. This action, which was necessary in order to carry out safety inspections, had automatically cut Japan's electric power production by more than 25 percent. Despite growing public opposition to nuclear power, by mid-2014 the government had completed most of its safety inspections and had begun the process of reactivating fifty-four closed reactors.

In early September of 2014, a panel of nuclear regulators had ruled that the Sendai power plant in southern Japan faced no risk from the several dormant volcanoes in its vicinity. On September 27, 2014, however, nearby Mount Ontake unexpectedly erupted, leading University of Tokyo professor and volcanologist Toshitsugu Fujii to warn that no one could accurately predict volcano eruptions, and that Japan was in danger of experiencing further volcanic disturbances that would endanger a number of nuclear power stations. Sure enough, in late 2016, Mount Sakurajima unexpectedly released a hot, fast-moving flow of gas and sediments that quickly knocked out both reactors at Sendai. This created overwhelming grassroots pressure to shut down any reactors even remotely under the threat of volcanic eruptions. Thus, Japan returned to a state of severely restricted nuclear power supply.

THE END OF THE PAX AMERICANA IN ASIA

The years 2012–2016 brought a fundamental shift in the balance of power in the entire Asia-Pacific region. China's economy had become arguably the world's largest. Previously, China had been content to pursue economic growth while largely ignoring geopolitical issues and ambitions. But all that started to change with its 2012 occupation of the Philippine-claimed Scarborough Shoal near the Philippine coast. Thereafter, China began to extend its growing power into the seas around it by asserting the "nine-dash line" of control (the sketched line segments on an old map now used by China to determine its area of rightful control), which included nearly all the islands and shoals of the South China Sea. In reaction to the 2012 purchase of the Senkaku Islands by the government of Japan, China asserted its own claim to the islands and began to challenge Japan's administration of them by sending fishing boats and other vessels into the islands' waters, as well as by practicing air-force fighter maneuvers in the area. In early 2014, China suddenly established a new Air Defense Identification Zone (ADIZ) that included the Senkakus, as well as reefs and islands claimed by South Korea. Later in the same year, it began oil-drilling operations in waters also claimed by Vietnam. These actions were accompanied by a rapid buildup of Chinese military forces, particularly shore-based anti-ship missile batteries aimed at eventually denying the US Pacific Command and allied forces committed to defending and maintaining stability in the region access to the waters within China's "first island chain" (Japan, Okinawa, the Ryukyus, the Senkakus, Taiwan, the Paracels, the Spratleys, and the Strait of Malacca).

All eyes had been on the United States to see how the long-time hegemon and guarantor of stability might respond, and a palpable unease could be felt in the region when Washington did not react strongly. In response to the Chinese occupation of the Scarborough Shoal in 2011, the White House had sent the secretary of state to Beijing and Manila to urge negotiations, but had taken no concrete steps to prevent or reverse the Chinese occupation. In what initially appeared to be a success for US diplomacy, China had agreed to talks with Manila. But as the talks dragged on and produced no result, China continued its occupation, and Washington continued to watch. In the case of Japan's long-disputed—and then, in 2012, openly challenged—sovereignty over the Senkaku Islands, the United States had always held a nuanced position. It had several times stated that it recognized Japan's present administration of the islands and that it therefore was obliged to defend them as part of Japanese territory under the US-Japan Mutual Security Treaty. In other words, the Senkakus were considered to be under the US nuclear umbrella. At the same time, however, Washington said that it had no opinion on whether China or Japan had rightful sovereignty over the islands, and that such final sovereignty should be determined by negotiation between those two countries. When China announced its new ADIZ, the US Air Force sent two B-2 bombers through the zone without giving prior notice to Chinese authorities, thereby indicating that Washington did not recognize the legitimacy of the zone. However, Washington also advised US airlines operating in the region to abide by the new Chinese ADIZ.

To be sure, Washington had announced it was "pivoting to Asia" in 2012, but in view of these developments, many in the region wondered what the "pivot" really meant. This concern was only heightened when word leaked out of the Pentagon in late 2013 that, in order to avoid a confrontation with China that might pose a direct threat to the United States, as well as to cut costs and avoid excessive US federal budget deficits, the US was considering a possible withdrawal of US forces to China's "second island chain" (Tokyo Bay, the Bonins, the Marianas, Guam, Palau, and the Sunda Strait). No one in the region was sure whether America really intended to maintain its dominance in the Asia-Pacific region or not.

Then, in late 2016, warning shots from Japanese Self-Defense Force pilots aimed at Chinese fighters overflying the Senkaku Islands accidentally resulted in the downing of one of the Chinese planes. China responded by occupying Uotsuri Island, the largest of the Senkakus. Washington condemned the action and sent ships from the Seventh Fleet to patrol the vicinity, but took no action to dislodge the occupying Chinese. Instead, it urged Japan to negotiate with Beijing for a deal to share administration of the islands. Nor did Washington respond strongly to intelligence leaks pointing to Chinese support for an Okinawan independence movement. Clearly, the US-Japan Mutual Security Treaty had its limits in the case of confrontation with China.

Adding to Japan's concerns was the growing quasi-alliance between China and South Korea. By 2014, China had become South Korea's largest trading and investment partner, and South Korea's largest *chaebol* corporate conglomerates were now heavily dependent not only on the Chinese market, but also on the country's technology and skilled labor. The United States, which still had formal command of the South Korean army under the terms of the US-Korea Mutual Defense Treaty of 1953, had been scheduled to transfer command to South Korean generals in 2015. But it advanced the transfer by a year to 2014, thus indicating that it wanted to be less directly responsible for the defense of South Korea. While these shifts were taking place, the relationship between Japan and South Korea was becoming more and more troubled. Korea continued to occupy the Takeshima chain of islets that Japan considered to be rightfully Japanese. Seoul continually rejected Tokyo's proposals for negotiation. A treaty negotiated in 2013–2014 to enable sharing of national security information by the two countries was rejected by Seoul at the last minute, meaning that the South Korean army could communicate with its putatively allied Japanese army only through the offices of the Pentagon. Underlying the growing coolness of the South Korea-Japan relationship were lingering issues from World War II, such as the drafting of Korean women by the Imperial Japanese Army to become sex slaves, or "comfort women," for Japanese troops. The flames of this and other wartime issues were fanned each time Japanese prime minister Shinzo Abe or his close associates paid homage at Tokyo's Yasukuni Shrine or appeared to be discussing the negation or rewording of Japan's apologies for the war.

The fact that China shared South Korea's resentment of Japan, and resented Abe's statements as much as—if not more than—Korea did greatly strengthened the growing bond between those two countries. The bond was further reinforced by the growing sense in South Korea that China was more important than the United States for keeping North Korea under control and for eventually opening that country to investment and production by South Korean firms. Thus, news from the Pentagon in late 2016 that the United States was planning to remove its troops from Korea virtually sealed the new China-South Korean alliance.

ABENOMICS IS NOT ENOUGH

By mid-2016, it was becoming clear that the economic policies of Prime Minister Abe—"Abenomics"—were not going to revive the Japanese economy from more than twenty years of stagnation and deflation. This bold program consisted of what Abe called the "three arrows." The first arrow was aggressive quantitative easing, under which the Bank of Japan essentially created huge quantities of money; the second arrow was increased fiscal stimulus through greater government spending on infrastructure; and the third arrow was structural reform aimed at opening the agricultural sector to greater competition, increasing and elevating the role of women in society and in the economy, stimulating start-up of new businesses through deregulation, and reforming stultified corporate structures and practices. This had all been aimed at generating an inflation rate of at least 2 percent while raising GDP and productivity growth. The success of this policy depended on economic growth surpassing the hoped-for level of inflation. Otherwise, rising interest rates in the wake of rising inflation would expand the interest payments on government bonds to such an extent that they would eat up virtually the entire government budget.

Initially Abe's strategy seemed to work, at least to some extent. The yen fell by 25 percent and exports surged, along with export-related employment and corporate profits. The Nikkei stock average rose higher than it had been in many years. What looked like the beginnings of a construction boom seemed to be underway, and a wave of hope coursed through the Japanese public. But problems arose as time passed. In order to reduce the huge government fiscal deficit that was threatening to undermine the health-care and retirement systems, consumption tax was increased, which had the unfortunate effect of undercutting the growth dynamic. In addition, the weak yen gave rise to retaliatory action. The South Korean government intervened frequently and massively in the global currency markets to offset the impact of a weaker yen on Korean exports. To a lesser extent, Taiwan, Singapore, Malaysia, and China did the same, while the US Congress threatened to pass legislation aimed at providing offsets to currency-related import surges. Suffering from a continuing euro crisis that saw unemployment in countries like Italy and France rise above 15 percent, the EU also undertook a series of tough actions against import surges related to currency movements.

More fundamental were two additional problems. Government spending on public construction in Japan no longer provided significant stimulus to growth or a very good return on investment. So much of such construction had been done over the years that, with a few exceptions, essentially only low-payoff projects were left. Even more important, however, was the increasingly apparent failure of the "third arrow" of structural reform. While the Abe proposals had been bolder than anything put forward in Japan in the preceding forty years, they were not bold enough, or at least not implemented in a bold enough way. Reducing corporate taxes, eliminating corporate cross-shareholdings, rationalizing the electricity production and distribution system, deregulating much agricultural production, reducing agricultural and a wide variety of other subsidies, increasing after-school activities for children so that mothers could work full-time, and trying to establish wages based on output rather than hours worked were all groundbreaking and necessary measures. Yet they proved difficult or impossible to achieve, and it was increasingly apparent that they would be insufficient to meet the goal of revitalizing the nation. Inflation had indeed risen, but there was little increase in real GDP growth, household incomes, or standards of living. New investment, production increases, and job growth remained sluggish. Citizens faced with rising costs and stagnant incomes were not happy. They began to fear that the aim of the government was to use inflation to reduce the cost of national debt. Because a large portion of citizens' wealth was invested in government bonds, this would threaten the real value of their savings and their retirement.

Fear caused pension funds, mutual funds, and other investors to sell off their holdings of Japanese government bonds and other yen-denominated assets. The government was reluctant to raise interest rates to stem the outflow, because with interest payments on public debt already eating up roughly 30 percent of government revenue, higher interest rates could threaten the government itself with bankruptcy. Instead, introduction of capital controls became a topic of discussion. Unfortunately, this had the effect of spurring further capital flight. The unthinkable possibility was becoming a reality: Japan would have to rely on borrowing from the International Monetary Fund (IMF) and put its economy effectively under IMF control.

UNADVENTUROUS YOUTH

Because it was a country with few natural resources and relatively little cultivatable land, modern Japan had been forced to fully exploit its human resources in order to achieve its position as one of the world's most advanced economies. Thus heavy emphasis had always been placed on education and maximum development of human capacity. As a result, Japanese students had always tended to do well on the standardized tests that are often used to make international educational comparisons. The best known of these tests was the Program for International Student Assessment, or PISA, which was taken every three years by fifteen-year-old students in many countries starting in 2000. In 2012, Japan placed seventh out of the seventy-eight entities where the PISA was administered. These included city-states or micro-states with very small populations such as Shanghai, Singapore, Hong Kong, and New Zealand; however, if these were discounted, Japan placed third. This was far better than, for example, the United States at number seventeen. Moreover, the United States had seen its position decline over the years, while Japan's had remained steadily near the top.

Yet, in 2015, as Japan approached a quarter century of economic stagnation, and the iconic Japanese companies and industries of long standing disappeared or paled into shadows of their former selves, many Japanese began to wonder whether the schools were teaching and measuring the right things. In short, was the education system preparing young people to deal successfully with the world they would face? Some astounding surveys and statistics suggested that the answer might well be *no*. For instance, in early 2015, the Institute of International Education found that the trend toward fewer and fewer Japanese going abroad to study was continuing. In 2008, the number of Japanese studying in America (30,000) was only about 60 percent of the number that had been there ten years previously. In 2015, this number fell by 50 percent. In other words, compared to the 50,000 Japanese students who had been studying in America in 1998, there were now only 15,000. This was not because more Japanese students were going to places like Australia or China; those countries also reported declining numbers of Japanese exchange students. The fact was that in an age of increasing internationalization and globalization, the young generation had less and less interest in learning about the outside world, and was not as well-equipped to deal with it.

Research between 2000 and 2010 by university analysts for publishers like Benesse indicated that Japan's young people were now less adventurous and less willing to take risks than their elders. There seemed to be fear that with widening gaps in society between rich and poor, making a mistake at a young age could prevent one from moving up or could even push one disastrously down. Thus ambition was muted.

Furthermore, as media strategist Mariko Sanchanta wrote in 2013, quoting a top executive of a Japanese bank, "It is impossible to persuade young bank executives to study abroad even if they are fully funded by the bank. They're concerned about falling behind their peers if they go overseas." Young people also seemed to think of Japan as safe and of other countries as dangerous. Books like Mitsuko Takahashi's *Don't Let Your Daughter Study Abroad*, published in 2007, fanned this fear. In a survey completed in 2012, the Ministry of Education, Culture, Sports, Science, and Technology had found that fully 60 percent of Japanese students were not interested in studying abroad. The main reason, cited by 52 percent of the students surveyed, was insufficient foreign language capability. This was closely related to the second reason, cited by 31 percent of students—inability to make friends and concern for the safety of the environment in which they might have to live. Thus, despite their high PISA scores, it seemed that a generation of Japanese students was being educated in such a way as to make them less capable of dealing with the outside world on which Japan's future depended.

This contrasted dramatically to the trends in most other countries, where the number of students studying abroad was multiplying rapidly. Thus, in 2011, even as the number of

Japanese students in America was declining, the number of Chinese students there rose by more than 40 percent to 156,000. The total number of international students in the United States in that year was 723,000, an increase of about 5 percent from the previous year. Japan seemed to be going against the flow. Significantly, the decline was more pronounced among male than female students, reflecting the fact that corporate sponsorship of overseas study had declined sharply. Men were led to view overseas study as a greater risk to their careers than did women, perhaps because the women knew that the big corporations were not going to hire them in any case.

SONY MERGES WITH SAMSUNG

Throughout the 1990s and the first decade of the twenty-first century, the once-fabled companies of Japan, Inc. had steadily lost ground to competitors in Asia, the United States, and Europe. Number two Japanese automaker Nissan had to be rescued by bringing in a foreign CEO and forging a close joint venture and partnership with France's Renault. In 2012, once-mighty Panasonic recorded the biggest losses of all time for any Japanese company. Sharp and Toshiba also recorded record losses; while Hitachi managed to revitalize itself, it did so only by dramatically downsizing. Former semiconductor stalwarts Elpida and Renesas came close to bankruptcy, and had to be rescued by some of their US competitors, along with the Japanese government.

Most significant, both symbolically and substantively, was the merger of Japan's fabled Sony with Korea's Samsung Electronics late in 2016. This was a huge shock for the Japanese public. Sony had for years epitomized Japanese industrial and technological leadership. While many old-guard Japanese companies had grown by establishing dominant positions in the relatively protected Japanese market and then branching out overseas, Sony had been global from the beginning. Its CEO and chairman, Akio Morita, had become fluent in English and prominent as an international statesman-CEO. While he had not always been in Japan's inner circle, he had always been in the world's inner circle; Sony, like Apple in its heyday, became synonymous with bold innovation, style, and quality.

By 2013, however, Sony had been looking and acting a lot like previously failing American companies such as Kodak and Motorola. It sold its headquarters building and began investing in new fields such as medical technology. It lost money in its traditional digital electronics, game, video, and mobile phone businesses, while making money on financial services and music. Traditionally regarded in the same way as a company like Apple, priding itself on the regular introduction of new hit products that created whole new industries, Sony hadn't had a hit in eighteen years, and seemed to be moving in a less global, more parochial, and less innovative direction.

A few hundred miles across the Sea of Japan in Korea, the situation was just the opposite. Whether it was smartphones, television sets, components, or flat-panel displays, Sony simply couldn't compete with the super-aggressive Korean giants. Rather than continuing to try to fight them, Sony decided to join them. In September of 2016, the company announced it was being taken over by Samsung and would henceforth be known as Samsung-Sony, or S&S for short.

INERTIA INTO ACTION

Since the Meiji Restoration in 1868, when Japan opened up to the West for the first time, the Japanese political system had evolved to resemble that of France. In both countries, a powerful central bureaucracy had come to monopolize taxation, spending, and regulatory powers at the expense of the regional prefectures over which it ruled. Indeed, the centralization in Tokyo was such that, in addition to central government and political parties, virtually all major business, labor, academic, and media organizations maintained their headquarters in the city.

While Japan's economy was collapsing, its energy supply disappearing, and its security becoming increasingly uncertain, life at the local level was also ever more difficult and unbearable. Changing the location of a stop sign in Osaka, for example, could require obtaining permission from several Tokyo-based agencies. Parents spent half the day getting their young children to and from the very limited number of government-approved child-care facilities available. Older children in elementary, middle, and high schools were not being well prepared for the modern world because centrally regulated curriculums were outdated. On top of all this, the fear of nuclear accidents in vulnerable local areas sparked a grassroots political reaction that quickly evolved into a broader movement opposing the central government.

Clearly Japan needed a fundamental revitalization program. Could it develop such a program in the face of deeply rooted inertial forces? No one really knew the answer to that question, but history suggested that it was possible. Twice in the past century and a half, Japan had reinvented itself: once in the Meiji Restoration of the 1860s, when Japan had been forced to open up by Commodore Matthew Perry and his Black Ships; and again in the wake of World War II and the US occupation of Japan.

The crises now facing Japan were every bit as existentially threatening as those of the Meiji and post–World War II periods. Thus any renaissance program would have to be as revolutionary as the two forerunners, if not more so. It had become clear that half measures and delay were only exacerbating the problems. In light of this consciousness, after the national elections of 2016, the Diet legislated the creation of a kind of new Iwakura Mission, the Meiji-era task force that traveled abroad to find ideas for reinventing Japan. To this body, called the Extraordinary National Revitalization Commission, were appointed representatives from all elements of Japanese society—political, business, academic, regional, media, social, agricultural—and even some foreigners familiar with Japan. Their task, like that of the Iwakura Mission, was to develop a program for revitalizing the country.

CHAPTER 3

Pax Pacifica

You were impressed yesterday on your arrival at Haneda and during your ride into Tokyo by the high sea walls that have been constructed around the airport and much of the rest of Tokyo Bay. Now, in 2050, there are no longer any doubts about the reality of global warming. It has been recognized as the major national security threat for many nations, including Japan. Rising sea levels have already substantially submerged the Maldives and the Seychelles, requiring mass evacuation of their populations. Along with Tokyo and Osaka, other major coastal cities such as Mumbai, Rotterdam, and New York are literally struggling to keep their heads above water.

Today, as you walk to breakfast through the lobby of the Imperial Hotel, you are asked to pause to let the Indian Minister of Defense and his entourage pass. They are on their way to join the US Secretary of Defense and the Ministers of Defense of Japan, Australia, Indonesia, and the Philippines in the semiannual meeting of the PacInd (Pacific and Indian Ocean) Mutual Security Alliance that has replaced the old network of unilateral American security guarantees as the main pillar of stability in the Asia-Pacific region. As you sit down at your breakfast table, you note the Chinese and Japanese flags on a table across the room reserved for the High Commissioners of the Senkaku-Diaoyu Islands Joint Government Commission, the body through which the Japanese and Chinese governments jointly administer the formerly contested island group.

This is a far cry from thirty-seven years ago when there was a serious threat of war between China and the Japan-US Alliance. Then, Japan was occupying and administering the obscure islands—really just bits of rock barely rising out of the water—known as Senkaku to the Japanese and Diaoyu to the Chinese, at the far end of the Ryukyu island chain near Taiwan. An increasingly powerful China was claiming that it had rightful sovereignty over these islets and that Japan was unlawfully occupying and preparing to colonize them. Beijing had begun sending fishing boats and naval ships into what Tokyo claimed as Japan's territorial waters, while also declaring an Air Defense Identification Zone (ADIZ) that just happened to cover the islands. Japan invoked the US-Japan Mutual Security Treaty saying that the island chain fell under the US security umbrella, and Washington reluctantly assented. The swords were at least halfway out of their scabbards.

Indeed, because of its immediacy and global significance, this was one of the first issues the Extraordinary National Revitalization Commission had found itself confronting. The response of the Commission set the tone for much that was to follow. Noting that the contested islands had only become part of Japan in 1895 after China's defeat in the Sino-Japanese War and had been administered by the United States from 1945 until 1972, the Commission called for settlement by arbitration through the World Court and offered Chinese energy companies the same rights to explore for and produce oil and gas as any Japanese or other international corporation.

In fact, in 2050, the Senkakus remain uninhabited and undeveloped under the shared Japanese-Chinese administration. With overlapping ADIZs that are minimally enforced by both governments, there have been no incidents for years. The islets have proven not to have significant gas and oil deposits. In any case, the whole energy issue has become insignificant for Japan as the country has become energy independent based on the development of methane hydrate, shale, clean nuclear, and renewable energy sources. Beyond that, 3-D printing, widespread use of labor-saving robots, and high carbon taxes on jet and bunker fuel have virtually ended the era of global supply chains and thus also the need for trading nations to defend them.

Beyond the acceleration of global warming and inexorably rising water levels, the main global security threats today include conflict in Europe arising from massive immigration from the disease-plagued regions of West Africa as well as from the continuing Shia-Sunni civil war in the Middle East; drug-resistant viruses; highly sophisticated and extremely wealthy international criminal groups; the destruction of the world's jungles in Brazil, Indonesia, and Africa; and cyber disruption.

THE DECLINE OF CHINA

China has become much less important in world affairs than seemed likely thirty-five years ago. Although it was not then apparent, the golden days of China's growth were over by 2015. Its labor force had started shrinking in 2012–2013, while the overall population began aging rapidly in 2015 and quickly became among the oldest in the world. The question had always been whether China would get rich before it became old; the answer, as it turned out, was that it would not. When that became apparent, the flaws in the Chinese system began to show. It was clear that the already wide gap between rich and poor was going to continue widening. The bill for past pollution, environmental degradation, and corruption began to come due. None of this had affected the Chinese high-growth GDP figures in the past, but now the results were clear: corrupt practices were choking growth, and pollution and environmental problems were resulting in ill health and premature deaths. Corruption in particular became a huge issue. Officials and Communist Party operatives who had become enormously rich while officially being paid normal salaries became the targets of investigation, public protest, and harassment. Such people hurried to get themselves and their money out of China and to obscure the funds they had already stashed away abroad. More important than this was the fact that China was increasingly unable to afford medical and elder care while also paying for the large military force it had been building and maintaining. Thus, like the United States before it, China began to downsize its security forces, a step that also induced it to be more cooperative with Japan and other leading countries.

Most important, however, was China's growing internal political tension and a loosening of national unity. Large areas like Guangdong Province were demanding more autonomy, and major political, business, academic, and media figures were calling for more participative politics with much more transparency and openness. China had become absorbed with its own internal difficulties while Japan's Revitalization Commission was leading its country toward restoration.

Now, in the middle of the twenty-first century, India has become far more important than China. As the Centre for Economics and Business Research forecast long ago, India has recently passed China to become the world's largest economy. Having become the world's most populous nation in 2025, it now has the youngest working population of the major countries. It also has a large, well-trained, and experienced military with its own nuclear weapons and delivery systems, as well as large modern naval, air, cyber, and drone forces. These forces were successful in compelling China to abandon its claims to Indian territory by 2025 with the Treaty of the Himalayas. It was the 2022 inclusion of India in what had been the US-Japan Mutual Security Treaty, and the extension of that alliance to include Australia, Indonesia, and the Philippines that turned the old bilateral US-Japan pact into what has come to be called the Grand Alliance. This treaty also includes many cooperative basing, training, and visiting arrangements with countries such as Singapore and Vietnam. The Grand Alliance has become more significant to world security than NATO, and—in combination with the inward turning of China—now assures peace and stability in the entire region spanning Asia-Pacific countries, the Indian Ocean, and the Persian Gulf. Importantly, it was not the United States but Japan that took the initiative to achieve this multilateral security system, and it is Japan, Australia, the Philippines, and India who take the primary first reaction responsibility for assuring security in their respective regions. Of course, US forces are always available if absolutely necessary, but they are the call of last rather than first resort.

Effectively, the mutual security system that grew out of the US occupation of Japan and the Cold War has been turned upside down. The Pax Americana has become the Pax Indo-Pacifica.

THE FADING OF THE PAX AMERICANA

The end of the Pax Americana in the Pacific had actually been foreshadowed as early as July, 1969, when then-president Richard Nixon announced the Nixon Doctrine. This stated that the

United States would provide a nuclear shield to allies under the threat of nuclear attack, and that the United States would provide appropriate security assistance to allies threatened by non-nuclear aggression. But it emphasized that the United States would expect the nation under threat to assume the primary responsibility for its own defense. Coming at the height of the Vietnam War, this was an early signal that the countries of Asia could not count on America to fight their battles if they were not prepared to fight for themselves.

Subsequently, the end of the Cold War removed much of the justification for the extensive network of US security alliances and military deployments. A "peace dividend" was widely expected, and most of the US forces in Europe were repatriated as Washington slashed defense expenditures.

The US Defense Strategy Reports of 1990 and 1992 also called for removal of most US forces from the Asia-Pacific region by the end of the decade. At the same time, leaders in Japan began to speak of the lessening need for the security alliance with the United States, and of greater reliance on the UN and on economic cooperation. It began to look as if Japan would reassume responsibility for its own foreign policy and bear a much greater burden for its own defense.

But that all changed in 1995 with the publication of the US Defense Department's new Security Strategy for the East Asia-Pacific Region. This document reversed previous statements by saying that although the Cold War was over, diverse conflicts posed threats to US interests and made it necessary for America to maintain its then-current troop levels (about 100,000) in the region for the foreseeable future. This was followed in April of 1996 by the US-Japan Joint Declaration reaffirming the "Alliance for the 21st Century," which essentially confirmed the unilateral US commitments of the US-Japan Mutual Security

Treaty while providing the basis for a potential broadening of Japan's support of US military-related actions. Thus, as far as the United States and Japan were concerned, the end of the Cold War changed nothing.

Behind this great reversal were three unexpected developments: the Gulf War of 1990–1991, North Korea's nuclear weapon and missile development, and the rapid rise of China's military spending. All of these created uncertainty that caused both Tokyo and Washington to postpone significant changes in the security arrangements. But this status-quo course posed several problems for America. The US was losing the overwhelming economic competitiveness that had supported its political and military superiority during the Cold War. China was becoming a formidable regional rival. With a rapidly growing economy and an authoritarian government that had no need of policy approval from the citizenry, it could easily bear the burden of an arms race. With a relatively declining economy, Washington would find engaging in such a race increasingly difficult. (By 2012 it had already become impossible for Washington to even contemplate sending its aircraft-carrier battle groups into the Taiwan Strait, as it had done in 1996 in response to Chinese threats of attack on Taiwan.) In addition, by carrying the major burden of defense for Japan and its other Asian allies, the United States was enabling Japan to postpone the long-term necessity of providing more of its own security. The arrangement allowed Tokyo to avoid serious consideration of its own circumstances. For instance, it could neglect settling disputes with South Korea and China over minor islands, antagonize neighbors with denials of certain facts of World War II, and postpone serious discussion of mutual defense arrangements with South Korea and other potential Asian allies. Finally, the understanding assumed a perfect and continuing congruence between the interests of

America and those of its Asian allies. In doing so, it potentially made the United States hostage to policies and actions of its allies that might not always be in its own best interests.

WAKE-UP TIME

The advent of the administration of Prime Minister Shinzo Abe in December of 2012 marked the beginning of the end of the Pax Americana. Abe himself recognized that the United States could not indefinitely maintain its hegemonic role, and that the arrangement had become a potential long-term trap: as US power declined, Japan would increasingly be unable to defend itself unless it took steps now to assure its future. Early in his term, Abe spoke of "breaking away from the postwar order."

Abe visited India in May of 2013, pledging greater defense cooperation between Japan and India and agreeing to conduct joint military exercises on a frequent basis. In July of that year, he visited the Philippines and offered ten patrol boats to help the Philippine coast guard better defend Manila's claims to some of the South China Sea islands also claimed by China. Said Abe, "For Japan, the Philippines is a strategic partner with whom we share fundamental values and many strategic interests. In order to further reinforce this relationship...we confirm continued assistance to the capacity-building of the Philippine coast guard."

Coming from the then junior security partner in the US-Japan alliance, these visits and statements were surprising to some. But Abe seemed to have understood that the continued presence of American power in the region could only be maintained on the basis of a stronger, more independent Japan. Many suspected Abe of dreaming of a revitalization of Japan's prewar nationalism. But, as Kazuhiko Togo, an ambassador in the Japanese Foreign Ministry noted in the Nelson Report in September,

2014, no American president could indefinitely justify unilateral American defense of Japan to the American public when the interests of the two countries might diverge. Ironically, the nationalist Abe was trying to keep the Americans in the Pacific as part of his effort to keep the Chinese out, or at least at bay.

Three issues were particularly indicative of the trend of the future of the Pax Americana: South Korea-Japan dissension; Chinese-Japanese confrontation over the Senkaku Islands; and a potential choice for America between the current Air-Sea Battle strategy of complete dominance over the East and South China Seas up to the shores of China, and the new, less confrontational Offshore Control strategy anchored on the second island chain rather than the first.

SOUTH KOREA AND JAPAN DON'T TALK TO EACH OTHER

Like Japan, South Korea had a mutual security treaty with the United States that committed America to its unilateral defense. As allies of the United States, South Korea and Japan were indirectly allies of each other, and shared many of the same security concerns. Nevertheless, neither country shared even routine national security intelligence with the other. All exchanges took place through American intermediaries. Finally, in June, 2013, it appeared that an agreement on intelligence sharing had been reached. At the last minute, however, the deal was tabled because of an intense anti-Japanese reaction by the South Korean parliament.

This was triggered by Tokyo's release of a public opinion survey showing that two-thirds of Japanese thought the Takeshima Islands, then administered by South Korea as its own sovereign territory, were rightfully Japanese territory. South Korean politicians saw the release of this survey as insultingly provocative and reneged on the intelligence deal.

To explain just how strange this situation was, some analysts noted that Japan's Self-Defense Forces were committed to defending the Takeshima Islands as Japanese territory, while South Korea's president emphasized that his country would defend them to the death, especially against Japan. The United States, as the most important ally of both countries, was bound by treaty to defend each. Did that mean that the US Navy would go to war with South Korea against Japan while the US Army went to war with Japan against South Korea? Obviously, this was kind of a joke question, but it carried an important hidden meaning. If South Korea and Japan didn't care enough about their own and regional security to settle the issue of these tiny, insignificant islands in order to share national security intelligence, perhaps America should also think differently about how it fulfilled its security treaty commitments.

THE SENKAKU ISLANDS

The second issue that had ramifications for the future of the Pax Americana was China's unilateral and unannounced establishment, on November 23, 2013, of an Air Defense Identification Zone (ADIZ) over the East China Sea that overlapped with Japan's ADIZ in the same area, covering the Senkaku Islands. Beijing required aircraft of any type passing through this zone to file a flight plan with the Chinese authorities and to notify them when entering the space.

Sovereignty disputes over the Senkakus between Japan and China were nothing new. In the wake of World War II, the islands had been kept under US Occupation authority and then turned over to Japan, along with Okinawa, when the islands reverted to Tokyo's authority in 1972. According to accounts by former Japanese diplomat Hiroshi Hashimoto, during their 1972 talks

on restoration of Japan-China diplomatic relations, Chinese Foreign Minister Zhou En Lai and Japanese Prime Minister Kakuei
Tanaka had agreed to leave resolution of the question of ultimate
sovereignty over the islands to later generations. Quiet then prevailed until September of 2012, when the Japanese government
bought three of the islands from their private owner. Ironically,
Tokyo did this to forestall any private plans for economic development of the islands that might antagonize China. Tokyo's
intent to the contrary notwithstanding, Beijing was antagonized,
claiming the purchase was a violation of the agreement between
Zhou and Tanaka, and responded aggressively by sending fishing
boats, patrol craft, and observation planes into the waters and
skies around the islands. At one point, Chinese naval guns even
locked their firing radar on Japanese Self-Defense Force planes.
All of this seemed to be aimed at calling into question Japan's
ability to administer the islands and at forcing Japan to agree to
negotiations over their eventual fate.

Japan had no interest in negotiating as this might have constituted an admission of the possible validity of China's claims.
In the eyes of Tokyo, Japan's ownership of the Senkakus could no
more be disputed than China's ownership of Taiwan.

In this regard, however, a crucial question was what the
United States thought. By treaty, it was obliged to come to Japan's
defense if Japanese territory were attacked. But did the Senkakus
count as Japanese territory? On one hand, Washington recognized that Japan was administering the islands, and said in press
statements in 2013 that it would defend against any effort to
change that administration by force. On the other hand, it repeat-
edly responded to press questions by saying that it had no opinion
on the question of which country's historical claims were most
valid. So the United States would not commit itself completely to
support Japan's position, and that gave a hint of danger to Tokyo.

The imposition of the ADIZ by Beijing probed at this possible gap between Washington and Tokyo. The immediate US reaction was to announce that it would not recognize the zone. To prove the point, it immediately sent two B-52 bombers through the zone without prior notice or flight plans. While that was encouraging for Japan, Washington also directed all US airlines to act in accordance with the Chinese demands. This was less encouraging, as Japan had told its airlines to ignore the Chinese zone requirements. In early December, 2013, Vice President Joe Biden visited first Japan and then China. His mission was to reassure Japan of America's strong commitment to its defense, while also not saying anything that might further disrupt US-China relations. In Beijing, he urged Chinese president Xi Jinping to administer the ADIZ passively, but did not suggest that China cancel the zone. To close observers, the message seemed clear. Washington was reluctant to risk offending China in defense of what Japan considered its right of sovereignty over the Senkakus. This became more worrying for Tokyo in May of 2013, when some Chinese generals stated that Japan also had no right of sovereignty over Okinawa and the other Ryukyu Islands.

In 2012, US President Barack Obama had announced what he called the "Pivot to Asia," indicating a major shift in US foreign policy priorities. The intention was to maintain American hegemony by shifting military resources to the area while also negotiating a web of trade and investment agreements. By the spring of 2014, however, the "pivot" was looking a bit like the pawing of a paper tiger. It wasn't clear what, if any action, the United States would take in defense of Japanese interests. Moreover, it appeared that Washington's reluctance to confront China would only grow as China became ever stronger. This realization opened Japanese eyes and forced Tokyo to reconsider its longtime strategy of relying solely on America for its ultimate defense.

Nor was Japan the only country with concerns. To the Tai-wanese, it had been apparent for some time that the United States was steadily withdrawing from their defense in the face of rising Chinese power. Similar views were also increasingly being expressed in South Korea, where lingering anti-Japanese senti-ments seemed to outweigh concern about China. Indeed, the increasing integration of the Chinese and South Korean econo-mies and a shared interest in avoiding a collapse of the North Korean regime seemed to be pushing China and South Korea into a new alignment.

In April of 2014, President Obama visited Japan and Korea and attempted to counter the doubts about American staying power. At a press conference in Tokyo, he specifically stated that the Senkaku Islands fell under the US defense umbrella. While this muted immediate rumblings of doubt, it did not really address the fundamental issue underlying the doubts: that the interests of the United States and Japan (and other Asian treaty allies) were increasingly divergent. It was a situation in which the treaty responsibilities for the United States to defend its allies tended to be at odds with America's fundamental national inter-ests. This was the issue on the mind of Prime Minister Abe and everyone else in the Asia-Pacific region, and it raised the question of whether everyone needed to develop a new strategy. Certainly that was what the Americans were doing.

AIR-SEA BATTLE OR OFFSHORE CONTROL

By the end of 2014, the third force driving the decline of the Pax Americana was becoming ever more powerful. There was growing confusion in Washington about America's interests in East Asia and the Pacific and about how to deal with the rise of China, which, as one Asian foreign minister said, was like "the appearance of a new sun in the solar system around which all the planets were readjusting their orbits."

One reality facing America was that its particular type of hegemony was peculiarly expensive. Whereas hegemons usually taxed their client states to finance the stability being provided, the United States actually paid for the "privilege" of providing security. It did so directly by employing its own forces to protect allies, but it also did so indirectly by incurring immense trade deficits. Because it was buying more than it was selling to its major allies while also acquiescing to the transfer of its technology as a condition of market access in many cases, it was effectively transferring American jobs to its Asian allies. These costs had long been obscured by the fact that the status of the US dollar as the world's main reserve and transaction currency allowed America to finance its international debt in its own money. Thus, for example, in order to buy oil (priced globally in dollars), Japan had first to make and sell something to earn the necessary dollars; America, on the other hand, had only to print more dollars. As long as the world accepted the dollars in payment and was willing to lend to the United States in dollars, America could remain the hegemon indefinitely. But at this moment, the world had become restive about the arrangement. China was promoting its RMB as a major transaction currency and eventually a reserve currency, and the euro had already displaced the dollar to a certain extent. If the dollar's position weakened further, America's ability to maintain a military establishment as large as the forces of the rest of the world combined would become an impossible burden.

Already a budget deficit arrangement between the White House and Congress that aimed to cut government spending had forced a reduction of US forces and raised the deeper question of whether maintaining the hegemony was worth the cost. A great debate had arisen between proponents of the traditional doctrine of forward dominance, now known as Air-Sea Battle (ASB), and those of a competing doctrine called Offshore Control (OSC).

Underlying this debate was the question of whether China posed a threat to vital American interests. Orthodox advocates of the Pax Americana said yes. They argued that a huge amount of America's trade and overseas investment was in Asia, that the prosperity of the region depended on secure supply routes for Middle East oil and for far-spread supply chains, and that America's treaty obligations compelled it to maintain credibility as the enforcer of regional security. This group saw China as a major potential threat—not a certain threat, but a powerful threat under various circumstances. In particular, the group pointed to the "Anti-Access/Area Denial" (A2/AD) strategy China had been deploying since the entrance of the US aircraft carrier battle groups into the Taiwan Strait in 1996. Under this strategy, China had now deployed extensive batteries of shore-based anti-ship and anti-missile missiles aimed at denying America operational capability as far out from China as the so-called second island chain. (This consisted of the Bonin Islands, the Marianas, and Guam—as opposed to the first island chain, which comprised Okinawa, the Ryukyus, the Philippines, and Malaysia, Singapore, and Indonesia; see map on page 74). If China could effectively push US forces beyond the first island chain to the second island chain, argued the traditionalists, it would render the various US security guarantees useless and spell an end to US hegemony.

To avoid this, the traditionalists claimed it was necessary for the United States to maintain total dominance in the air and sea around China with the ability to strike devastating blows within China if necessary. Thus, the traditionalists developed the concept of ASB. It was essentially an offensive strategy which included the integration of air and naval units using cyber technology with smart weapons and munitions in a networked

MAP SHOWING THE FIRST ISLAND CHAIN
AND THE SECOND ISLAND CHAIN

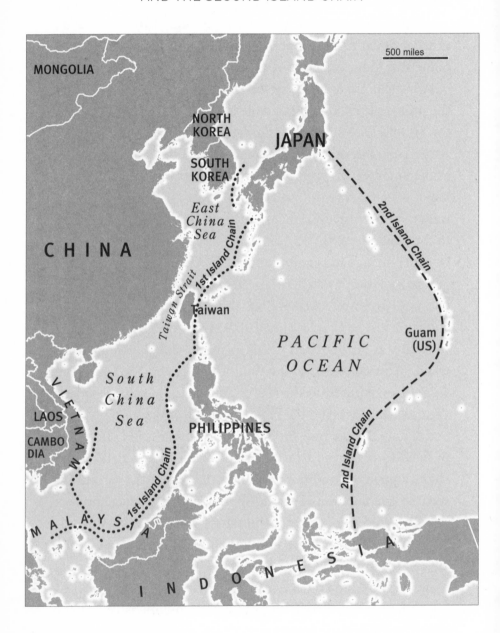

environment visible at all times to commanders in the field as well as to decision-makers in Washington. The objective would be to destroy enemy forces both abroad and at their home bases by penetrating their defenses and obliterating their command and communications systems. It involved the most high-tech and expensive kind of warfare, and it had been adopted as part of US national security doctrine around 2009, before the full effects of the Great Recession of 2008–2010 and the full implications of the long-term US economic outlook were recognized.

By 2014, however, the unorthodox OSC concept had begun to gain consideration. Its proponents began by questioning old premises. They asked what the real threat from China to the United States and Japan was. Aside from eventually recovering Taiwan in some kind of Hong Kong–like arrangement, and possibly gaining the Senkakus and certain islets in the South China Sea, Beijing in 2014 was demonstrating no interest in expanding its territory. It no longer really believed in communism and certainly was no longer bent on spreading communist doctrine around Asia. While the oil lanes through the Strait of Malacca and the South China Sea to Japan and Korea might be vulnerable to Chinese intervention, this was not a problem for the United States, whose oil did not come across the Pacific. Traditionalists voiced concern for US trade and investment in the region. But the unorthodox asked whether these were really being threatened. Would China undermine its own economic growth by cutting off its exports to America or to Japan and South Korea? When they really looked at things, the unorthodox said, they didn't see much of a threat to America or even to its Asian allies. Moreover, to the extent that there might be a threat to the allies, most of them were rich, powerful countries perfectly capable of dealing with all but the most extreme threats themselves.

In the absence of an aggressive threat, the unorthodox pointed out that the ASB approach was itself threatening, and could well become a self-fulfilling prophecy by sparking development of a Chinese threat that did not now exist. In place of ASB, they called for OSC. The idea was to adopt a nonthreatening strategy by abandoning the objective of absolute dominance within the first island chain. Rather than attacking China directly and trying to outgun its massive anti-ship missile arrays in a crisis, the OSC approach, while maintaining contestability within the first island chain by means of submarines, drones, and stealth aircraft, would mainly impose a blockade from the second island chain by cutting off the key inlet and outlet straits. This concept, said the nonconformists, would be far less expensive, far less likely to be perceived by the Chinese as a threat, and far less likely to make America hostage to intra-Asian squabbles when it had no particular interest in their outcome.

OSC was essentially a resurrection of Nixon's Guam doctrine, but at a moment when China was both far more powerful and far less militant than it had been in 1972. In proposing it, the unorthodox made the point that while the US Seventh Fleet and the US Air Force constantly patrolled the waters and airspace just outside China's territorial limits, and while they purposely triggered Chinese electronic warning mechanisms and kept US nuclear-armed submarines lurking in waters close to China, China did not reciprocate. It didn't patrol, for example, the Maui Straits in Hawaii or keep nuclear-armed submarines close to the Golden Gate Bridge in California, or fly aerial patrols from Seattle to San Diego just outside US territorial limits. How, the nonconformists asked, would Americans react if China deployed forces and adopted the same doctrines that the United States had deployed and was using? —Not in a welcoming manner, it was agreed. So why should the Chinese react differently? That question was actually a powerful argument for reconfiguring the old Nixon doctrine under the new rubric of OSC.

REALIGNMENTS AND REBALANCING

While ASB remained the official US doctrine in 2015, and Washington increased the number of ships and weapons systems operating in the western Pacific theater, over the next few years four major developments completely changed the game. One was the accelerating erosion of the American's standard of living. While the richest 1 percent of the population got richer, the relative wages, pensions, and medical care of the rest of the people fell; meanwhile, the aging American infrastructure continued crumbling. It thus became politically impossible to maintain spending on national security when such spending already accounted for half of the world's total. The American people increasingly asked why they should pay to maintain far-flung forces rather than building schools and hospitals at home. In response, political leaders began to cut the defense budget and the size of the military establishment dramatically. Thus the Africa and Southern Commands that oversaw all US national security activity in Africa and Latin America were eliminated, and defense spending was cut from 4.7 percent of GDP to 2.5 percent to bring it more in line with the spending of US allies, most of whom were budgeting from 1 to 2 percent of GDP on defense. Of course, this significantly reduced the capabilities and ambitions of the US national security community. One result was a decision to adopt the OSC strategy and to start moving most US troop and ship deployments from South Korea and Japan to Guam, Hawaii, and San Diego.

The second significant occurrence was China's creation of new ADIZs over large areas of the South China Sea and its

increasing interference with the flights of Japanese civilian airliners in all of the ADIZs. In some cases, Chinese authorities
would refuse to accept Japanese flight plans, causing delays. In
others, Chinese fighter planes would be scrambled and directed
to fly close to the civilian airliners, frightening their passengers. Meanwhile, Chinese harassment of the Senkaku Islands
continued; two of the islands were occupied for several days by
Chinese coastal forces claiming that the Chinese coastguard was
searching for lost fishermen. This again raised the question of
what the United States would do to defend the islands. Of course,
Washington repeated its pledge to fulfill treaty obligations in the
event of an invasion and occupation of Japanese territory. But
what did "invasion" mean, and what did "Japanese territory"
mean, and what did "defend" mean? The Chinese navy said it was
just rescuing stranded fishermen and installing warning signals
to prevent future accidents. Did Washington understand that as
an invasion? Finally, while most people thought "defend" meant
armed intervention to stop aggression, most of Washington
seemed to think it consisted of sending emissaries to Beijing
to beg for withdrawal. In any case, Washington made it clear
to Tokyo that it was not going to risk confrontation with China
over the Senkakus, and that Tokyo could either go to war with
China itself or seek a negotiated or arbitrated deal with China.
Eventually, the Chinese did withdraw, but not before the whole
event had starkly demonstrated the shift in the balance of power
in Asia and the erosion of the Pax Americana.

The third important shift occurred between South Korea,
China, and North Korea. It had actually been presaged at the
time of China's imposition of its ADIZ over the Senkakus in
2013. Initially, this ADIZ had also included Socotra, a submerged
rock claimed by South Korea, which used it for a research station and helipad. Although China had not warned Japan of the

pending ADIZ announcement, it had made an effort to warn South Korea. The initial South Korean reaction had been to tell its airlines to ignore the zone and not to comply with Chinese directives, while creating a new zone of its own that overlapped with the Chinese zone. South Korea also announced new naval exercises in the area of Socotra rock just to emphasize its jurisdiction. At the time, China said that it would work things out with South Korea through quiet consultations. Eventually the two countries did agree to rearrange their zones to avoid overlapping. This was obviously a very different path than that taken by China and Japan.

In fact, for some time South Korea's interests had been diverging from those of both Japan and the United States. While formally allied with the United States, South Korea continued to harbor ill will toward Japan over the events of the Second World War. It also received preferential treatment from China, with whose economy it was highly integrated as a result of vast cross-border investment and mutual supply chains. South Korea was a key source of high technology for China, as well as of parts and components, and China was South Korea's largest single market. But with Chinese wages rising rapidly, South Korea's giant business conglomerates, the *chaebol*, needed a new source of inexpensive labor to keep their products competitive in global markets. The rise of the new North Korean leader Kim Jong-un presented an opportunity to both China and South Korea. Neither country liked the North Korean regime, and both feared its potential for doing something really dangerous. On the other hand, neither of them wanted North Korea to collapse, nor did they want to occupy the country and take responsibility for rebuilding it.

Chinese president Xi Jinping took the lead in facilitating a three-cornered arrangement that China and South Korea hoped would solve their problems. China made clear to Kim that it would guarantee his security and buy North Korean exports. But this was under the condition that Kim would mothball his nukes, under the threat of personal elimination. South Korea would offer an open market, and would undertake to have its companies invest and move production of things like autos and smartphones to the north in a common-market type of arrangement. In this way, the total Korean economy would have almost as many people as the Japanese economy and, with a combination of advanced technology and low average wages, would be far more competitive. Of course, this alignment greatly diminished the rationale for the US-South Korea Mutual Defense Treaty.

The fourth and final event was Okinawa's 2017 vote for independence from Japan. While it came as a shock to Tokyo, this action had been brewing for a long time. The largest of the Ryukyu Islands and the center of the old Ryukyu kingdom and civilization, Okinawa had not been fully integrated into Japan until 1879, and after the conclusion of World War II had not been returned to Japan by the US Occupation until 1972. It had always been considered to be outside the main Japanese islands, and "mainlanders" tended to view Okinawans as inferior, a view strengthened by the fact that Okinawa was the poorest of Japan's prefectures and significantly dependent on subsidies from Tokyo. A major cause of unhappiness in Okinawa had been that the bulk of the US bases in Japan had been crammed into Okinawa, where their operations, noise, and the behavior of their troops were major disturbances. Promises from Tokyo and long negotiations between local governors, US generals, and Japanese political leaders never seemed to result in any action.

For a long time, the citizens of Okinawa had put up with this because they needed the revenue generated by the US troops and by the subsidies from Tokyo. But with the growth of the Chinese economy, Okinawa had become a major destination for Chinese tourists, as well as for Chinese investors in the real-estate and leisure industries. Confident that Okinawa could do well economically on its own, frustrated by the repeated non-fulfillment of a series of promises by the US to remove its bases, and quietly encouraged by suggestions from Beijing that China might be interested in paying for the occasional use of military bases there, the long latent Okinawa independence movement gained control of the legislature and pushed the independence vote through. The immediate reaction in Tokyo was to consider sending in the Self-Defense Forces, but warnings from both Washington and Beijing cooled that instinct. Eventually, a real deal to shift US bases and to give Okinawa more autonomy was worked out and the legislature rescinded the independence vote. But the whole episode clearly foreshadowed the direction in which affairs were likely to move.

WHITHER AMERICA, WHITHER JAPAN?

In the wake of these events and of a balanced budget agreement in the US Congress that drastically reduced military spending, Washington made the decision to shift away from the ASB formula and fully adopt the OSC concept. This meant the withdrawal of US troops from South Korea and Okinawa and from all bases on the main islands of Japan by 2022. The home port of the Seventh Fleet would be moved from Yokosuka, near Tokyo, to Guam; but the United States would also make visiting and repair-base arrangements with the Philippines, Vietnam, and Singapore so that some of the fleet would always be in those locations.

Japan's initial response to these decisions was fear, anger, and a sense of abandonment. There was much talk of Japan developing nuclear weapons. But the Revitalization Commission forged a middle path between the initially nationalistic reaction and the continued devotion to the pacifism prioritized by most Japanese. It proposed in 2017 to abolish Article 9 (the "no-war" clause of Japan's constitution) and to give Japan the same security powers as all other countries. It also called for a doubling of defense spending to a little over 2 percent of GDP annually, and suggested that the country dramatically increase the size of its naval and air forces. Japan's rocket technology was already advanced, and merely needed to be tweaked a bit to be militarily ready; and, of course, the country had access to the latest US weapons. Despite all the discussion of going nuclear, the Commission advised against doing so for the moment. That decision could always be revisited, but the Commission felt that quickly becoming a nuclear power could prove more risky than beneficial for Japan.

Rather than focusing too much attention on military affairs, the Commission called for diplomacy. Japan, it said, should seek broader and deeper alliance arrangements rather than relying solely on the United States. Commission emissaries visited South Korea, the Philippines, Vietnam, Indonesia, Singapore, Malaysia, Thailand, Australia, and India to take soundings. In most cases, they found cautious interest but also lingering doubts. The South Koreans, for example, were in a strange position. Culturally and economically, they were more like Japan and the Japanese than any other country or people. Yet they had become partially aligned with China, their ancient enemy. Still, they did not want to be dominated by China. Some kind of arrangement with Japan sounded potentially good to them. —But how, they asked, could they ally with Japan as long as some Japanese school textbooks denied key facts of World War II, or as long as leading Japanese politicians and commentators either denied or justified the complicity of the Japanese Imperial Army in the compulsion of Korean women to act as "comfort women" during World War II. Yes, the South Koreans agreed, Japan had apologized numerous times, and they also agreed that their own politicians were guilty of keeping old resentments alive for political purposes. And while they agreed that such posturing should be stopped, they also emphasized how Japan's apologies had too often been followed by actions such as reinterpretation of the wording of those apologies. Take some dramatic steps to reverse all this, they urged, and we will be very interested in stronger ties with you. While the South Korean case was different from others, all of the countries the emissaries visited expressed doubts of some sort about closer ties with Japan.

After hearing and considering the reports of the emissaries, the Commission suggested four steps. The first was to copy the German-French example. To overcome ill will after World War II, France and Germany had created a joint panel of scholars and experts to write the history textbooks that would be used in the schools of both countries. In this way, potential disputes over the past had been avoided. The Commission felt that in a similar way, Japan could overcome lingering resentment about the war in Asia by also establishing binational or multinational expert panels to write new textbooks. The Commission called for having these completed before 2025.

The second recommendation was to create an International Memorial for World War II that would demonstrate the origins, actions, and settlement of the war in full detail and from the viewpoints of the key antagonists. Like the textbooks, this memorial was to be created by an international panel of experts from all the countries touched by the war, as a way of preventing past history from overshadowing present negotiations and possible alliances. The memorial was also to be completed by 2025, and was to subsume all other war-memorial shrines in Japan.

The third step was for Japan to renounce claims to the Take-shima Islands. The fourth was the previously mentioned offer to submit the issue of sovereignty over the Senkaku Islands to the World Court for arbitration. As the Takeshimas had little value, by agreeing to recognize South Korean authority over them, Japan would remove a big obstacle to cooperation with South Korea at little real cost. By suggesting arbitration on the Senkakus, Japan would be seen as reasonable and peace-seeking and might arrive at an acceptable agreement with China.

These measures immediately unleashed a vast wave of relief, gratitude, warmth, and good feeling toward Japan from all of Asia. It was this attitudinal shift, more than anything else, that made it possible for Japan to conclude the cooperation and mutual security treaties with South Korea, the Philippines, Vietnam, Malaysia, and Indonesia that are in effect today. With the strong assistance of the United States, what has emerged today in 2050 is a much more conventional and equal alliance system, as well as a stronger one than that which prevailed under the American hegemony. The US security treaties with Japan, South Korea, the Philippines, and others have all been maintained, and the South Korean and Japanese army, naval, and air force establishments have continued their cooperation and joint training with the US forces. But now the Japanese forces are fully capable of taking action in all arenas. So Japan has become a "normal" country that equally shares risk and vulnerability with its allies and is thereby a more valuable ally itself.

The final new development was the evolution of security cooperation between the United States, India, Indonesia, Australia and Japan, and the conclusion of mutual security treaties between these powers in the late 2020s. This completed the Grand Alliance that has secured peace and growth over half the world for the past quarter century.

CHAPTER 4

Women to The Rescue

A s you have been traveling around Japan and enjoying the spectacular cherry-blossom season of this mid-century year of 2050, you have noticed that something about the Japanese population looks different since the last time you were here, in 2015. There are many more children and youths crowding the stations and riding their bicycles along the streets, zipping past healthy-looking elderly men and women who dodge the bikes with an agility that belies their age. In the evenings, when the sidewalks are crowded with workers leaving their offices, you notice that there are as many women in smart business suits as there are men, something that had already made an impression on you when you attended a conference with a Japanese client company yesterday. That conference had been chaired by a female CEO, and you were surprised to see that women and non-Japanese employees of the company outnumbered the Japanese men around the conference table. Your Japanese host at the company declined your suggestion of an after-work beer because he had to collect his children from the daycare center. So you left the office alone and went in search of a drink by yourself, but instead of streets lined with bars, you could only find streets lined with family restaurants, where mothers, fathers, and young children were enjoying dinner together.

Of course, this is all in stark contrast to the situation that faced the Extraordinary National Revitalization Commission back in 2016. The nation had started to shrink in 2005, when it ended the year with 10,000 fewer persons than it had had at the year's start. By 2011, the population had fallen by 202,000 per year. From there, the decline only continued to accelerate, because each year there were fewer women of childbearing age, fewer couples getting married, and a steady increase in the average age at which women were having their first child—at about the age of thirty-one in 2016. As noted in chapter 2, official forecasts in 2015 suggested the population might fall to as low as 85 million by 2050. That forecast suggested the theoretical possibility that the annual population decline could reach one million, and that the last Japanese person could die in the year 2135. Long before that time, however, Japan would cease to function as a viable society.

This was particularly true because the only thing aging and shrinking faster than Japan's overall population was its workforce. From 87 million workers in 2010, this figure was on track to fall to 52 million by 2050, about the same number of workers as at the end of World War II. With that rate of shrinkage, just maintaining standards of living, let alone achieving any increase, would require unbelievable increases in productivity. Pension funds would quickly be exhausted. There would be ever fewer consumers, and the number of young people available to fill the ranks of the Self-Defense Forces would fall just at the moment when the potential for military conflict with China appeared to be rising and the relative strength of the United States declining. The problem had both immediate and longer-term aspects, but in both cases the Revitalization Commission realized that the key to the future was in the hands of Japan's women.

WOMEN, WORK, AND BIRTH

To maintain its economic growth and standards of living in the immediate future, Japan badly needed more of its women to both join the workforce and have more children. In this regard, Japan lagged badly behind all other advanced countries with the exception of South Korea. For instance, the average female participation rate in the workforce for the member countries of the Organization for Economic Cooperation and Development (OECD) in 2011 was about 70 percent, while Japan's was only about 62 percent. It was calculated that raising the Japanese level to the OECD average would increase GDP by about 4 percent. Raising it further to the 76–78 percent level of northern European countries would add another 4 percent to the GDP. According to a 2013 Goldman Sachs estimate, Japan's GDP would be 15 percent larger if women of prime age (twenty-five to fifty-four) participated in the labor force at the same 80 percent level as its men.

The need for more women in the workforce had been discussed and researched around the world for decades. Many developed countries had begun experiencing declining birthrates and a shrinking workforce since the advent of the contraceptive pill in the 1960s. At the same time, the rising costs of raising and educating children adequately for the modern era had made two-income families a necessity. Yet most countries had avoided providing assistance to working mothers, with the result that women were not able to have as many children as they might like.

However, beginning with Sweden in the 1980s and then with France in the mid-1990s, some countries had managed to stabilize and even reverse these demographic trends. Partly they did so through increased family assistance such as child-support payments, child-care programs, and generous maternal and paternal work leave periods. Partly it was also due to the adoption of civil unions and of legislation to ensure equal rights for children whether born in or out of wedlock. In view of these trends, it seemed logical that Japan should also focus on promoting and getting rid of all impediments to the participation of women in the workforce while they were also having children. In other words, making it easy for women to work during their childbearing years would make them likely to bear more children. Of course, it was also true that Sweden, France, the UK, and the United States also benefited from a significant inflow of immigrants who tended to have somewhat higher birthrates.

ISSUES IN JAPAN

The Revitalization Commission was aware that the biggest complaint of virtually all Japanese women and of many professional men was lack of adequate child care. Exhausted parents complained of endless hours spent dropping one child at one center and then another child at another center in the morning, and then reversing the route in the evening. This was a manifestation of the fragmented but highly regulated child-care system. In fact, there were two well-established systems. The state-run day-care centers, known as *hoikuen*, provided full day care for working mothers of children up to age six. These were administered and funded by the Ministry of Health, Labor, and Welfare. Alongside these day-care centers were state-run preschools, known as *yochien*, that provided care for only part of the day for children from three to six years of age. These were administered and funded by the Ministry of Education and Science, and were primarily intended for children of traditional single-earner families with a stay-at-home mother. Both systems were highly regulated, with requirements for a certain amount of floor space, specified training of personnel, designated equipment, and so forth. The result was a combination of crowding in the *hoikuen* and under-utilization of the *yochien*, where only 70 percent of the seats were actually taken. But for bureaucratic reasons it was impossible to switch *hoikuen* users to the *yochien*. Furthermore, in spite of maintaining two separate systems, Japan was actually spending less than the United States, Germany, or the UK, and far less than Sweden or France, on care for children up to the age of six.

All the evidence showed that the availability of child care played a major role in the decision of women to work or not to work. Studies indicated that the birth of a child reduced women's labor-force participation rates by 30 percent. For women living with parents or other relatives who could help care for the child, workforce participation rates were far higher. Thus, these reports emphasized the need for greatly expanded child-care capacity.

To its credit, the Abe administration had introduced plans for expansion of child-care programs in 2014. But a real-life lesson on how to do this was actually provided by an experiment in Yokohama. In 2010, the city had defied central government authorities, taking matters into its own hands. It had set a target of reducing child-care waiting lists to zero by 2013. To do so, it had established its own liberal regulations for day-care centers and allowed for privatization, enabling entrepreneurs to establish privately run centers so long as they met certain broad basic standards. The result was an explosion in the number of new day-care centers and the elimination of the waiting lists by the target date; the city's budget increased by only 1.7 percent, while the number of children in child-care facilities rose by more than 25 percent. In response to this, in July 2014 the Abe administration had announced the Gakudo program. This would include provisions for increased after-school activities so that as many as 300,000 students could be kept at school until the end of the workday, when parents could pick them up after leaving their offices. The measures also included recognition of parents as "supporting child-care professionals," authorized to conduct certain school-related activities.

As important as it was, child care was only the first and most obvious obstacle to female labor-force participation. Further study had revealed that a second barrier was the structure of the tax system. Like many countries, Japan had long indirectly compensated women for being housewives by taxing families rather than individuals and providing tax exemptions for the heads of household as long as spousal income did not exceed ¥1.03 million (roughly US$8,000). This was also the income level that many private companies set as the threshold for pension and other benefits. This pay level was often referred to as the "barrier to full-time female employment." In a significant forward step, the Abe administration had largely removed this part of the tax law in 2014 to encourage more employment of women outside the home.

Nevertheless, strong disincentives for women to work remained beyond the lack of child care and the outdated tax policy, such as ingrained corporate practices and societal attitudes. For example, in various surveys, long, inflexible working hours and lack of employer support were actually the second most important reasons cited by women for not working. As Japan continued to age and more women needed to care for elderly parents, this problem of lack of support was bound to become worse.

Almost equally problematic was the extremely low percentage of female managers in Japanese companies. Only 9 percent of Japanese managers were women, compared to, for example, 43 percent in the United States. This meant a huge lack of role models for women and thus a lack of encouragement for women to take or stay with full-time professional employment. There were several causes for this discrepancy, but a key one was the structure of Japanese careers. Upon graduation from university or professional school, young people in Japan were recruited by companies for what were implicitly lifelong jobs. For women, the key decision at this juncture was between the career-track positions usually taken by men, and non-career-track positions. Career-track positions paid more, entailed an investment in training during a lifetime of work, and came with a lump-sum retirement payment, a pension, and other benefits. Non-career-track jobs paid less, came with no guarantees and entailed simpler tasks with much less training; these were mostly filled by women. For career-track employees, there were long-term binding arrangements which provided employment security but also obligated the employee to stay with the company and to move wherever they were sent by the company.

The whole system was predicated on the assumption that women generally would not enter a full-time business or profes-sional career, and was designed to minimize the potential cost to the company of early retirement by women. It was a male-centric system in every respect. And, of course, it had become a self-ful-filling prophecy. Because the system operated on the assumption that women would not be a central part of it, they weren't—even when they were desperately needed. And even when women did get into career-track positions with the same employment con-tracts as men, advancement tended to be slower. Surveys showed that a majority of top-performing male employees were one or more steps ahead of top-performing female employees in the promotion cycle. The result of all this was that median wages for Japanese women were 28 percent less than those of men, a dif-ference that was twice as great as that found in other advanced economies. While it had become global common sense that firms with more women and a diversified mix of board members tended to outperform those made up mostly of men, Japan continued to lag behind in female participation.

Actually, Japan's labor-force participation by females in their early to mid twenties was similar to that of other advanced economies. But the participation rate dropped sharply as Japanese women reached their late twenties and thirties, reflecting the fact that roughly 60 percent of Japanese women quit the workforce entirely after giving birth to their first child. Partly this was because of the factors noted above, but it was also due to the very weak support system for working mothers. In the first place, laws and corporate policies regarding maternity leave and child-care leave in Japan provided far shorter leave times than in most other advanced economies. In 2013, Abe had announced three years of maternity leave, but this was to be available only to one parent. In Japanese society, such a long leave would almost surely be taken by the mother, who would then have difficulty returning to work at the end of the leave because she no longer "fit" into the work group, having been seen by co-workers to have left it. Moreover, leave was only available to "regular" workers—those with permanent contracts. "Irregular" workers, meaning those with temporary contracts, were not eligible. As women made up a large percentage of irregular workers, and because the number of irregular workers in the workforce was growing, this meant that fewer and fewer mothers were getting paid leave periods, and that those leave periods were becoming shorter and shorter. If the mothers exceeded their leave limits, their jobs would not be held for them. Beyond this was the problem of lack of support from husbands. Parental leave was also available to fathers, but less than 3 percent of Japanese fathers actually took the leave available to them, as it was considered unmanly and somewhat disloyal to the company to do so. By comparison, 70 percent of Swedish fathers took the full extent of their legal leave. Further-more, Japanese fathers spent less time helping around the home than fathers in many other advanced economies. This reflected not only male attitudes toward gender roles, but also the fact that the long-established custom at Japanese corporations was for executives to work far beyond the limit of the legally established hours and to engage in social activities after leaving the office. This, in turn, reflected the lack of adequate employee evalua-tion systems at Japanese corporations. In lieu of such systems, employees were judged on the amount of time they spent on work and work-related activities. That their time might be better spent in supporting their wives and children was not a consideration. Yet the Revitalization Commission came to see from the expe-rience of other advanced countries such as Sweden, France, and the United States that longer parental leaves and higher home support by fathers greatly increased the rate of long-term female workforce participation. Of course, this was in the context of a legal structure that provided rights for the worker to return to his or her job after a long leave period. This highlighted for the Commission the need for such mandatory rules in Japan.

CHILDBEARING AND IMMIGRATION

An obvious matter of attention in any consideration of falling birth rates is abortion. About 200,000 abortions were performed in Japan in 2011. About 1.05 million Japanese babies were born every year at that time. Thus if there had been no abortions, the Japanese fertility rate would automatically have increased by about 20 percent. Of course, the Revitalization Commission knew it would be impossible to bring the abortion rate to zero, but investigation of the circumstances and causes of abortion showed that it often involved young, unmarried women wishing to avoid the social stigma of single motherhood and discrimination from Japanese employment, taxation, housing, social services, and other systems.

The fact that child adoption was rare in Japan also contributed to the problem. For example, in the United States the rate was 170 adoptions per 10,000 births. In Japan it was six. An important element in this was the traditional *koseki* family registration system. This ancient system recorded all the significant events in one's life, such as birth, marriage, and divorce, in a village or town registry. This registry was organized by family under the name of the father or male head of each household. Children with no legal father, for example, were registered in the household of the mother's father. Much of the genealogical record of the family was stored in this system and the information was readily available to outsiders. The *koseki* system thus acted as a powerful force preventing the changes Japan so desperately needed to avoid a demographic disaster.

Another issue was that of extending the actual fertility period of women. On the one hand, women needed to delay marriage and childbearing in order to establish an employment and professional record. On the other, they had a finite period of time before menopause, and by delaying childbearing they minimized the time during which they could have children. One way to extend that time, however, was to create commercial egg banks where women could take some of their healthy eggs when they were young and store them frozen for use in their forties or even fifties. Then, having established themselves in jobs and careers, they could later withdraw the eggs and give birth to the number of children they desired. Indeed, by 2015 some Japanese women were donating eggs to egg banks in Thailand; other Japanese women would obtain them in order to carry out a late pregnancy. These women were going to Thailand to do this because the procedure, while not illegal in Japan, was frowned upon and discouraged there.

There was a further aspect of the negative demographic trends affecting women. A foreigner living in Japan could obtain a visa for a young woman to come to Japan from a place like the Philippines and to live in his or her household as a domestic help. But no Japanese could obtain the same visa for a household help. The obvious assumption behind this policy was that foreigners and their helps would be temporary residents, while helps living with Japanese were likely to be permanent residents who would become a burden on Japanese society. Of course, another way of looking at it was that a foreign help living with a Japanese household could free the woman of the household to join the workforce. But this was not the thinking that prevailed in Japan, which had always strictly limited immigration. By 2014 the country had begun suffering an actual net outflow of emigrants, as its young people—especially its young women—left at an accelerating rate, sometimes looking for a more open work environment and sometimes taking children for schooling to countries like Australia, New Zealand, Canada, and the United States, where they could learn to speak English fluently.

These trends posed a large question to the study groups sent by the Commission to investigate the practices and experiences of other highly developed countries. Should Japan consider changing its long historical taboo on any significant permanent entry of non-Japanese into its society? There was great fear of disruption to the homogeneous, tightly knit, delicately balanced Japanese social structure. Would foreign immigrants have the same sense of community, shared destiny, mutual obligation, and the need for self-sacrifice in the face of crisis and disaster? Japan had experimented a bit in the late twentieth century with bringing in immigrants from among the Japanese who had emigrated to Brazil long ago. But it had turned out that the Japanese Brazilians seemed to be more Brazilian than Japanese, and the experiment had proven difficult. It was clear, however, that immigration was playing a major role in revitalizing stagnating societies and economies like those of the UK, France, Germany, and Scandinavia. Indeed, there was even evidence that slightly increased rates of immigration were playing a very positive role in South Korea, especially in bringing technological and business talent, as well as inexpensive health- and elder-care providers.

Yet further consideration revealed another very interesting and potentially important detail. Population projections in 2015 showed France eclipsing Germany by 2030. How could this be possible when both countries were experiencing about the same rate of immigration and Germany's current total population was 25 percent larger than that of France? The answer was that France, through various family support policies, had succeeded in raising its domestic fertility rate to 2.03 children per woman, or just about the 2.1 needed for population replacement. But Germany's fertility rate had fallen to 1.36, far below the replacement rate. Thus, Germany would have needed a higher rate of immigration just to keep its total population from declining.

THE SITUATION ABROAD

These kinds of data, along with the fact that many other countries faced problems similar to those of Japan, led the Commission to send study groups to thoroughly investigate the experiences of France, the Scandinavian countries, the UK, Germany, Italy, the Netherlands, and the United States. France had the longest experience with trying to stimulate greater family formation, among the highest rates of female workforce participation, and the highest birthrates. Prompted by national security concerns about a gap between German and French birthrates, France had fully launched a system of state payments to parents in the 1930s; by the 1960s, the French fertility rate of 2.87 was well above Germany's 2.51. But, like most other advanced countries in the late 1960s, France experienced a steadily falling birthrate, which reached 1.73 in 1993. This was still far above Germany's 1.24, but it was well below the 2.1 rate of population replacement.

Fearing short- to medium-term economic stagnation and long-term extinction, Paris adopted perhaps the world's most generous package of family support measures. For one thing, it greatly liberalized the definition of family to include unmarried people living together, and even a mother and child living with no father present, or a father and child with no mother present. This was of great significance in a society in which more than 50 percent of children were born out of wedlock. Thus, mothers in 2016 received the equivalent of about US$1,300 as a kind of bonus payment in the seventh month of every pregnancy. Then there were smaller annual payments until the child's third birthday. Fully paid maternity leave from work—with the guarantee of a return to the same position—was available for sixteen weeks per child for the first two children and twenty-six weeks in the case of a third child. Mothers could split the time, if they wished, with their partners, but the father received an additional eleven days of paid leave that only he could take. Mothers also received a monthly stipend that varied from about US$200 per month to as much as US$450 per month, depending on the number of children. Any mother who left the workforce in order to stay at home to care for a third child received a monthly stipend of about US$1200 per month on top of the other standard payments and benefits. A mother who desired more time off after the sixteen or twenty-six weeks of paid maternity leave could receive further leave of up to two and a half years without pay, but with the guarantee of being able to return to her job. If she had a second child in the meantime, she could receive as much as five years of unpaid leave, with the ability to return to her job still guaranteed.

When French mothers returned to work, a national child-care program (*crèche*) was available for all children between the ages of two months and three years. There was a fee, but it was on a sliding scale based on income, and ranged from about US$6 per hour to around US$.50 per hour. Each *crèche* had a child psychologist and pediatrician either on staff or on call, and at least 50 percent of the staff was required to have a diploma in early child care and education. The *crèches* were open from 7:30 a.m. until 7 or even 8 p.m. The program was so popular that it was used by a very large percentage of French families, of all income levels, with a child under three years old. However, for those who preferred not to use it or to use it part-time, there was a program under which the government provided tax incentives to support the hiring of a nanny to care for the child at home.

For children aged three to six, the government provided a preschool program (*école maternelle*) from 8:30 a.m. until 4:30 p.m., which was often connected to a *crèche* that provided care until later in the evening. In addition to these benefits, there was an income tax deduction that rose according to the number of children a person had. The tax benefit for a third child was twice the amount credited for the first two. Couples with three children also received a 10 percent increase in their pension benefits, and railway ticket prices were reduced by three-fourths for couples with three or more children. This all came on top of the national health-care service that provided what had been ranked by health-care professionals as the world's best overall health care at very low cost. Furthermore, the French system prorated all pay and benefits for part-time work, so that a part-time worker would be included in the pension, health care, unemployment, and paid sick leave benefits in the same way as a full-time worker, although at a lower rate. Finally, everyone in France was guaranteed five weeks of paid vacation every year.

In sum, the French support system guaranteed that a person with a child did not have to worry that taking care of the child could mean losing a job or losing welfare, educational, health, or pension benefits. Indeed, a mother or father could be assured of always having sufficient financial support and the opportunity of employment regardless of marital or family status.

But there was more than just government support. In France, businesses generally did not discriminate against hiring women—indeed, quite the opposite. It had been mandated by law in the 1990s that at least 40 percent of the directors of major corporations be women. And even at smaller corporations, the number of women directors could not be fewer than the number of men minus two. Thus, if the board consisted of three people, at least one of them had to be a woman. It had been inculcated into the general culture of the country to accept young women starting a career and interrupting it several times while having children and raising a family. It was understood that French women would take time off before and after they gave birth, and that they could elect to remain at home for six months or longer if circumstances warranted that. Businesses accepted this pattern simply as the cost of keeping qualified women in their employ. The rhythm of the French workweek also helped women with families. They were allowed to work Mondays and Tuesdays; take Wednesdays off to be with their children, because this day was typically a half-day in French schools; and then work Thursdays and Fridays.

One possible weakness of the French system was that it was heavily focused on women's role in family formation and did very little to foster men's responsibility to participate in child rearing. Perhaps some might have argued that this was unnecessary in view of the close-knit family relationships in France and the relatively wide distribution of child-rearing responsibilities. Still, in terms of creating an environment supportive of child rearing, it was notable that French men were, overall, less engaged than their wives.

Here was where the Nordic formula (referring to Norway, Sweden, Denmark, Finland, and the Netherlands) offered a better example. All over Scandinavia there was a strong emphasis on gender equality. For example, since the turn of the twenty-first century Norway had required that corporate boards of directors consist of 50 percent women. Similar standards prevailed in the other Nordic countries. Importantly, taxes were levied and benefits granted on an individual basis rather than on the traditional family basis. Thus, a wife was not dependent on her husband's income. Indeed, in these countries as in France, children were treated equally whether or not the mother was formally married. At the same time, the father received benefits similar to those of the mother. In Norway, for example, he would receive ten weeks of paid paternity leave, while in Sweden each parent was expected to take at least two months of the thirteen-month paid maternity and paternity leave. In other words, if they wished, the parents could each take six months of leave and then decide which one would get the extra month. Here again, taxation was on an individual rather than on a family basis, and all over Scandinavia there was a strong emphasis on the need for fathers to share the work of the household and of rearing the children. In this way, it was thought, women would be as able as men to work and contribute to the economy, while also being willing to have more children because the economic penalties related to bearing and rearing children would be greatly reduced. In short, the Scandinavians believed that making it easy and attractive for women to be in the workforce also naturally led to a higher birthrate.

When the study team turned to the example of the UK, it found that a country's fertility rate is not forever fixed, and can even change quite quickly. The UK had entered the twenty-first century with a fertility rate of only 1.6, but this had risen rapidly to about 2.0 by 2012. To some extent, this reflected the adoption by Britain of many of the elements of the French and Scandinavian plans. But mainly it was a manifestation of the wave of immigration that had occurred in Britain in the late twentieth century, when the UK essentially threw its borders open. The new immigrants included many young women from societies that tended to have larger families than the British norm, and this dramatically increased the overall fertility rate.

At first glance, the example of the United States appeared to teach the same lesson as that of the UK, namely that relatively easy immigration can raise a nation's fertility rates. But at second glance, there was another element that confirmed some of the Nordic success. Much more than most other countries, perhaps owing to its pioneer heritage, the United States had a tradition of husbands sharing the household and child-rearing chores. The United States also had widely available and relatively affordable child care and preschool program availability. This was not because there were strong publicly funded programs, but rather because there was no particular regulation of these services, so the private sector could provide them in a for-profit, competitive environment. Thus, even though it had nothing like the French and Scandinavian family support programs, and spent only a fraction of what those governments spent on child and family support, the United States had a relatively high female labor-force participation rate—about 70 percent—and a relatively high fertility rate of 2.04. It was also true, however, that this rate was somewhat dependent on recent immigrants having more children than the average of the country as a whole.

The study team found that the German example was important in that it supplied a kind of negative confirmation. While Germany had adopted many of the generous parental leave systems and tax- and child-benefit practices of France and the Scandinavian countries, it did not have anything like the extensive public child care and preschool programs of those countries. Consequently, the risk and costs of having children were higher and the fertility rate was much lower. This was especially telling because, as noted earlier, Germany and France both had about the same rate of immigration. So the effect of immigrants having more children sooner than longtime citizens would be about the same in each country. Yet Germany had a far lower fertility rate than France, suggesting that, even if it were acceptable, immigration alone might not be sufficient to turn around the fertility trajectory without the availability of adequate child care.

The importance of inexpensive child care and availability of preschool programs was also reinforced by the Italian example. Italy's fertility rate of 1.41 was just barely ahead of Japan's 1.39, and it had much the same family and child policies and programs as Japan. To be sure, it provided long parental leave periods with full pay, and even longer periods with partial pay. It also provided some cash payments for having children, along with some tax benefits, although these were not as generous as those of Germany, France, and the Nordic countries. But inexpensive child-care and preschool facilities were not widely available in Italy—even less so than in Germany. And like Japan, Italy placed the lion's share of the work of taking care of elders on married women, who were expected to care not only for their own parents but also for their parents-in-law. Thus, as in Japan, the costs to women of marriage and childbearing were relatively high, while at the same time their education level and the potential career rewards for that education was also high. As in Japan, women were increasingly tending to opt for higher pay without the burdens of marriage and child rearing.

Because of the expressed desire of many Japanese women for part-time work, the Commission looked with particular interest at the example of the Netherlands, where the female labor-force participation rate, which had been lower than that of Japan in 1970, was now one of the highest in the world. What the Dutch had done, the Commission discovered, was to dramatically reduce the differences between part-time and full-time workers, beginning in 1980. Thus, for example, the median hourly wage was the same for part- and full-time workers, as were social security benefits, employment protection, and work rules. In addition, it was easy to shift from full-time to part-time work or from part-time to full-time. Indeed, under the Working Hours Adjustment Act of 2000, Dutch workers, after one year of continuous employment with the same employer, had the right to change their working hours. Thus there was almost complete flexibility in the Netherlands between full-time and part-time work, and that led to a dramatic increase in female labor-force participation.

An obvious question was the cost of all these different programs and systems. In France, if all of the direct and indirect forms of family aid were counted, the country was spending over 5 percent of its GDP. This was twice what it was spending on defense and nearly three times what it was spending on research and development. Clearly the French approach was working to some extent, but it was very expensive—as was that of the Nordic countries, although Sweden had reduced its costs to about 3.7 percent of its GDP by privatizing parts of the child-care and preschool programs. The Commission found it very interesting that the British system was also quite expensive, consuming by some estimates as much as 25 percent and certainly not less than 10 percent of the British government budget. These payments amounted to three to six times more than the country was spending on defense or research and development.

The study group obviously wondered whether there was a way to get the French result without the French level of spending. The Nordic variant indicated that it might be possible, and the different examples of Germany and the United States, as well as some academic studies, seemed to confirm this. Germany spent almost as much as France, but had a much weaker system of child care and preschool training. The United States, in contrast, spent only about 1.3 percent of its GDP on family-oriented programs, but it had a robust private system of child care and preschool programs. The conclusion, which was backed up by several academic studies, seemed to be that countries with some degree of immigration, good child-care and preschool provision, flexible work schedules, high status for women workers and managers, and security for women, in conjunction with the sharing of household and family responsibilities by men, tended to be the countries with the highest fertility rates.

RECOMMENDATIONS: NEW LAWS AND NEW POLICIES

In the light of all of its investigations and findings, the Commission at the end of 2016 proposed a comprehensive reform package with three primary sets of new laws and policies. One was aimed at making it easier and more attractive for women to work, and at encouraging more workers of both genders to join the workforce in Japan. This included creating role models for women by having corporations hire more women as lifelong employees and appointing more women to their boards. The second was aimed particularly at fostering childbearing by elimi-nating social and economic burdens on women. These measures included abolishing the *koseki* system, lifting restrictions on visas for domestic helpers, making adoption easier, and giving women the right to return to work after a long maternity leave. The third set of regulations focused on measures to attract more foreign workers to Japan. This reform package saw Japan's spending in these areas rise from 1.2 percent of GDP to 3 percent.

The Commission understood the key lesson that higher female participation in the workforce actually led to higher fertility if that participation was based primarily on women having the desire and flexibility to work, rather than being forced to work for the family to survive. Thus a major part of the package, which was mandated by law, included Nordic-style parental leave periods and very flexible provisions for full-time or part-time work. Specifically, it called for shared parental leave of twelve months at full pay from the company, with another twelve months available at one-third pay. Here, the Commission also added something uniquely Japanese. It called for elder-care leave with provisions similar to those of parental leave. In both cases, the leave could be divided as partners saw fit. Further-more, at least three months of paternity leave was made man-datory. Dutch-style flexible work provisions were also included. Thus, Japanese women or men could work part time with the same benefits and guarantees as full-time workers—prorated according to the hours they worked. Part-time workers also had the possibility of switching to full-time work at any time, while full-timers could change to part time.

The package also included elimination of tax distortions that effectively discriminated against women, and changed the structure of the tax system from one that levied taxes on fami-lies to one that levied taxes on individuals. In addition, vacation times were lengthened to four weeks annually, and the taking of vacation was made mandatory. Large companies were required to close work at 5 p.m., with penalties for supervisors who kept employees longer than an hour after closing time.

This package not only required commitment from corporations, it also required the community to create a child-friendly environment. For example, it was mandated that no restaurant could refuse a customer with small children, and railroad companies were required to reserve a car for the sole use of mothers with small children. Perhaps most important was the reform of the child-care and preschool system, which transferred authority for these from the central government to the municipalities. Operating under broad guidelines, local authorities were to privatize child care by contracting the actual provision of services to private-sector agents. The aim of these measures was to give all parents of children under the age of six many inexpensive choices for child care.

Another key element was borrowed from Norway. To create role models for women and more diversified corporate governance, this part of the package mandated that by the year 2030 one-half of a company's directors be women. Wider recommended changes relating to corporate practices and labor relations also had an impact on women. These changes included basing advancement on merit rather than seniority, and using formal job descriptions and employee evaluations to avoid conscious or unconscious discrimination.

The Commission also called for legislation to abolish the *koseki* family registration system in favor of a simple birth-certificate system like that of the United States. Again, the prefectures and municipalities were empowered within broad guidelines to issue their own certificates of birth. Thus resident registration for the local municipality would be sufficient, and there would be no need for the *koseki* system. These birth certificates were to be issued to each child at birth without reference to families beyond the names of the mother and father, or of just the mother in the event of an unknown father. All children born of parents domiciled in Japan were to be granted Japanese nationality. The certificates were not to be made available to the public, and were to be used only for such things as obtaining a driver's license, passport, or marriage license. In other words, society would have to judge and make decisions about people based on their own record of accomplishment rather than on family relationships and origins. Now, in 2050, these measures have resulted in the disappearance of the old stigma against unmarried mothers and adopted children.

THE IMPORTANCE OF IMMIGRATION

Regarding attracting more foreign workers to Japan to boost female participation in the workforce, the study group and the Commission concluded that the best solution for Japan would be to allow for somewhat increased but selective and controlled immigration, while making all efforts to increase the domestic fertility rate and to create an attractive environment that would make Japanese—especially young, female Japanese—want to stay in or return to Japan.

At the time of the investigation in 2015, non-Japanese residents constituted about 2 percent of the total population of Japan. The Commission called for a policy of gradually increasing this number to 6 percent by 2040, with the focus on particular types of immigrants. First, it said, every effort would be made to recruit foreign technologists and experts in fields such as software engineering, biotech research, and systems analysis: all areas where Japan was relatively weak. This aspect of the immigration policy also included a special entry visa for those foreigners who promised to invest in and start new businesses in Japan, which was similar to policies in Canada and the United States. In these ways, it was hoped that Japan would attract talent, innovation, and investment from all over the world. Chinese engineers proved to be particularly enthusiastic entrepreneurs, and brought not only new ideas to Japan but also opportunities for dealing directly with the Chinese home market. At the same time, Japan was an ideal place for them because it provided the start-up funding and incentives they needed to get new projects off the ground.

The Commission also called for the recruitment of young people from neighboring Asian countries to fill positions in the exploding fields of housekeeping, nursing, elder care, and health care, which were not especially attractive jobs for Japanese because of their relatively low pay and sometimes unpleasant tasks. Philippine nationals had a history of providing domestic help to Japan's foreign residents; now visa regulations were changed to allow Japanese to also have resident housekeeping staff from overseas. Philippine nurses, along with nurses from other southeast Asian countries, also benefitted from a new ruling that accepted nursing certifications from abroad as valid in Japan, and which granted immigrants falling into this category time to study and learn Japanese. Nurses certified in Indonesia, for instance, were no longer required to pass complicated Japanese medical exams, but had only to take basic Japanese language classes as appropriate.

As well as actively recruiting people with special talents from developing countries, Japan looked to Europe and the United States. France was especially targeted. Because it had not liberalized its labor markets following the financial crisis of 2008–2010, the country hemorrhaged an incredible number of its best engineers as they sought better opportunities, at first in the UK and the United States, but then also in Japan. For instance, by 2020 the number of newly graduated engineers leaving France had risen to nearly one in two. Experienced engineers were leaving as well. But France's loss was Japan's opportunity.

Having witnessed the success of Australia in recruiting American miners during the commodity boom of 2000–2008, Tokyo decided in 2015 to set up a recruiting office in Paris just off the Champs-Élysées, along with branches in Toulouse and Lyon, both centers of industry teeming with the talent Japan's companies needed. These efforts quickly led to a large inflow of skilled professional immigrants into Japan. Its eminent technology base made it an attractive destination for French engineers; in addition, Tokyo had more Michelin three-star restaurants than Paris, something Japan's talent recruiters found to be a strong selling point. Japan was able to attract engineers who had worked with Airbus and its principal suppliers for the A380 program, which facilitated a rapid and effective absorption of Boeing know-how in the wake of the Mitsubishi takeover of Boeing. And Japan's computer-aided design and graphics industries attracted key talent from the highly advanced French 3-D software industry. With the aid of the French software engineers now working in the R&D centers of Japan's major automakers, Japan was able quickly to move to a dominant position in this critically important niche of the market.

Japan also gained an unexpected benefit from the impact of global warming on France. The steady increase in temperatures was adversely affecting the quality of wines from such famous French regions as Bordeaux and Burgundy. Young French wine-makers found that many of Japan's former rice-growing regions could be turned profitably into vineyards. Their unique French training allowed these young wine-makers to rapidly improve the quality of Japan's wines and bring them to world-class levels.

For example, today, in 2050, Chateau Yoshida is considered one of the world's most sought-after Burgundies.

In addition to France, Japan also established recruitment centers in the major cities of India and China. As a result, the number of Indian and Chinese engineers living and working in Japan jumped dramatically. Indeed, so much did the Indian community expand that it built Indian-run schools and professional institutions where many Japanese students are now enrolled as they strive to learn advanced IT technologies in English.

The young engineers and entrepreneurs gathering in Japan from all over the world acted as a synergistic stimulus that multiplied innovation geometrically, integrating their talents and financial means with the small and medium-sized firms already working in new technologies in Japan. They were natural allies. The established firms had been slow to move away from their rigid polices of mandatory retirement at sixty and their step-function pay scales tied mainly to longevity with the firm. The wave of foreign entrepreneurs came with very different visions of how to manage things. Not everyone thought the newcomers were right, but younger Japanese—especially young women—flourished in an environment where merit drove compensation. Another aspect of the new firms was their flexibility with regard to work schedules, the location of work, and the way their employees worked. Everything possible was done to accommodate the special needs of the workers. It was these smaller firms that eventually became the model for creating high-productivity work environments that simultaneously fostered a change of lifestyle and values that further encouraged the growth of families.

THIRTY-FIVE YEARS LATER

Now, thirty-five years later in 2050, the wisdom of the Commission is evident. Its new policies have produced the intended positive results, and even some unintended ones. The number of women in the workforce is now 85 percent, among the highest in the world. Moreover, women now account for just under half of the directors of corporate boards, about 75 percent of all doctors, and 35 percent of CEOs. About 99 percent of children under the age of six are in privatized childcare facilities. Some municipalities have introduced a system under which parents can use municipally funded vouchers to obtain childcare services. This has resulted in a decline in overall municipal spending as the efficient service providers have proven most popular with voucher holders and have gotten most of the payments, while inefficient or unpopular facilities have exited the market or made their services more attractive. Because of the reduced spending and rising quality of services, many more municipalities are adopting this voucher system today.

One of the unintended results of the new policies is that the number of bars in Tokyo and other metropolitan centers has declined dramatically. Because of lifestyle changes, as well as the introduction of more flexible working hours, men no longer linger at work and in the bars socializing with their superiors and colleagues. On the other hand, the number of family restaurants has mushroomed, as has the number of newborns. Now no restaurant is refusing service to small children; rather, they generally offer them special favors such as crayons and extra cake.

Thanks to easily available egg banks, it is now not uncommon for women in their mid-forties to be having children. The new rules have also resulted in a dramatic increase in the number of infants and young children being adopted both within Japan and from abroad. At the same time, the rate of abortion has fallen to nearly zero and the fertility rate has risen to 2.3. After a fairly sharp decline to about 115 million people in 2025, the population began to grow again and is now approaching 140 million people.

The face of that population has also changed. Thirty-five years ago, foreign residents of Japan accounted for roughly 2 percent of the population. Today, that proportion is just under 6 percent. It is noticeable, but not to such an extent that there is any sense of the Japanese being overwhelmed. The pattern of immigration has been very interesting to observe. More than half of the annual inflow consists of Chinese, who assimilate quickly because they can learn Japanese faster than other immigrants. But others have assimilated more rapidly than was expected because the increasingly bilingual nature of Japanese society has made English a true second language in Japan. The influx of young women from southeast Asia to work in the health-care sector has been critical to the staffing of the increasing numbers of large retirement and assisted-living homes built outside major centers like Tokyo and Osaka. This has followed a pattern of immigration observed in northern Europe and the United States. Some of these women have ultimately married Japanese men and had Japanese children, while others stay for five or ten years before returning to their home countries.

Just as the rate of net immigration has steadily risen, so too has the longevity of Japan's men and women. Medical advances and general improvements in the environment as the Japanese economy has become increasingly green and sustainable have contributed to the continued lengthening of the Japanese healthy lifespan, which remains by far the world's longest. Mortality rates in early twenty-first century Japan declined faster than had been expected, with life expectancy today in 2050 for men rising from around eighty to nearly ninety years, and for women from eighty-six years to ninety-five years.

But what these statistics do not show is the corresponding improvement in the health of most men and women well into their early eighties. For example, beginning in 2020, all elders of seventy and above have been required to take various community exercise classes to earn "health points" that could be used in exchange for free flu shots. Improved vitality allowed Japan's government gradually to raise the full-pension retirement age to eighty. In parallel with this increase, the government loosened the restrictions around continuing to work and allowed older workers the flexibility to adapt their work schedules to their needs. Both developments were important to preventing Japan's social security system from being completely overwhelmed. Social security contributions—which had been 15 percent of national income—did rise, but by 2040 the increase stopped and the social security contributions as a fraction of national income declined. Older Japanese typically changed their professions after sixty-five, moving into less physically demanding roles. For example, many were retrained to become teaching assistants in elementary schools and to share their working experiences with young students in their communities. Thus, extending a healthy lifespan resulted in more labor participation by elders and in overall higher national productivity.

Thus has Japan proven that the demographic future of a nation is not necessarily immutable. While most of the rest of Asia—especially South Korea and China—is becoming older and more enfeebled every day, Japan in 2050 is becoming younger and more robust.

CHAPTER 5

Japan Becomes an English-Speaking Country

You wake in the morning and turn on the TV for the news. You click the channel selector in search of CNN or the BBC or some other English-language broadcast, but you keep hitting the Japanese-language stations. Then you see it—the scrolling English subtitle line at the bottom of the screen. You don't need CNN. In fact, you can already feel your limited Japanese improving as you listen to the news presenter speaking Japanese and follow his words in English in the subtitle line. But you do want to hear the news in English as well, so finally you find the CNN channel. Surprise—here you get the opposite. A Japanese scrolling subtitle runs at the bottom of the screen. Now you can feel your Japanese reading ability improving.

Today you have a breakfast meeting across town, so you click off the TV, take the elevator downstairs, and catch a cab for Roppongi Hills. Your cabdriver greets you with a nice "Good morning" and then proceeds to tell you in fluent English all about his son's baseball team, his wife's gardening hobby, and the big fish his father just caught. You are astonished by the cosmopolitanism of Tokyo as it celebrates the mid-twenty-first-century mark, and you are surprised by the diversity of faces and languages you encounter. Actually, it was in the 2030s that a palpable shift began, as global corporations began moving their Asia headquarters from Hong Kong, Singapore, and even Sydney to Tokyo, Osaka, Yokohama, and Fukuoka. Of course, Tokyo had always been an attractive city to foreigners because of its high level of public safety, good flight connections to other major centers in Asia, flawless public services, unparalleled infrastructure, and good educational services. But it had always been behind Hong Kong and Singapore as an Asian headquarters city for global corporations, largely because of the language issue. Both Singapore and Hong Kong were English-speaking cities where global business executives and their wives and children could easily fit in and adapt to local conditions. They could even become active in the local community. Not so in Tokyo and other major Japanese cities.

In the past, not many Japanese spoke English well enough to get beyond simple conversation, and very few of the foreigners living in Japan spoke any Japanese at all. In addition, written Japanese was so difficult that very few non-Japanese could live comfortably outside the expatriate community with its special clubs and go-betweens. Now, however, the situation is completely different, because Japan has become for all practical purposes an English-speaking country. Communication is now as easy as it is in Singapore, and perhaps easier than in Hong Kong. As a result, a wave of American, European, Southeast Asian, South American, Indian, and Chinese executive expatriates and their families now live in Japan. Indeed, because of the air pollution in Beijing and Shanghai, many global executives stationed in China leave their families in Japan and visit on weekends. All this has created demand for housing, autos, office space, schools, financial services, restaurants, and a multitude of other services that has contributed to Japan's economic revival.

ENGLISHNIZATION

The effort to vastly improve Japan's English-speaking capability became a top national priority as the 2020 Tokyo Olympics neared. At the forefront of this effort were several of the business and technology leaders on the Extraordinary National Revitalization Commission—people such as Masayoshi Son, chairman of telecommunications corporation Softbank, and Hiroshi Mikitani, founder of e-commerce company Rakuten. Mikitani had hit the headlines in 2010 with his decision to make English the official language of his company, a process that was coined "Englishnization." Son, Mikitani, and their colleagues in the Commission realized how isolated and distanced Japan had become from the main streams of global innovation, discourse, and economic advance. They feared that this so-called Galapagos syndrome (a term originally used to refer to Japanese cell phones, which were so advanced that they had little commonality with mobile phones elsewhere in the world, and so did not actually serve as a means of communication except among Japanese) would eventually not only isolate but actually undermine the nation.

These Commission members argued that it was crucial to expand and improve English-language education, pointing to the research and activity of the Education First (EF) language-training company, which had identified a high correlation between a country's English-language capability (as measured by EF's English Proficiency Index [EPI]) and its economic performance (see graphs overleaf). EF's calculations showed that English skills improve innovation, communication with suppliers

ENGLISH AND INCOME

Gross National Income per Capita (USD)

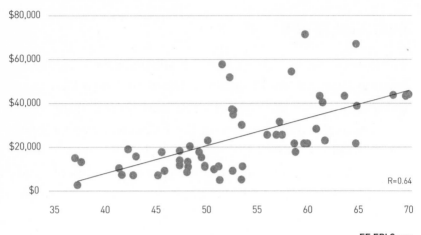

R=0.64

EF EPI Score

Source: World Bank, GNI per capita PPP($), 2012

ENGLISH AND THE EASE OF DOING BUSINESS

Ease of Doing Business Score

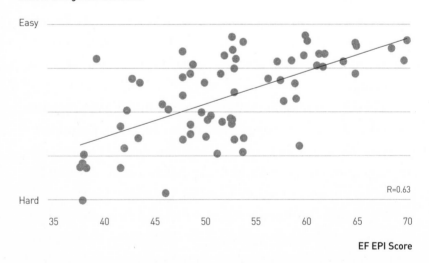

R=0.63

EF EPI Score

Source: World Bank and IFC Ease of Doing Business Index, 2013

ENGLISH AND DEVELOPMENT

Human Development Index (HDI)

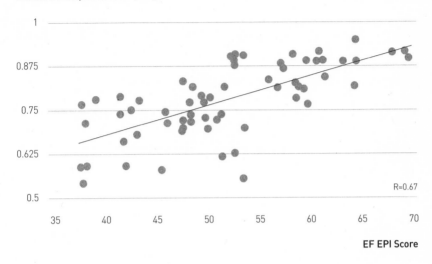

EF EPI Score

R=0.67

Source: United Nations Human Development Report, 2012

ENGLISH AND PROSPERITY

Legatum Prosperity Index

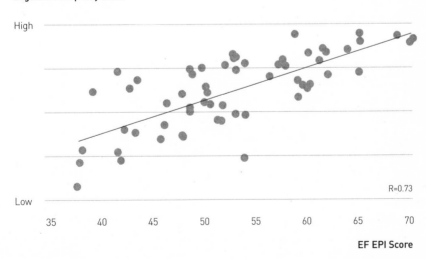

EF EPI Score

R=0.73

Source: Legatum Institute, 2013

ENGLISH AND INTERNET PENETRATION

Internet Users per 100 People

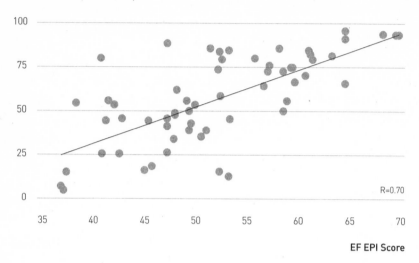

R=0.70

EF EPI Score

Source: World Bank, 2012

ENGLISH AND SCHOOLING

Average Years of Schooling

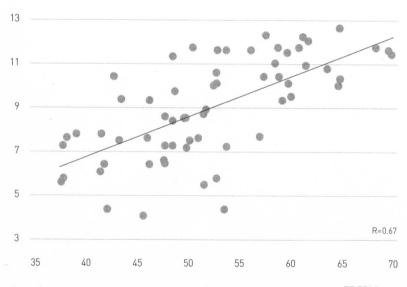

R=0.67

EF EPI Score

Source: United Nations Development Program, 2012

and customers, and recruiting power—all of which contribute to a better export environment. Thus, with the exception of a few commodity-exporting countries like Saudi Arabia, the GDP grows and individuals enjoy a higher standard of living as English-language capability rises. Not surprisingly, EF demonstrated that, aside from those where English was the mother tongue, countries with the greatest English-speaking capability were largely European. However, it also made the surprising discovery that despite the lack of similarity between Asian languages and English, a number of Asian school systems were successfully turning out students who were very proficient in English.

The EF EPI chart overleaf, published in 2014, shows Japan ranking twenty-sixth out of the sixty-three countries surveyed for English-speaking capability. This was not a terribly poor placement; Japan was ahead of France (twenty-ninth) and China (thirty-seventh). However, what the chart does not show—but what some of the Commission members were acutely aware of— is the fact that China, South Korea, Vietnam and others were making great efforts and were seen to be moving rapidly up the proficiency scale each year the survey was published. But Japan was not making any efforts to improve. Potential costs were enormous: difficulty in doing global business; reduced understanding of the global, political, economic, social, and technological environment; lack of awareness and subsequent undertaking of R&D and innovation; lower educational achievement; and less overall human development.

Of course, many in Japan had been aware of these kinds of correlations for some time but had never strongly felt the need to react. What the business and technology leaders among the Commission members now emphasized was that the problem was not just a matter of communication but also a matter of stimulating thought, discussion, problem solving, and new ideas

EF EPI 2014 RANKINGS

VERY HIGH PROFICIENCY

01	Denmark	69.30
02	Netherlands	68.99
03	Sweden	67.80
04	Finland	64.40
05	Norway	64.33
06	Poland	64.26
07	Austria	63.21

HIGH PROFICIENCY

08	Estonia	61.39
09	Belgium	61.21
10	Germany	60.89
11	Slovenia	60.60
12	Malaysia	59.73
13	Singapore	59.58
14	Latvia	59.43
15	Argentina	59.02
16	Romania	58.63
17	Hungary	58.55
18	Switzerland	58.29

MODERATE PROFICIENCY

19	Czech Republic	57.42
20	Spain	57.18
21	Portugal	56.83
22	Slovakia	55.96
23	Dominican Republic	53.66
24	South Korea	53.62
25	India	53.54
26	Japan	52.88
27	Italy	52.80
28	Indonesia	52.74
29	France	52.69
30	Taiwan	52.56
31	Hong Kong	52.50

LOW PROFICIENCY

32	U.A.E.	51.80
33	Vietnam	51.57
34	Peru	51.46
35	Ecuador	51.05
36	Russia	50.44
37	China	50.15
38	Brazil	49.96
39	Mexico	49.83
40	Uruguay	49.61
41	Chile	48.75
42	Colombia	48.54
43	Costa Rica	48.53
44	Ukraine	48.50

VERY LOW PROFICIENCY

45	Jordan	47.82
46	Qatar	47.81
47	Turkey	47.80
48	Thailand	47.79
49	Sri Lanka	46.37
50	Venezuela	46.12
51	Guatemala	45.77
52	Panama	43.70
53	El Salvador	43.46
54	Kazakhstan	42.97
55	Morocco	42.43
56	Egypt	42.13
57	Iran	41.83
58	Kuwait	41.80
59	Saudi Arabia	39.48
60	Algeria	38.51
61	Cambodia	38.25
62	Libya	38.19
63	Iraq	38.02

8

Source: EF English Proficiency Index 2014

through socializing. For example, they explained, the Japanese language was informed by Confucian principles and tended to compel a certain degree of indirection and deference in discussion between people of unequal status, whether the disparity was one of age, gender, or social position. Argumentation in Japanese could easily be interpreted as a slight, or even a personal attack. Using the Japanese language made for consensus and social harmony, but perhaps also contributed to stagnation by impeding the innovation that comes out of the free, uninhibited exchange of ideas and opinions that is possible in a more egalitarian, practically oriented language like English.

Some of the Commission members also had another aspect of the situation in mind. While manga had quickly spread to overseas markets, only a few Japanese novels, such as those of Haruki Murakami, were ever translated for foreign audiences. The Commission knew that there were great Japanese novelists and thinkers whose ideas were never communicated to the outside world. They knew that locked in Japan was the potential for great innovation, great new products and services, and great spiritual comfort. They also knew that the interaction of these Japanese concepts with those of other peoples around the world would unleash unexpected discoveries and benefits. All this, they argued, could be unlocked by English.

THE PROBLEM

Thus, the truth the Commission faced in 2016 was that Japan's level of English ability was inadequate for the country's future needs. Of course, the issue of how to improve Japan's English capability was not a new one. Indeed, it was a topic that had been addressed over and over again. Prime Minister Abe had called for making scores on the Test of English as a Foreign Language

(TOEFL) an important part of the requirements for university entrance in early 2014. While this was a bold proposal at the time, it was only the beginning of what was really needed. There seemed to be two fundamental issues. One was that the focus of English teaching in schools had always been on grammar, reading, and translation of texts rather than on speaking, listening, understanding, and communicating. The main point was to pass the written language requirements of the university entrance examinations. So students were not really taught the language as a means of communication. The second issue merely compounded the failings of the first. It was that the vast majority of English teachers in Japanese schools could not speak English. They might be able to read it and translate it, but they could not readily understand spoken English or respond in spoken English, so their English instruction and explanations were all conducted in Japanese. The worst aspect of this problem was that it had been known for a long time. But each time suggestions were made to change the method and focus of teaching, the teachers themselves, perhaps fearful of losing their jobs, had strongly opposed any reform. A Ministry of Education survey in 2009 showed that of 29,524 English teachers in 10,029 middle schools, only 201 were native English speakers. If part-time teachers were excluded, there were only 49 native English speakers out of 25,449 full-time English teachers at middle school.

To get around this problem, the government had initiated the JET (Japan Exchange Teaching) and ALT (Assistant Language Teacher) programs beginning in the late 1980s. These brought new university graduates from English-speaking countries to Japan to work as assistant teachers in preschools and elementary and high schools. In the peak year of 2002, a total of 6,273 foreign assistants participated in the program. While they were useful for purposes of teaching proper pronunciation and for interacting informally with students out of the classroom, they were not conducting the classes, and in most cases had no teaching experience. So the focus of most English classes remained grammar and translation, and the instruction continued to be mainly in Japanese. Some observers argued that the JET and ALT programs were wonderful for teaching foreigners about Japan, but not much use for teaching Japanese how to speak English.

The Commission again sent study teams abroad to find out what other countries were doing and found enormous emphasis on English teaching and learning virtually everywhere. They discovered that the countries with the highest English proficiency included Norway, Sweden, Denmark, Finland, Poland, Austria, and the Netherlands. With the exception of Poland, these were all small countries, and, with the additional exception of Finland, they all spoke a Germanic language with a relatively close relationship to English. Nevertheless, they all carried out comprehensive programs to achieve English proficiency. To begin with, all English teachers were fluent in the language. Instruction often began at preschool, and had in all cases begun by the third year of elementary school. It continued through all high school grades until age seventeen or eighteen. English classes were conducted mainly in English, and the emphasis was on total communication performance, so that by the time of graduation from high school, students were capable of reading, writing, translating, speaking, and understanding the spoken language.

Perhaps more important than classroom instruction, the study group found, was the contact that young people in these countries had with English in their everyday lives. In most non-English-speaking countries, American, British, Canadian, and Australian movies, TV programs, and news events that were broadcast domestically were dubbed from English into the national language. But in the Netherlands, the Scandinavian countries, and Finland, the programs were often broadcast in their original English with Dutch, Finnish, Danish, Norwegian, or Swedish subtitles. Thus the citizens of these countries were constantly listening to English in a wide variety of circumstances while simultaneously reading the translation in their native language. It was as if they had a constant twenty-four-hour language-laboratory session. In addition, because computer games, pop music, Internet activity, and mobile phone apps in these countries were often in English without translation, young people were practically living in a bilingual environment. Indeed, many of them actually were, because their parents, having been educated in the same way, were fluent in English and would often speak English at home. Many universities in these countries also gave instruction in English to the extent that a degree in almost any discipline could be obtained entirely in classes conducted in English. In other words, a student from any country could obtain a university degree from, for example, a Swedish university, without any knowledge of Swedish.

A final point with regard to the countries most proficient in English was that most of their students traveled or studied abroad at some point during their education, either to the United States or some other English-speaking country, or to a country in which the common language for the students and the locals was English. For example, Swedish students studying in Germany would probably converse with Germans in English. So there was a great opportunity and necessity for speaking English just in the course of everyday living.

The Commission discovered that other countries that were highly proficient in English included Belgium, Estonia, Hungary, Germany, Poland, Singapore, Malaysia, Slovenia, Latvia, Argentina, Romania, and Switzerland. All of these countries shared many of the attributes of the most proficient countries. While (with the exception of Belgium) they did not show original English-language movies and TV programs in English with subtitles in the national language, they did put great emphasis on English teaching by English-speaking teachers, and their students also traveled extensively abroad.

The Commission was particularly interested in the cases of Singapore, Malaysia, and India, as these were Asian countries whose native languages were not at all similar to English; their cultures also varied substantially from Western cultures and from each other. All of them, of course, shared the legacy of having been part of the British Empire, but other countries like Myanmar and South Africa that had also been part of the empire lacked the same level of English proficiency. What all the high-proficiency countries had done, however, was to make English an official language of the state. Thus, in Singapore, English, Malay, and Chinese were all official languages. In India, official languages included English, Hindi, and a few others. This meant that all official documents and statements were issued in English, that all interactions between citizens and the offices of the government had to be available in English, and that the media of the country had to publish and broadcast at least partially in English. In fact, all these countries were multi-ethnic, multi-religious, and multi-lingual, and English had become their lingua franca. In particular, English was the language of business in those countries—in fact, this was the case in most countries, as the world economy had become increasingly globalized and integrated.

The Commission found South Korea's approach to English education extraordinarily interesting. In the first half of the twentieth century, the majority of Koreans had been unable to read or write even in their own language, let alone a foreign language. Beginning in the late 1940s, Korea had launched a massive literacy and education catch-up effort that carried it to the top of the international education sweepstakes, with over 70 percent of its students entering university—far more than in any other country. With regard to English learning, South Korea had early on recognized that English ability was a key to global business competitiveness, and had made massive efforts to improve English teaching at home and to send as many students as possible for at least some study time abroad. Thus the number of South Koreans studying abroad had grown from practically none in the 1960s to 250,000 in 2013. Indeed, so anxious were South Koreans to have their children become fluent English speakers that it was common practice for South Korean mothers to move with their children to Australia, New Zealand, or the United States during the school year, while fathers stayed at home to work. Nor was South Korea the only example. The annual number of Chinese studying at universities in the United States, Britain, Australia, Canada, and New Zealand topped 350,000 by 2013. This was in stark contrast to Japan, where the number of Japanese students studying abroad was falling dramatically, from 82,945 in 2004 to only 58,060 in 2010. Indeed, it seemed that as other nations became more globalized, Japan focused ever more inwardly.

One of the members of the Commission was actually an American who had had long experience as a trade negotiator with Japan, and who had been appointed in order to lend an outside perspective to the Commission's work. He also had substantial experience in South Korea as well as elsewhere in Asia, Europe, and Latin America. He noted that as a result of their emphasis on English and their study periods abroad, South Koreans and South Korean businesses were not only better able to interact with foreigners than Japanese, but were also better able to integrate non-Koreans into the Korean business environment than Japanese could integrate non-Japanese into the Japanese business environment. Samsung, for example, could readily incorporate

American engineers and executives into its development and marketing teams in Seoul. Moreover, educated South Koreans were avid readers of the English-language press and technical journals, and could easily exchange views with people in other countries. They could easily establish contacts and relationships in new markets and with new organizations. The consequences of all this became apparent in the loss of Japan's leadership in key global industries as companies like Panasonic, Nissan, Toyota, NEC, Sony, and Toshiba found it increasingly difficult to compete with their South Korean rivals. It was this phenomenon that prompted Rakuten founder and CEO Hiroshi Mikitani to sound an urgent warning in 2012 in his book *Taka ga Eigo*, or "Englishnization." There he signaled the dire facts of twenty-first-century life to his countrymen, pointing out that competition of all types, but especially economic competition, was more and more global. In order to be competitive, corporations would have to hire not just the best Japanese workers, but the best global workers. They would have to exploit not just the best Japanese ideas, but the best global ideas. He noted that Japan's population was shrinking, and that its economy as a share of the global economy was also shrinking. Just to remain alive, therefore, Japanese companies would have to do more and more of their business outside of Japan. If they were going to be successful in foreign markets, Japanese executives would have to be very capable in English. Mikitani further explained that Japan's past success as an exporter in the global market had been based on its ability to supply outstanding manufactured products. In this case, the products were the main interface with the customer, and their good quality, good design, and fast delivery were self-evident. But in the future, the economy would become more and more service-oriented, and the services wouldn't explain themselves so easily. They would have to be introduced and maintained through more personal interaction. At the global level, that would require much better and broader English capability than Japan had at the time.

In his book, Mikitani used his experience with his own company to show what could and must be done. He described in detail how in the early years of the twenty-first century Rakuten had adopted English as its corporate language, even for internal communications and presentations that took place in Japan among only Japanese. He showed how his company had undertaken to train all its employees in English and to move them to the green zone of proficiency on the Test of English for International Communication (TOEIC) within two years. He had concluded the book by urging other companies—and, indeed, the whole nation—to adopt a similar drive.

THE CURSE OF ENGLISH

While Mikitani didn't say so, it was well known that historically there had always been a feeling in Japan of essential and unbridgeable differentness from other countries with regard to language and culture. This sense had been accompanied by a strong concern for the need to protect Japanese culture and the Japanese way of life from erosion or contamination by contact with foreign elements. Indeed, Mikitani himself had often suggested that one reason the Tokyo authorities established the Japanese English-learning system in its nonfunctional form was actually to prevent Japanese from learning it well enough to enable them to escape from the "Galapagos" environment of Japan. So, in a way, the Japanese language in itself had been used as a means of preventing the "Japanese way" from being overwhelmed by Western influence over the past two hundred years.

Yet it was increasingly clear that Japanese culture and the "Japanese way" had their own exportable and overwhelming elements. Sushi had become a global dish, karaoke was as popular in New York as in Tokyo, and *kanban* (just-in-time delivery) had become an English word widely used in manufacturing operations around the world. Japan had become virtually synonymous with outstanding quality control, while the whole concept of fast food that had originated in Japan (think sushi, instant noodles, baked potato-wagons) had now swept the world (even France). Japan was widely admired as a safe society in which things worked and ran on time. It may have been prudent to think about protecting Japanese culture and national mores from sudden inundation by Western ideas and values in the nineteenth and early twentieth centuries. But in the twenty-first century the challenge was not protection but revitalization and globalization; for this, the mastery of English was as essential, just as the mastery of Western science had been during the Meiji period.

WHAT HAD TO BE DONE

Based on these findings, the Commission made a series of recommendations aimed at achieving the goal of equaling Germany in English-speaking proficiency by mid-century. Germany was chosen because it was a large, advanced country like Japan with a level of English capability that was good, but not impossibly high. There seemed little hope that Japan could equal Scandinavia's English-language capability. But maybe it could come close to Germany.

The first step was to have all English teachers in Japan take the TOEIC or the TOEFL. Those who scored in the green level, indicating good proficiency, were cleared to continue teaching. All others were either asked to take retirement or to undergo intensive training to elevate their scores to the green level within one year. To replace retiring teachers, Japanese who had lived and studied abroad in English-speaking environments were recruited by municipal governments and assigned to help with teaching at local schools. They were assisted in this recruiting by the Keidanren (Japan Business Federation) and the Japan External Trade Organization (JETRO), which had extensive ties to Japanese people living abroad.

At the same time, the JET program was revitalized to bring not only thousands of native English-speaking college graduates to Japan as teacher assistants, but also to bring a large number of fully qualified professional English teachers from English-speaking countries. In addition, online programs for teaching English were made widely available to schools and students so they could take advantage of the resources and native language speakers available worldwide. The school curriculum was modified so that simple English instruction began in child-care centers and continued through the entire twelve years of elementary, middle, and high school. Online teaching programs also made it possible for students to undertake extra English study at any time. With financial support from domestic and overseas foundations, each Japanese second-year high school student was offered the opportunity to study for one year at an English-speaking high school abroad. Whether or not the students availed themselves of the opportunity, they were required to reach the TOEIC proficiency level as a condition of graduation from high school.

In the corporate world, each company with more than 100 employees was urged to adopt a five-year plan for making English the corporate language, and the government set a target of having all such corporations conduct most of their day-to-day business in English by 2020. By the same token, the ministries and other

Japanese government bodies were directed to implement the same kinds of measures. Proficiency in English was also made a requirement for obtaining a job in the Japanese bureaucracy.

As the 2020 Tokyo Olympics approached and the practical need for greater English capability in conjunction with the games became evident, legislation was adopted to establish English as an official language of Japan by 2025. This meant that all publications, forms, public signs, and other official statements had to be available in English as well as Japanese. It also meant that speeches in the Diet and at other official events could be made in either English or Japanese. Universities were required gradually to teach more courses in English, until by 2025 they reached the goal of being able to grant their degrees to students who had followed the curriculum in either English or Japanese. This would be in imitation of Beppu's Ritsumeikan University, which had already been offering such an opportunity in 2013. Non-Japanese students were encouraged to enroll and take their degrees at Japanese universities along with Japanese students who were doing their studies in the English language.

Perhaps most revolutionary was the Commission's recommendation to do away with dubbing and to emulate the Dutch and the Scandinavians in their practice of subtitling television programs, movies, and other broadcast and Internet productions. Thus programs in Japanese would have English subtitles, and those in English would have Japanese subtitles. In this way, Japanese viewers, like their counterparts in the Netherlands and the Nordic countries, would be fed a constant diet of English in one of the most easily digestible forms.

It took a while to get this organized, not least because there was initially just a huge shortage of translators and subtitle writers. But automated translation evolved to help enormously, and by the early 2020s most Japanese were finding it much easier to understand and be understood while traveling abroad. As a consequence, the number of Japanese taking overseas trips and extended stays abroad rose dramatically. At the same time, non-Japanese-speaking people could travel virtually anywhere in Japan and be fully conversant with what was happening in the country by reading the subtitles and listening to Japanese media.

THE UNEXPECTED BLESSINGS OF ENGLISH

By 2030 Japan had made enormous steps toward becoming a more or less completely bilingual country. This was already having unexpected and revolutionary ramifications—most significantly for the Japanese government bureaucracy, the Diet, and the overall governance of Japan.

The bureaucracy had always had great discretionary power in Japan. This was partly because the traditional philosophy of governance was that anything not specifically authorized was forbidden, which compelled the citizenry to be always asking permission. This kind of thinking was in contrast to systems such as those of the United States and the United Kingdom, where no permission was required unless something was specifically forbidden. The Japanese bureaucracy was also powerful because Japanese laws tended to be written by the bureaucracy, and were drafted with broad provisions to be filled in with specific ordinances later by, of course, the bureaucracy. The power of the bureaucracy was also partly a result of the fact that Japanese citizens customarily did not question their lawmakers and bureaucrats: the inoffensive vagueness of the Japanese language and the Confucian principles embedded in it inhibited questioning of the high-status Diet members and bureaucrats by mere lowly citizens. The bureaucracy was also immune to pressure from outside Japan because most foreigners didn't understand

and couldn't read the antiquated and complex Japanese of the law and legal documents. Indeed, many Japanese complained that even they could not fully understand such writing.

By the 2040s, the widespread knowledge and use of English and the requirement that all laws and regulations be published in English had changed all that. When they wished to be direct but non-confrontational, Diet members sometimes debated and asked questions in English. Ordinary citizens and journalists did the same thing, as, of course, did foreigners. Because leaders were now debating and publishing in English, it had become much easier to point out illogical statements and ambiguous discretionary decisions. Now there was nowhere for the politicians and the bureaucrats to hide.

More broadly, the change in Japanese society was remarkable. Japanese leaders became very polished in their discussions and presentations in international gatherings. Japanese entrants in global debate contests became numerous, and frequently won. More Japanese papers were cited in academic journals and articles. Japanese prime ministers became major figures at the G20 and G7 meetings; Japan was admitted as a full permanent member of the UN Security Council, while Japanese also began to fill the top spots of many other international organizations.

The widespread use of English also helped business discussions become more frank and productive, and business collaboration both within Japan and between Japan and other countries unlocked unexpected innovation and growth, just as some of the Commission members had anticipated. Furthermore, as anticipated, Japanese authors, teachers, writers, athletes, medical doctors, entertainers, and others found a global market for their talents.

This all created a tsunami of money into Japan that helped fill the government coffers as well as private accounts. Because of the strength of its institutions, its open and transparent system, and its convertible currency, Tokyo surpassed Hong Kong and Singapore to become the major hub of Asian finance, just as London was the hub of European finance.

Now that English had become a viable medium of communication for serious business in Japan, the demand for Japanese medical services exploded. Japan's medical system was already known as one of the world's best, and the country was famous for the longevity of its people. But, as with finance, the difficulties of language and communication had always inhibited non-Japanese from seeking medical help in Japan and kept the Japanese from offering it. But now, sophisticated medical facilities that had been overbuilt and substantially underused for many years in major cities were in high demand. For a long time, so-called medical tourists (patients seeking treatment outside their home country) had been traveling to Asian centers such as Singapore, Bangkok, New Delhi, and Bangalore. Now these centers suffered a decline in patients as those seeking treatment increasingly took the road to Japan. Furthermore, students and practitioners followed suit: Japan's medical schools were suddenly full of students from all over the world who were bent on getting their medical degrees from world-class Japanese institutions. Drawn by the excellence of Japan's laboratories, technicians, high-speed communications, and other support facilities, many of the world's leading doctors and medical scientists moved their practices and main offices to Japan.

What was true of bankers and doctors was also true of scientific researchers more generally. Since the mid-1990s, Japan had been spending more than 3 percent of its GDP on R&D, putting it among the top two or three countries in terms of support for science and engineering. Despite the huge investment, Japan had gotten relatively meager returns. With the increase in English-language capability, however, this changed dramatically. Global companies rushed to establish labs in Japan, and the number of scientific papers co-authored by Japanese and non-Japanese researchers soared, as did global Japanese patent applications along with all other indices of scientific and engineering activity.

The situation was similar with regard to food. Always a center of culinary excellence, Japan became the unquestioned mecca of global gourmets. No self-respecting chef could neglect a period of training in Japan, and no restaurant with any hope of world recognition could afford not to have Japan-trained people in its kitchen.

As noted in the previous chapter, Japan had adopted a policy of regulated but more open immigration, and had even begun to recruit immigrants with special talents from other nations. This would have been impossible without the Englishnization policy. Not only did it facilitate recruiting, but many of the people who came for educational, medical, or business reasons ended up staying in Japan because of its comfortable living environment. Many of them took Japanese spouses and had children who, thanks to the abolition of the old *koseki* family registration system and the implementation of the new rules for citizenship (see chapter 4), were granted Japanese citizenship and became part of the new population wave.

In spite of its longstanding fear that its culture might be overwhelmed by outside influences, Japan found that English was not only the means by which Japanese culture could be defended, but was also a way for Japan's culture to be globalized and thereby contribute to at least the partial "Japanization" of other societies. English was not a threat but a vital key to the survival, revitalization, and new success of Japan and Japanese culture. Rather than being a curse, English turned out to be a blessing.

CHAPTER 6

Innovation Nation

As you read the news on your Takeuchi glasses, you are struck by the number of articles dealing with venture capital, start-ups, and entrepreneurs. Of course you already knew that Japan had become a hub for innovators and new technology development. But being here is giving you a whole different level of understanding. You are constantly amazed at the innovations that surround you, from the robots at the hotel that open the doors and put you into the smart taxis to the way the your hotel-room door opens automatically upon sensing your presence. But the volume of daily news reports on new entrepreneurial activity amazes you as much as the technological innovations you see. Is this really the country where, not so long ago, the last thing anyone wanted to be was an entrepreneur? Where almost no one did start-ups? The rule in the old days was that the nail sticking up would be hammered down. How did this happen, you ask yourself.

Well, for one thing, in a speech early in 2013, Prime Minister Abe had called on Japan to become the world's "most innovation-friendly nation," and had declared that he would conduct vigorous regulatory reforms and prepare a research environment that would attract researchers from around the world to

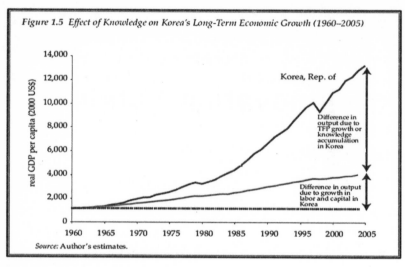

Figure 1.5 *Effect of Knowledge on Korea's Long-Term Economic Growth (1960–2005)*

Source: Author's estimates.

Source: Joonghae Suh and Derek H.C. Chen.
"Korea as a Knowledge Economy: Evolutionary Process and Lessons Learned."
Korea Development Institute and the World Bank Institute, 2007.

come work in Japan. This had followed similar South Korean announcements made in 2007, when the World Bank Institute and the Korea Development Institute had mapped the effect of knowledge, technology, and innovation on the South Korean GDP since 1960, as shown in the graph above. They had concluded that the effect of knowledge on Korean economic growth was rising at close to an exponential rate.

Faced with an aging population, low birthrate, and increasing competition from the likes of China, Singapore, Taiwan, Finland, Sweden, and Vietnam, South Korea had recognized that only knowledge and innovation could enable it to maintain and increase its standard of living. What was true for South Korea, which still had relatively inexpensive labor and the potential to tap very cheap labor in North Korea, was doubly true for Japan, with its extremely high wages and living costs. The prime minister had, of course, sensed this in making his 2013 declaration. But the new Extraordinary National Revitalization Commission made the point more strongly by presenting a unanimous conclusion that accelerating Japanese innovation was second in importance only to reversing the country's demographic trends, and that such acceleration should be given the same kind of emphasis that had been proposed for changing the role of women.

THE GOLDEN ERA

To many, this was a startling conclusion. After all, Japan was already an acknowledged global leader in a wide range of technologies and industries. The 2014 Battelle Institute R&D Funding Forecast (see overleaf) had listed Japan as number two in automotive, information and communications, and instruments and electronics technologies; number three in nanomaterials, composite materials, and environmental and sustainability technologies; number four in health care, life science, and energy technologies; and number five in commercial aerospace and non-automotive transport technologies.

Furthermore, Japan accounted for eleven of the world's fifty top R&D-investing companies in the ranking of the European Commission's Industrial R&D Investment Scoreboard of 2013. By comparison, the United States, whose population and GDP were almost three times that of Japan, had nineteen; and the EU, with a population more than four times greater and a GDP more than three times larger than Japan's, had eighteen. Indeed, according to OECD statistics, at 3.39 percent, Japan's total R&D spending as a percentage of GDP was third in the world, exceeded only by Israel at 4.38 percent and South Korea at 4.03 percent. By contrast, the United States spent only 2.77 percent of GDP on R&D; for China, the number was about 2 percent (although this was up from 1 percent only a few years previously). In terms of spending per scientist and engineer, Japan was number three

GLOBAL RESEARCHER VIEWS OF LEADING COUNTRIES IN R&D BY RESEARCH/TECHNOLOGY AREA

	1	2	3	4	5
Agriculture & Food Production	US	China	Germany	Brazil	Australia
Automotive & Other Motor Vehicle	Germany	Japan	US	China	South Korea
Commercial Aerospace, Rail, & Other Non-Automotive Transport	US	France	Germany	China	Japan
Military Aerospace, Defense & Security Technologies	US	Russia	China	Israel	U.K.
Composite, Nanotech, & Other Advanced Materials	US	Germany	Japan	China	U.K.
Energy Generation & Efficiency	Germany	US	China	Japan	Denmark
Environmental and Sustainability	Germany	US	Japan	Sweden	U.K.
Health-care, Medical, Life Science & Biotech	US	U.K.	Germany	Japan	China
Information & Communication (ICT)	US	Japan	China	Germany	South Korea
Instruments & Other Non-ICT Electronics	US	Japan	Germany	China	U.K.

2014 Global R&D Funding Forecast, December 2014, p. 34.
"Global Researcher Views of Leading Countries in R&D by Research/Technology Area."
Source: Battelle/R&D Magazine 2014 Global R&D Funding Forecast.

in the world, behind only Finland and Sweden. In this regard it surpassed the United States, South Korea, China, and all the large European R&D-intensive countries. With these facts in mind, it was possible to suggest that Japan might actually be the most technology-intensive country in the world.

This strong performance had not happened by accident. To begin with, the Japanese are inherently among the world's most creative people, with a keen sense of the practical and a refined elegance in design. One need only consider the style of Japanese bartenders (whose unique tools have spread around the world) mixing drinks, or watch a Japanese construction company demolish an obsolete high-rise building, to perceive this. Added to this innate inventiveness was a long history of importing advanced technologies from abroad and improving them for Japanese use as well as for export in modified form. The Japanese had imported their writing system from China in the sixth century, but had combined it with the native *kana* syllabary to create their own more flexible and more easily learned system. Between the time of the Meiji Restoration in 1868 and World War II, Japan had made an enormous effort to import, master, improve, and modify the technology and industrial know-how of the West. In later years, people tended to forget that at the beginning of the war, the Mitsubishi Zero had been by far the world's best fighter plane, while the Yamato had been the most advanced battleship. Japan had ceased being a developing country well before the Second World War.

The unparalleled destruction wrought by the war had caused unprecedented suffering. But with defeat and the subsequent seven-year US occupation of Japan also came two positive phenomena. One was an opening up of social and business structures. Relatively young people could advance rapidly, based on their talent, because in the postwar environment talent was in far higher demand than seniority and relationships. Also, entrepreneurs, who in normal times might have hesitated to take the financial risk of trying a start-up venture, now had little to lose by trying to launch new businesses. At the same time, old businesses were willing to deal with new businesses because old suppliers had disappeared or no longer had enough capacity to meet demand. Thus it was that in the twenty years after 1945 a number of companies—Sony, Honda, Kyocera, and others—were founded and met with success after success.

The second positive phenomenon was the revival and strengthening of a process that had started in the late nineteenth century, when government and industry had joined forces to scour the world for technology that would enable Japan to catch up to the West. After the Second World War, this drive was renewed as Japan sought to recover from destruction and overtake America in technological and industrial development as well as in overall standard of living. Beginning with basic industries such as steel, textiles, shipbuilding, chemicals, and machinery, Japan quickly learned the latest technologies and rebuilt its systems to use them effectively. By doing so, it rapidly achieved world-class productivity with low costs and began reconquering the world markets it had previously dominated, while also making large inroads into new markets. By the 1960s, total national spending on R&D as a percentage of GDP had doubled, and technology development contributed powerfully to rapidly rising productivity, increased income, and world-class competitiveness in key industries. This was when Japan's R&D machine really began running at top speed. Companies like Sony, Hitachi, Toshiba, and others entered and quickly dominated the global markets for radios, cameras, recording devices, and audio equipment. Then they moved into production of television sets, quickly displacing the major US and European manufacturers. Japanese makers moved from consumer electronics to dominate machine tools, semiconductors, semiconductor production equipment, ceramics, and many other areas. In short, Japan seemed to have become industrially and technologically unbeatable.

An important fact of this period was that Japan's development and especially its productivity gains were strongly linked to the output of US R&D, which underpinned Japan's innovation, allowing it rapidly to become competitive in a wide variety of high-tech industries. The effectiveness of Japanese companies in commercializing technology developed outside of Japan—a sort of reverse engineering skill—was widely studied and admired. Indeed, in a survey of sixteen major industrial countries at the time, Japan ranked first in this capability. But the Japanese companies did not just rely on reverse engineering. They also added important improvements, such as better design and miniaturization, the latter making such products as the transistor radio possible. Japan's producers also put great emphasis on designing to facilitate more efficient manufacturing, a step that made their commercialization processes far more effective than those of American companies. As a consequence, by the late twentieth century, Japan was number one in rapidly commercializing new products and processes flowing from the global R&D pipeline. The result was a growing and often dominant market share for its high-tech companies across a broad range of global markets.

THEN IT ALL CHANGED

In 1990, seven of the world's top twelve electronics firms were Japanese. By 2012, only two remained in the top rankings. The number one spot had been taken by South Korea's Samsung, followed by Apple and Google of the United States, and then by Taiwan's Foxconn. Particularly striking was the fact that Apple, after much success in the 1980s, had nearly gone bankrupt in the early 1990s, while, until 1998, Google had been only an idea in the heads of two college students. Their sudden rise to the top ranks of global electronics firms illustrated both the speed at which innovation can unleash change and the unusual strength of the United States in fostering such changes and companies.

Japan's loss of leadership in these fields was both broad and deep. Just as the Japanese semiconductor producers had displaced their US competitors in the past, South Korean and Taiwanese producers were now displacing the Japanese; the Chinese also began to get into the race. Surprisingly, the Dutch company ASML rose to become the leader in the production of key semiconductor equipment items. The Japanese auto industry also lost some of its momentum. While Toyota powered ahead, number two Nissan fell into deep trouble and had to be rescued in the late 1990s by Renault. The boom products, like the early transistor radios, color televisions, and the Sony Walkmans that Japanese industry had become accustomed to became fewer and Japan's market share in many industries began to erode.

Japanese industry was slow to recognize the importance of the Internet. As a whole new generation of Internet equipment-oriented companies like Cisco, Juniper Networks, and Huawei emerged, the absence of Japanese firms among them was noteworthy. China, meanwhile, was rapidly advancing in many core computing and information technologies, and the IT network capabilities of its companies were world class—far superior to the fragmented, domestically focused Japanese network equipment providers.

To combat this loss of momentum, Japanese business and government leaders doubled the nation's R&D spending in the late 1990s and early 2000s. Yet it seemed that the more they spent, the worse the situation became. For instance, while software

inexorably gained critical importance, in the face of competitors like Microsoft, SAP, Oracle, and others, Japanese industry
remained a marginal competitor. Because software is an enabling
technology, weakness in its development had ramifications for
many other industries. Take the e-reader industry as an example.
In most respects, Japanese e-reader technology matched that of
Amazon. But the embedded software of the Japanese producers
had limited search capability. The result was that Amazon's
Kindle won most of the market. Nor was Japanese industry ready
to introduce or compete with products such as the Apple iPad
and iPhone, or to develop alternative operating systems like the
Google Android system, which quickly came to run most of the
world's smartphones and which South Korea's Samsung used as
a springboard to leadership in the industry.

The lack of these kinds of completely new products was perhaps most disturbing to Japanese leaders. In 2013, while the list
of the world's top fifty R&D companies contained many Japanese
names, the list of companies that had doubled their sales while
also entering the top R&D ranks had none. Eight such companies were US corporations such as Google, Apple, Amazon, and
Caterpillar. Others included China's Huawei, Brazil's Vale, Germany's Continental (auto parts), and Denmark's Novo Nordisk
(pharmaceuticals). If one looked at the entire list of companies
on the EU Industrial R&D Investment Scoreboard, 21 percent
were Japanese. But, if one looked at the list of high-performance
companies (those with ten-year annual growth rates of 8 percent
and R&D spending in excess of 2 percent of sales), only 2 percent
were Japanese, and there were no Japanese names among the top
fifty. Of course, it was to be expected that some Japanese companies would lose momentum. This was a common phenomenon
among companies in all countries. But the paucity of newcomers
to replace those that were faltering was deeply troubling.

It was clear that Japan's innovation had decelerated in the early 1990s, even as the government's R&D spending had doubled. Some of this slowdown could be attributed to a general reduction in the benefits of innovation that was also observed in Europe and the United States. But even taking this overall negative trend into account, Japan's innovation slowdown was unexpectedly severe. The bottom line, as the Commission saw very quickly, was that Japan's vast investment in R&D was simply not paying off.

SOMETHING WAS NOT WORKING

The easy explanation was that an overvalued yen was undermining Japan's competitiveness. In fact, this widely held view was not entirely wrong. It was true that since the mid-1990s, the yen had been relatively strong, as the Japanese government had greatly reduced its interventions in currency markets while China, South Korea, Taiwan, Singapore, and others had carefully managed the value of their currencies to keep their exports competitive. Less often mentioned, but implicitly linked with the currency policy, was the broader question of industry-government coordination and cooperation to achieve competitiveness. Although Japan's traditionally close government-business link was still widely referred to as Japan, Inc. in the West, the truth was that since the 1992 bursting of the great Japan asset bubble, this link had largely become a thing of the past. The Asian Tigers and China, however, all continued to imitate the old Japan, Inc. way. This, no doubt, partly explained why Japanese technology companies were less bold in their programs and investments than many of their Asian competitors.

But there were other, more compelling explanations. In the 1960s, '70s, and '80s, Japan had been mostly alone in Asia as a technologically capable country, but in the '90s, South Korea, Taiwan, China, and even India had emerged as increasingly world-class players. China's R&D spending, which had been growing at nearly 30 percent annually for a number of years, had outpaced Japan's by 2010, and was second only to the United States—which it was also expected to surpass in this regard around the year 2022. As a result, China had already become a major participant in the global technology competition. Chinese companies like ZTE, Petro China, and Huawei were now among the top investors in technology development in the world. South Korea had also entered the top ranks. Samsung Electronics and LG were both among the top fifty R&D companies in the world according to the EU Scoreboard, while India and Taiwan had also achieved notice as being among the countries with the most rapidly rising R&D spending. Moreover, two Taiwanese companies and two Indian companies were listed among the EU Scoreboard's top fifty high-performance companies for the years 2002–2011.

The significance of these developments is well illustrated by a comparison of the reactions of Samsung and its Japanese rivals to the Asian financial crisis at the end of the 1990s, as illustrated in the graph overleaf. As the markets weakened at the end of the twentieth century, Samsung continued to invest, while its Japanese competitors hesitated. This cycle was constantly repeated over ten years, with Samsung moving aggressively and Japanese firms holding back, until Samsung had pushed Japanese companies out of their leadership positions in semiconductors, personal computers, and television sets, and then finally left them behind as merely marginal players in the global smartphone market.

Of course, the new Asian competitors, especially the Chinese, benefited from cheaper labor, but they didn't compete only on cost. They also gained an advantage on the basis of their

COMPARISON OF SEMICONDUCTOR-RELATED INVESTMENT BY SAMSUNG AND FIVE JAPANESE FIRMS

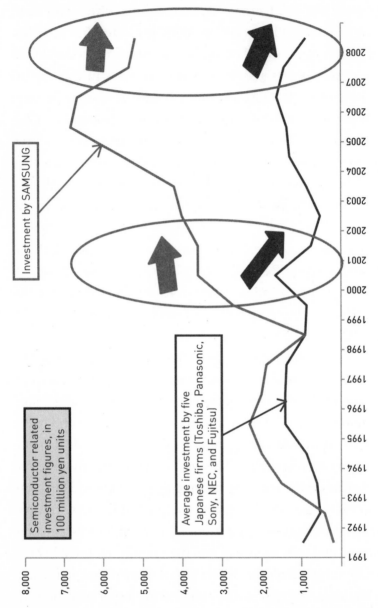

Source: Commerce and Information Policy Bureau, Ministry of Economy, Trade, and Industry (METI). Economics of Information and Innovation Strategy, May 2010; Mitsubishi UFJ Research & Consulting, Research on International Dissemination of IT Industry in Social Systems.

advanced technology. The emergence of these aggressive Asian competitors prevented the Japanese from waiting and carefully gauging where the latest technologies were heading before deciding how to enter the new markets with winning, high-quality, sophisticated, low-cost products. South Korean, Taiwanese, and Chinese competitors were now aggressively taking bold risks and making large first-mover investments to stake out positions in global high-tech markets, while Japanese companies were shut out and relegated to fighting only over a share of Japan's domestic market. Even in that once completely secure citadel, strong foreign firms were now gaining significant positions and depriving the Japanese of their longtime stronghold. Japan now found that China and the Asian Tigers had taken its own business methods and improved on them, just as Japan had previously improved on American methods.

Equal in significance to developments in Asia was the fact that the United States had staged a strong comeback from its technology defeats by Japan between 1970 and 1990. Fields like biotech, nanotech, and cloud computing, which had been only concepts in the 1970s, were now significantly dominated by US companies. While much of the Japanese semiconductor industry went bankrupt and lost market share to South Korean and Taiwanese producers, US makers came to dominate mobile-phone processors and other key market segments. Of the ten key technology areas listed by Battelle in 2012, the United States was rated as number one in eight. On the EU Scoreboard's list of the top fifty high-performance R&D companies, thirty-three were US companies. On Battelle's 2012 list of twelve major R&D companies whose sales had increased by more than 100 percent over the previous ten years, eight were US corporations.

Beyond the increase in global competitors, Japan also suffered from the fact that its R&D investment tended to be concentrated in a relatively few manufacturing sectors, and in a few companies within those sectors. Globally speaking, the sectors in which the highest R&D investment had been made from 1995 until 2014 had been pharmaceuticals and biotechnology, technology hardware and equipment, autos and auto parts, software and computer services, and electronics and electrical equipment. While Japan was strongly represented in the auto and electronics sectors, it invested much less in pharmaceuticals, biotech, software, and computer services. It had long had a *monozukuri*, or "making things," culture that valued production of hard goods over services and software. In the postwar era, Japan had focused intently on producing manufactured goods for export. Its competitiveness had become dependent on a relatively few manufacturing companies that employed a large share of Japan's technologists, and, because of lifetime employment policies, kept them tied up for thirty or forty years.

But as the world changed in the 1990s, this system had proved inflexible. In part, this was due to the industry-centered structure of Japanese R&D investment. The Japanese government accounted for only about 20 percent of the country's total R&D spending, with the rest being spent by major corporations. This was quite different from the United States and other leading technology countries, where the government accounted for a third to a half of the national R&D spending. Thus Japan had nothing to match America's National Institute of Health (which alone accounted for nearly half of total global spending on biotech research), its National Aeronautic and Space Administration (NASA), or its military R&D establishment. Nor did Japan have the extensive government-university network of the United States and of countries like Finland and Sweden. To be sure, Japan's universities did a lot of interesting research, but not in the same industry-government-coordinated context as the United States and other countries. Moreover, because of the lifetime employment system and the high risks associated with new ventures in Japan, there was no tradition of or system for stimulating start-up companies. As a result, R&D funding was heavily weighted toward the established sectors that had benefitted Japan in the past. Within these sectors, a relatively small number of companies, including Toyota, Sony, Hitachi, Nissan, Panasonic, Fujitsu, and Toshiba, accounted for the bulk of the technology development activity. Not only did this structure tend to continue directing resources to older and less rapidly evolving technology, it also tended to limit Japanese involvement in rapidly expanding new technologies.

At the same time, the need of Japanese corporations to achieve a broad consensus before making big decisions, combined with the impact of the collapse of the financial bubble in 1992 and the evaporation of industry-government cooperation, made leading companies hesitant to invest in research. Intent on avoiding excessive risk, the companies had focused mainly on incremental development of "me-too" products rather than on breakthroughs. Further, within large companies, projects had often had to fit the requirements of sister divisions rather than those of the general markets. In addition, there had been a decline in the capacity of the companies, in cooperation with key government ministries, to scan the world and identify and commercialize promising new ideas ahead of competitors. Thus, rather than exploiting their huge R&D investments, Japan's biggest companies were holding back.

The disdain for services and software had also become a huge handicap. Productivity in Japan's finance, transportation, retailing, and other service industries was among the lowest of the OECD countries. Especially glaring was the poor performance in the communications and information technology sector. Here there was no Japanese Google, no Japanese iOS or Android operating system, and, even considering hardware, no Japanese equivalent of China's Huawei or ZTE. Japan's communications and information technology (CIT) sector simply wasn't delivering anything like the productivity gains that the United States and some other national CIT sectors were achieving. According to the OECD, Japan's innovation rate (that is, the number of enterprises demonstrating some degree of innovation) in CIT was one-fifth that of the United States and some European countries.

Although global software solutions had become essential in the Internet era, few Japanese companies were on the leading edge. A great deal of the problem arose from Japan's longstanding structural weakness in this area. In the global industry of independent software producers, Japan was a minor participant. While some areas, such as the auto industry, could thrive in the absence of a strong domestic software capability, others, such as electronics, could not. Over the years, various solutions, including outsourcing of development to India and China, had been tried. But nothing had worked, because companies were unwilling to risk revealing their technology secrets; cultural and linguistic communication problems were also a factor. Here was one of the instances in which that lack of adequate capability in English, the language of global software, concretely harmed Japan. But the biggest problem was simply a general misunderstanding throughout traditional Japanese industry of what it really means to be a software developer. Truly proficient software developers not only understand software systems and how to code them, but they also understand the user's needs and business model. As a consequence, they can provide state-of-the-art solutions that the user is either unaware of or doesn't completely understand. While a few Japanese companies, such as Toyota, fully appreciated the importance of software development, most still equated software developers with simple code writers working to preset specifications. It must be emphasized that this was not true in nontraditional Japanese industries such as video games, where Japan was a leader, perhaps because this type of industry accepted idiosyncratic workers. In most of Japanese industry, however, the ignorance of the importance of software development as a competitive tool was having disastrous consequences for Japan in the digital age.

Finally, there was the problem of the universities. Based on the American example, university-led research in support of advanced corporate R&D had become an important component of high-tech competitiveness around the globe. This link was well understood in Japan's science and technology (S&T) community, and a number of plans aimed at strengthening the role of the universities had been issued by the Science and Technology Council in the years between 1980 and 2015. These included programs for upgrading university infrastructure and for developing stronger links between university and corporate R&D labs. While a step in the right direction, these efforts were hampered by the sanctity of long-term relationships and the strong resistance of interlocking bureaucracies. The same old professors tended to continue to receive the majority of the government's grants from the same old ministries for funding the same old favorite projects that had usually not yielded results. In this context, it was noteworthy that some of the world's leading companies in a wide range of fields had established advanced research facilities in China in order to take advantage of the large number of high-quality researchers coming out of China's rapidly improving universities. In 2013, China was second only to the US with respect to the number of its universities ranked in the top 500 in the world. This figure had more than doubled since 2003, while Japan's ranking had tumbled from fourth to sixth.

As China's universities grew in global stature, two troubling trends for Japanese universities became apparent. First, despite a major push by its S&T community to increase research collaboration with US universities, Japan found its scientific collaboration with Chinese universities increasing more rapidly, with many Chinese scientists coming to Japan. Second, Chinese graduate students in the science and engineering fields came to constitute by far the greatest number of foreign students participating in Japan's leading graduate programs. These twin trends posed a dilemma. Japan was seeking to place more and more emphasis on university-led basic and applied research as the source of innovative ideas. Yet its major Asian competitor, China, was more and more tightly plugged into this research, and had a more flexible business and industrial structure that was better able to turn new ideas into new products and services. In the past, utilizing the US technology base had dramatically accelerated the growth of Japanese productivity. Now China was doing the same thing with Japan's technology base, but without the element of reciprocity that had become one of the defining characteristics of the Japan-US relationship. Thus Japan was losing ground to China even as it strove to multiply and strengthen its ties to the United States.

An important event that summed up both the sad state of Japanese technology and the causes thereof had been the precipitate decline of Nippon Electric Company (NEC) in the first decade of the twenty-first century. Twenty years earlier, the company had been one of the world's largest CIT firms, with advanced R&D labs considered to be among the world's finest. The company had been so prosperous that it had decorated its executive floors with Greek statuary. But after the turn of the century, it had lost its footing and begun turning out "me-too" products adapted only to the demands of Japanese consumers rather than the global marketplace. Indeed, even in Japan, NEC found it increasingly difficult to compete. It rapidly lost market share in the semiconductor, telecommunications, and consumer electronics markets. As a result, its once cutting-edge labs were forced to shrink by more than half. The problem was not that NEC had been spending too little on R&D; it was that all the R&D spending had not produced anything very new that could conquer world markets. It seemed that either the labs were producing nothing or that the good ideas they produced were being bottled up in the corporation. Either way, the future did not look bright.

THE IMPACT OF DISRUPTIVE TECHNOLOGY

A positive aspect of the high-technology field is that it is usually changing rapidly, thereby offering new opportunities for recovery even if companies have lost their positions in older markets. In 2013, the McKinsey Global Institute had identified twelve technologies as being potentially "disruptive," meaning that they were developing rapidly and had the potential to cause major breakthroughs whose impact would probably result in significant market disruptions in the near future. These offered a golden opportunity for halting and reversing the decline of Japan's high-tech competitiveness. The good news was that Japan was already quite competitive in about half the technologies on the list. These included advanced robotics, autonomous vehicles, next-generation genomics, energy storage, 3-D printing, advanced materials (including nanotechnology), oil and gas exploration and recovery, and renewable energy. Japan's leading high-tech companies were already closely monitoring these areas and, in principle, were fully capable of becoming first movers in turning them into commercial products and services. Moreover, the

Japanese government's long-term S&T plan included significant long-range investment in each of the twelve disruptive technologies. Thus, the country seemed well positioned to capitalize on its R&D investments. Unfortunately, the four economically most important technologies on McKinsey's list were mobile Internet, automation of knowledge work, the Internet of Things, and cloud technology. It was precisely in these areas that Japan's R&D position was weakest. A major reason was that complementary capabilities in embedded software development were a prerequisite for successfully competing in any of these four areas, and, as noted previously, Japan was not good at embedded software.

Moreover, Japanese companies were mostly ill suited to compete in disruptive environments in which old companies and technologies were pushed aside in successive waves. In the United States, for example, Intel, once the foremost producer of microprocessors, had found entry into the markets for mobile processors extremely difficult. Likewise, Microsoft had failed badly in getting into mobile communications. But these giants had quickly been upstaged by younger, rising companies, and the United States remained highly competitive in advanced information and communications technology. This same phenomenon of old companies being quickly replaced by new ones did not occur nearly so often in Japan. But to compete successfully in the new disruptive technology environment would require such agility. In an evolutionary R&D environment, the risk of being completely wrong about the direction of a technological trend is not great, but neither is the potential reward. In a more revolutionary, discontinuous environment, the risk is higher, but so is the reward. To escape continuing decline, the Japanese technology establishment had to find breakthrough solutions and develop a way to make big bets on uncertain technologies.

Fortunately, three aspects of the situation indicated how Japan might reverse its technology slide. First, Japanese companies and researchers had a strong position in nanotechnology. This was especially valuable because, by its very nature, nanotechnology matched up well with Japan's tradition of precise, high-quality manufacturing. Nanotechnology also had the enormous advantage of being an enabling technology. It could be applied to health care, instrumentation, electronics (e.g., new forms of computing techniques), and many other fields. It was thus critically important that Japan use its advantages here to open the door for competitive entry into a wide variety of other industries.

The problem in achieving success in nanotechnology lay in overcoming the traditional segmentation of most Japanese R&D organizations and bringing them together to work on integrated solutions, so that new nanotechnology formats could be tested quickly in the marketplace. Japan too often encountered the Valley of Death phenomenon, in which a good idea tended to die inside the lab or inside the larger organization because it wasn't compatible with the traditional way of thinking and of doing things, and thus could not obtain sufficient funding to make the transition from lab to commercialization. Similarly, traditional university organizations structured around the classic engineering fields tended to be inflexible. This tendency was strengthened by the Ministry of Education, Culture, Sports, Science and Technology (MEXT)'s preference for funding incumbent researchers working on traditional science and engineering topics rather than on truly innovative and potentially disruptive research.

A second area of special potential for Japan was in health and medicine, especially gerontechnology, in which Japanese research was quite advanced because of the needs of its aging population. In these fields there were important potential synergies with nanotechnology that could be used, for example, in targeted drug delivery for treatment of cancer. Similarly, nanotechnology could be used to open avenues to biotechnology, where Japan was relatively weak, through its application to regenerative medicine. For years, the relative weakness of the universities in the sciences had forced pharmaceutical companies to rely on their own R&D programs and on licenses from and tie-ups with foreign companies for new drugs and devices. But gradually the cost of new developments had grown to threaten the survival of the companies. Now there was potential not only to stay alive, but to thrive.

Finally, there were innovations in software that held promise for Japan. For decades, the country had tried a variety of measures to solve its competitive weaknesses in this area without much success. But the advent of open-source software such as Google's Android operating system in the early 2000s provided the opportunity for escaping from the tyranny of Microsoft, Oracle, and the other software giants, as well as for overcoming the weaknesses of traditional corporate software development teams. Particularly important was the fact that this open-source trend fit nicely with the unique structure of the Japanese software industry. While the traditional Japanese high-tech companies had found software a handicap, the global business of gaming software was dominated by Japanese companies. Open-source software made it possible for developers at smaller, nontraditional companies to leapfrog old barriers, and for the big tech companies to exploit the talents of the independent developers.

Thus, if Japan could see disruptive technologies as an opportunity rather than a threat, its future would be bright indeed.

WHAT HAD TO BE DONE

After reviewing all of the analysis, the Commission made two background observations and then proposed a comprehensive action plan to make Japan a truly innovation-friendly country. The first observation was that innovation was flowering most abundantly outside the main university and corporate research departments, in what might be called fringe areas like manga and video games, where nonconformists were allowed to thrive.

The second was that, according to a well-known Booz & Company study of innovation, there is little evidence of an immediate close correlation between increased corporate R&D spending and increasing innovation. Booz concluded that businesses with the highest R&D spending levels were not necessarily the most innovative. Thus, reversing Japan's declining inventiveness was not a matter of simply spending more on R&D. Indeed, it seemed to be quite the opposite. As noted above, some of the most innovative areas of Japanese business were to be found in the small to mid-sized companies operating in businesses outside the mainstream and without big R&D budgets.

Next, the Commission proposed the actions it considered essential for transforming Japan's innovation and technology position. The first was a reiteration of their call for greater English-language competence. Because the language of technology was English, the Commission emphasized again that gaining a high level of English speaking ability would greatly facilitate communication and collaborative activity with the entire high-tech world.

The second was a reiteration of their recommendations on immigration. In this case, the Commission called for allowing at least 100,000 foreign researchers and software development engineers to come and work in Japan, as well to teach at Japanese universities. This number was gradually to be expanded to

500,000 over a decade, with special attention being paid to software development engineers.

The third recommendation was to reduce MEXT's funding of R&D to only 10 percent of its 2015 level. MEXT's role in fostering innovation through university research had proven counterproductive. Sustained efforts had been made to reduce its influence, but it still controlled well over half of the government's S&T budget. Japan, said the Commission, needed to build teaching and research capacity in the disruptive technologies important to the nation's future, while slashing the funding of legacy programs that were being sustained because of strong personal and institutional connections.

The fourth recommendation was based on the Commission's conclusion that too much R&D was taking place in large firms that fostered a "me-too" climate of imitation with little or no real innovation. In 2013–2014, the Abe administration had introduced a kind of state-sponsored venture capital program that called on *otaku*—a word for "weird guys" closely associated with those involved in the world of video games, manga, and anime—to submit research and business proposals for possible funding. This had obtained a strong response. The Commission therefore built on the proposal by calling for the R&D tax credit to be reduced for large companies and increased for small and medium-sized firms that met certain criteria regarding the global potential of their business and its linkage to other Japanese technology and business development. This increased credit would also be made available to divisions of large companies that split off from their parent firms and formed independent technology companies. In addition to the increased tax credit, such new companies would also have access to low-cost start-up loans, and would pay only half the standard corporate income tax rate for the first three years.

The fifth recommendation was to turn the salary system upside down by giving large salaries to young scientists and engineers. Young people would be allowed great freedom to pursue high-risk projects that also had potentially high rewards. This, after all, was what the young people in the successful fringe companies were already doing. So the idea was to encourage the same kind of thinking and activity in larger corporations. As they progressed in their careers, these young people would be subject to performance reviews; their compensation would be maintained, raised, or lowered depending on the results of their work. As time passed and they became older, it was expected that, in general, their compensation would decline.

The sixth recommendation was that the S&T Council, in conjunction with the Ministry of Economy, Trade and Industry (METI), should establish a technology monitoring office that would constantly scan the world to observe activity in cutting-edge technology and compare Japan to the world leaders in each critical sector. The office would publish its findings and comparisons on a regular basis so that everyone could easily know where Japan ranked in key technology capabilities, market share, numbers of researchers, and amounts being spent in various areas.

The seventh recommendation was for development of a government agency like America's Defense Advanced Research Projects Agency (DARPA) that would pull together various innovative technology elements in Japan from the universities, small companies, large companies, and the government to fill important gaps in Japan's technology base.

The eighth and final recommendation was for the government to give high national priority to increasing Japan's technological competitiveness.

INNOVATION HEAVEN

Now, in 2050, Japan has indisputably become the most innovation-friendly nation on earth. Implementation of the Commission's recommendations has completely restructured Japan's twentieth-century-era R&D complex into a sleek new twenty-first-century model based on Japan's intrinsic creativity and inventiveness. Japan is now an exciting place for scientists and engineers from all over the world to invent new things and to see their ideas tested in the ultimate proving lab—the global marketplace. What was only a vague dream forty years ago has become reality. Japan is attracting young, motivated engineers, researchers, and entrepreneurs from all over the world to learn, invent, and build exciting new businesses by working with Japan's leading science and engineering teams.

Today there are hundreds of thousands of non-Japanese software engineers and developers embedded in Japan's R&D establishment at all levels. This is partly a direct result of immigration reforms, but also of the fact that English is now the official second language of Japan and the unofficial first language of Japan's R&D world. Innovation is flourishing, as language and distance no longer create communications problems. Indian software developers have filled an important deficiency, allowing Japan to leap ahead in Internet and mobile platform developments. One example is autonomous car software. Using open-source platforms, Japanese engineers have been able to marry their concrete product design capability with the talents of Indian and US software developers to transpose original engineering designs into software code. In this way, the design can actually be implemented in code and can easily be changed to produce a variety of products. No other country in the world has combined these sorts of skill sets in this way and achieved such incredible results.

Japanese women are now heading a large proportion of the major science and engineering programs at universities and corporate labs. And enrollment in university science and engineering programs has been steadily growing over the past forty years, in large part because of woman-friendly policies. Furthermore, five of the world's top ten engineering universities are now in Japan. This is partly a result of generous government funding that has given Japan research facilities that few other countries can equal. In addition, as Japan's global reputation in advanced materials, 3-D design and testing, and many other engineering specialties has grown, many global companies have decided to co-locate laboratories with major Japanese university research complexes. Although China is no longer Japan's major source of foreign graduate students—they now flock to Japan from all over the world—ties to China's enormous R&D establishment are carefully monitored to ensure a balanced flow of knowledge that benefits both countries.

None of this should surprise anyone who was aware of Japan's latent capabilities in the early 2000s. Take energy, for example. In 2015, Japan could produce a dollar of GDP with half the energy of the United States and two-thirds that of Europe. Today, despite dramatic advances in Europe, America, and China, Japan can produce a dollar of GDP with only one-third the energy of China and about half that of Europe and the United States. This is because Japan has been able to capitalize on the renewable energy research that was already in the R&D pipeline more than three decades ago.

Or take architecture and engineering. As long ago as the 1980s, Japan had the strongest civil engineering programs in the world. Now, in the mid-twenty-first century, Japanese construction companies have been able to exploit this strength by overseeing the destruction of older, energy-inefficient high-rise towers, while helping the United States and Middle Eastern countries renew their older cities by creating greener, denser population centers around highly energy-efficient, super-tall towers. Chinese and South Korean construction firms have sought to copy Japan's methods, but the Japanese industry's strong intellectual property position, combined with its mastery of the integration of advanced materials and designs, has made it difficult for these competitors to advance.

Another example would be the autonomous vehicles now gliding through the cities and along the expressways of Japan. While Germany and the United States have also strongly supported development of this technology, large-scale demand appeared first in Japan, where urban planners, for reasons of safety and energy efficiency, specifically designed cities to make the best use of these vehicles.

Building super-tall structures and using autonomous vehicles as the backbone of the urban transport system have proven highly effective in addressing the rapid growth of the elderly population and its concentration in central urban areas. This kind of urban planning was social innovation on a massive scale; it allowed Japan to become a sort of test site for demonstrating best practice to the rest of the world in how smart cities should be developed.

Japan's investment in gerontechnology has also had a huge payoff. Like Japan, China has experienced the rapid aging of its population. But unlike Japan, China's elderly are not very healthy. They have huge medical problems resulting from years of breathing polluted air and drinking polluted water. These elderly Chinese have become an enormous market for Japan's gerontechnology. Japanese medical companies are greatly aided in tapping this market by the Chinese doctors and technologists who have been educated at Japanese universities and who have worked in the labs of Japanese medical technology companies.

But these are only a few examples of the dynamism of the new Japan. The fact is that the old dinosaur Japanese companies like NEC, Mitsui & Co., Nippon Steel, Toshiba, and others have been transformed by the new rules and the new social-work environment. They experienced a rebirth even as new start-up companies were undergoing their first birth. Together the old and new firms have succeeded in making Japan the world's most innovation-friendly country.

CHAPTER 7

Energy Independence

A few weeks into your trip, it's dawned on you that in the new Japan no one seems ever to turn out the lights or mention the price of oil. It's obvious, too, that all the whizbang technology and the highly automated living environment require an enormous amount of energy. Yet, you've hardly seen or heard the word "energy" anywhere in the media, nor have any of the people you've been meeting and talking with mentioned it. Indeed, all of their discussion indicates that they more or less take the ready availability and low cost of energy for granted.

That certainly was not always the case. On the contrary, energy had been Japan's Achilles' heel. It was concern for oil supplies that led to Japan's attack on Pearl Harbor and its entry into the conflict that became World War II. For nearly thirty years after that conflict, America remained the world's major oil producer and price setter. It kept oil relatively inexpensive to boost its own prosperity and that of its allies in Europe and Japan. Thus the "Japanese Miracle" of postwar economic recovery was fueled by cheap oil-based energy, despite Japan's oil scarcity. For example, in 1950, the country's energy mix was 50 percent coal, 33 percent hydroelectric, and only 17 percent oil. By the early 1970s, that had switched to 77 percent oil, 17 percent coal, and 5 percent hydroelectric. But in 1970, US production began slowly to decline, and Middle East producers took over the role of balancing global supply and setting prices. The formation of their cartel (Organization of the Petroleum Exporting Countries, or OPEC) and its embargo on oil exports to certain countries in 1973 resulted in the "first oil crisis" that drove prices to very high levels. This was followed by the "second oil crisis" in the wake of the 1979 Iranian revolution, which drove prices even higher. With global demand rising and supply being artificially depressed by producers, it was clear that Japan's future competitiveness, prosperity, and national security would depend on developing inexpensive and preferably domestically supplied alternative energy sources.

JAPAN'S NEW MODEL

In response to this crisis, Japan adopted a policy of diversification by switching away from oil to coal (imported mostly from Australia and the United States), nuclear power, and natural gas or liquefied natural gas (LNG). It also emphasized energy conservation. Thus, over the next thirty years, as its GDP tripled, Japan's energy consumption rose by only 1.5 times. Also over that period, the country's energy authorities constructed about forty-five nuclear reactors, mostly along its rugged, sometimes seismically active coastline. As a result, by the turn of the century, oil had fallen from more than 70 percent of Japan's primary energy supply to about 50 percent, with nuclear power, natural gas, coal, and renewable energy sources rising from 30 to 50 percent of the total. Of total electricity demand, nuclear power was supplying about 25 percent, up from 1 to 2 percent at the time of the crisis.

By 2002, the energy issue had become linked to the problem of global warming and reduction of carbon-dioxide emissions.

This led to renewed emphasis on nuclear energy, with the enthusiastic support of all elements of the politically and bureaucratically powerful nuclear power industry. A ten-year energy plan calling for a 30 percent increase in nuclear power and the installation of nine to twelve new plants by 2011 was endorsed by the cabinet. In 2004, the Japan Atomic Industrial Forum called for a 60 percent reduction in carbon dioxide emissions and a doubling of nuclear generating capacity, so that nuclear plants would supply 60 percent of the nation's total power by 2050. In October 2005, the Atomic Energy Commission reaffirmed policy directions for nuclear to achieve a 30 to 40 percent share of primary energy generation by 2030.

Then, the Strategic Energy Plan (SEP) released in 2010 recommended that the nuclear share of the nation's electric power generation be increased from 34 to over 50 percent by 2020, so that Japan, like France, would derive more than 50 percent of its electric power from nuclear generation. This plan called for adding at least nine and perhaps as many as fifteen new reactors to the fifty-four that already existed. Of course, nuclear energy was not the only focus of attention. The Ministry of Economy Trade and Industry (METI) had introduced a feed-in tariff for solar and other renewable electric power sources in 2009, and research and development continued on methane hydrate, biomass, geothermal, and tidal energy sources. But the main thrust was for achieving near- to medium-term reduction of greenhouse gas emissions and reduction of energy imports by emphasizing nuclear power generation.

It is important to understand that this planning was strongly influenced by what was collectively known as "Japan's Nuclear Money Tree." This was the combination of the ten electric power companies, the nuclear equipment makers, the nuclear construction companies, the regulatory authorities in METI, and a web of nonprofit nuclear-power promotion associations and foundations created and maintained by the companies and regulatory agencies. The power companies, known as EPCOs (Electric Power Companies), were vertically integrated (i.e., they generated the power and also distributed it over their own wholly-owned grid) regional monopolies that were only weakly and partially connected to each other. They had historically maintained a virtual stranglehold over all elements of the electricity market. Beginning in the mid-1990s, deregulation was supposed to unbundle the EPCO monopolies and allow competition at all levels—power generation, transmission, distribution, and retailing. Wholesale power bidding was permitted in 1996, and this was followed by other ostensible liberalizations such as the retailing of electricity by distribution companies other than the EPCOs in 1999. But these reforms were never comprehensive, and the power industry remained an extremely influential political force that was able to develop a kind of apparent unbundling under rules of "competitive conduct" overseen by METI, while maintaining an actual situation under which the market share of each EPCO remained essentially the same. An important reason for this was the fact that power could not readily be moved from one part of the country to another, both because the grids were only slightly interconnected, if at all, and because one part of the country used electricity at 50 hertz, while the other part used it at 60 hertz. Government policy (strongly influenced by the electric power lobby) had effectively required each EPCO to achieve power self-sufficiency in its geographical area without much interconnection to other regions, more or less forcing Japan to follow a nuclear-power roadmap. Introduction of renewable and alternative energy was limited because the lack of grid interconnection made it difficult or impossible to move energy from where it might be generated (whether by solar-power installations in

Hokkaido or conventional plants in other remote areas) to the urban markets where it was in demand.

On March 11, 2011, all of these plans fell apart, along with a large portion of the nuclear power complex at Fukushima, in the wake of a huge earthquake and subsequent tsunami that breached the plant's sea walls. The accumulated weaknesses of the structure of the power system were made glaringly apparent. The Fukushima reactor did not fail directly because of the tsunami, but rather because the Tokyo Electric Power Company (TEPCO) had not established and enforced proper safety measures, and government regulators (probably anticipating possible post-retirement jobs in the industry) had chosen to overlook the omission. Exacerbating the problem of the loss of power to Tokyo from Fukushima was the fact that the grid would not allow easy transfer of power from western Japan—which had plenty—to metropolitan Tokyo, where there was very little.

Of course, the costs resulting from the Fukushima disaster were enormous. The Fujitsu Research Institute estimated that increased imports of oil and LNG alone cost about ¥4 trillion (US$ 3.3 billion) annually; on top of that, the price of electricity rose by about 15 percent per year between 2011 and 2014. The Japan Center for Economic Research estimated the total cost of the cleanup of the Fukushima site at up to ¥25 trillion (US$20 billion)—roughly the same as the economic cost of the first oil crisis of the 1970s. When all the elements were added up, they demonstrated dramatically that even though the probability of an event like Fukushima was low, its enormous potential cost required that Japan completely rethink its energy strategy. Indeed, the issues associated with the nuclear calamity at Fukushima were a significant part of the reason for the establishment of the Extraordinary National Revitalization Commission, and the Commission paid a great deal of attention to them.

GOALS

The energy situation the Commission confronted at its inception was extremely complex. Nuclear energy had seemed an ideal solution for Japan. Although it entailed a big initial investment, thereafter it was inexpensive, domestically produced, had no emissions, and ran constantly day and night in all weather, providing an ideal base load for the entire electric grid. Ironically, however, what had begun as a way of protecting Japan from external threats evolved into an unexpected internal threat of immensely costly accidents that demanded a whole new set of protective measures and perhaps development of a whole new energy supply.

Despite its virtues, nuclear energy had always carried the risk of a meltdown, leakage of radiation, or some other disastrous event. The risk of such an event occurring at any particular moment was low. But, if it did occur, the impact would be catastrophic. Furthermore, over a long period of time, some significant accident was almost a certainty. Now that Japan had experienced one of history's worst nuclear accidents, it became very cautious about adding further nuclear power plants or even continuing to use the existing reactors. The only immediate alternative was to import enormous quantities of oil, coal, and LNG, and that was what Japan had done after the Fukushima disaster, while keeping its reactors shut for safety inspections and because of strong public opposition to restarting them. In 2014, the Abe administration had succeeded in completing safety inspections and beginning a gradual restart of a number of reactors. The government's plan was to get as many reactors back on line as possible while also working diligently to develop alternative power sources. However, the eruption of Mount Ontake in that year, along with the ensuing volcanic activity, forced a renewed shutdown of many reactors. Furthermore, the Israeli attack on Iran in 2016 had resulted in the closure of the Strait of Hormuz.

The Strait had quickly been reopened by the US Navy, but for Japan everything was back to square one. With the price of oil at US$200 per barrel, energy costs were making Japan's industries increasingly uncompetitive while dramatically raising its trade and current account deficits. This, in turn, was forcing it to liquidate its large US dollar reserves and little by little to fund more of its budget deficit by borrowing from non-Japanese sources. At the same time, the fifty-four existing nuclear power plants represented an enormous investment. If they could not be used, the loss of the investment would cost society a great deal. On the other hand, restarting them carried the risk of further accidents of unknown proportions, unknown but possibly grave consequences, and further prohibitive costs.

In confronting the situation, the Commission began by reviewing the country's key goals with respect to energy generation and supply. It reaffirmed that these were to achieve the maximum possible degree of energy independence while also keeping energy prices at a level commensurate with maintaining Japan's economic competitiveness, and to reduce greenhouse gas emissions ultimately to zero. It then turned to the question of options. In considering these, the Commission not only looked at domestic energy development activity, but also sent delegations abroad to observe the goals of other countries and how they were planning to meet them.

FRANCE: ALL NUCLEAR, ALL THE TIME

Because France and Japan were very similar in terms of energy strategy and development, Paris was the logical first stop. The Japanese delegation found that France was sticking with its nuclear expansion plans. The accidents in Chernobyl and Fukushima, along with the 2011 German decision to decommission all seventeen of its reactors had sparked debate and even proposals in the French Parliament calling for dramatic reduction of reliance on nuclear energy. But these suggestions went nowhere, and French energy policy remained as it had been since the mid-1970s.

Many factors lay behind this decision. One was the fact France had never had a serious nuclear accident. There was also fear that decommissioning a lot of reactors could bankrupt Électricité de France (EDF), the government-owned power monopoly, and thereby cause serious financial problems for the state. Moreover, France had also created surplus generating capacity (relative to domestic demand) and had designed its power grid to support efficient transfer of power between deficit and surplus regions not only within France, but also between France and most other countries in Europe. This had resulted in large exports of French electricity. As the monopoly operator, EDF became enormously skilled at balancing supply and demand across the interconnected European power grids. Because it had excess generating capacity, EDF was also always searching for new ways to utilize its surplus. Thus, France was increasingly relying on electricity for residential heating, and was aiming to put 2 million electric vehicles on its roads by the early 2020s. To handle these changes, France was planning to upgrade its grid with smart technology over the next twenty-five years. One drawback to the new renewable energy sources being developed was their lack of flexibility to meet peak demands when the sun didn't shine or the wind didn't blow, or when Germany might have a power failure in some part of its grid. Thus, as France planned for the future it realized that its grid needed to be modernized, with sufficient short-term storage capacity to handle the increasingly varied demand patterns arising from the multiplication of uses for and sources of electric power.

Here were some lessons for Japan, whether or not it moved forward with nuclear power. The quality and sophistication of the grid had to be a critical component of investment, regardless of the ultimate energy supply scenario. Like France, Japan had set an ambitious target for having electric vehicles on the road by the 2020s. Along with the proliferation of other electric devices, this would only cause greater fluctuations in demand. In this kind of environment, no matter what the primary energy source (nuclear, coal, oil, gas, solar, or other renewables) a smart, flexible grid would be necessary to manage the widely varying load requirements. Some form of new storage technology integrated into the grid would be extremely desirable.

LESSONS FROM DENMARK AND GERMANY

In Copenhagen and Berlin, the delegation found that energy intensity (that is, the total primary energy consumed measured in caloric content per unit of real GDP) in Denmark was 20 percent less than Japan's 8,400 kilowatt-hours, while Germany's was about 14 percent less. The reason was not hard to determine: Denmark had the highest household electricity prices in the world, and Germany had the second highest. Residential end-user electricity prices in Denmark were over 50 percent higher than the EU average, and roughly 20 percent higher even than in Germany. These differences were the result of deliberate government policies to promote conservation in the household and commercial sectors. Direct energy taxes accounted for 35 percent of Denmark's end-user electricity tariffs, three times the EU average. If value-added and other taxes were included, taxes accounted for 55 percent of the final price of electricity. Of course, these prices did not apply to industrial users, who paid far lower rates. German industry also paid similarly lower rates.

This divided-rate policy was aimed at maintaining industrial competitiveness while promoting domestic energy conservation. And it produced the intended result: Denmark's newer houses consumed 50 percent less energy per square meter than houses built before the policy was implemented, partly as a result of the high price of electricity and partly as a result of the application of high building-efficiency standards.

In both Denmark and Germany, the emphasis on conservation was just part of a broader policy aimed at rapidly expanding renewable energy supplies. Denmark had begun working on development of wind power in the wake of the oil crises of the 1970s. It redoubled these efforts in the 1980s and 1990s in response to concerns about greenhouse gases, and also to address legislation prohibiting the installation of nuclear power. It used feed-in tariffs (FIT) and initial 30 percent capital subsidies to promote wind energy production, and by the year 2000, wind energy accounted for 12 percent of Denmark's electric energy production. That nearly doubled to 22 percent by 2010, and then rose to 30 percent in 2012. Denmark's goal was to hit 50 percent in 2020.

Germany also was pursuing a very ambitious move to renewable energy. In the immediate wake of the Fukushima disaster, the German government had announced that it would close eight of its nuclear power plants immediately and the remaining nine by 2022. Chancellor Angela Merkel stated that this would give Germany a competitive lead in adopting and developing renewable energy sources. Indeed, in an interview with the Associated Press, Merkel specifically noted Japan's "helplessness in the face of its nuclear disaster, despite the fact that it is an industrialized, technologically advanced nation." Between 2002 and 2012, renewable sources had already quadrupled their delivery of power in Germany from about 6 percent to 25 percent of the electricity supply. The objective was to reach 35 percent in 2020, 50 percent in 2030, and 80 percent by 2050. It also aimed to reduce consumption by 10 percent in 2020 and 25 percent in 2050. Like Denmark, Germany used FIT and investment subsidies to stimulate development of renewables. However, the German program focused on a wide range of renewables that included not only wind and solar energy, but also hydropower, biomass, and geothermal sources.

There was a price tag for all of this. The Japanese delegation reported that the cost of replacing Germany's nuclear energy with renewable energy was officially estimated at the equivalent of about US$70 billion, in addition to the US$17 billion already devoted to subsidizing renewables. However, unofficial estimates put the cost at about US$340 billion between the years 2011–2021, and one German environment minister said the total cost of restructuring the energy industry could be US$1.3 trillion.

These findings had important implications for Japan. Because its population was expected inevitably to decline in the near future, Japan's SEP already included a fall in total energy consumption of about 15 percent. If Japan could achieve even Germany's rate of electricity conservation—let alone Denmark's—by 2030, it could reduce its electric needs by 30 percent. This alone would suffice to replace the energy lost from shutting down all of Japan's nuclear stations. Of course, it might result in some increase in electricity prices, but the total cost of nuclear accidents would also cause electricity prices to rise. So, in the end, it could be argued that renewables were no more expensive in real terms than nuclear energy. The Danish and German experiences had made it clear that a relatively rapid expansion of renewable energy production was technically feasible. It was also clear that Japan was lagging far behind other OECD countries in shifting to renewable energy. Indeed, the renewable share of

Japan's energy supply was only half the OECD average. Japan's 2015 goal—to obtain 20 percent or its energy from renewable sources by 2030—was what the OECD average had been in 2010.

THE UNITED STATES AND THE FRACKING REVOLUTION

Although the United States was the world's biggest generator of nuclear power, it had not built a new nuclear power plant since the Three Mile Island disaster in 1979. When the Revitalization Commission delegation arrived in Washington to carry out its study, the country's nuclear power production as a percentage of total electric production was only about 19 percent. The United States generated about half its electricity from coal and about 25 percent from natural gas, with small amounts from hydropower, biomass, solar, and wind. Japan, by comparison, was producing 28 percent of its power from coal and about the same from natural gas, with about 8 percent from hydropower and another 5 or 6 percent from renewable sources. Of course, there was also a huge difference between the two countries. The United States was a major oil and gas producer, while Japan was not. But the most important element of the US experience that held possible lessons for Japan was the recent emergence of the technology of hydraulic fracturing, or fracking, to produce oil and gas from shale rock. This had made America the world's largest oil and gas producer for the first time in forty years.

Particularly striking was the fact that in the early 2000s, very few had been aware of fracking technology; in fact, US energy companies and policy makers had been planning to build large ports for the importation of LNG, as it was anticipated that America's domestic gas production had already entered a long decline. But new drilling techniques had suddenly made fracking a commercially viable technology, completely changing the energy picture both in the US and globally. The LNG ports that had been expected to receive imports were now preparing to ship exports. OPEC had been dramatically weakened. It was an amazing reversal, and it demonstrated to Japanese observers that the potential for unusual technological solutions should never be discounted.

IT'S THE GRID, STUPID

After consideration of domestic investigations and of all the reports from abroad, it became obvious to the Commission that there was one central obstacle to a safe, balanced, economical, and environmentally friendly energy-supply system for Japan, an obstacle that needed to be tackled regardless of what policy Japan decided to pursue regarding nuclear energy or other technologies. That obstacle was its power grid.

Japan's ten EPCOs proudly pointed to how efficiently they had been running their grids, and emphasized that Japan was the world leader in minimizing transmission power losses. While this was true, it ignored the most important problem, which was that the grid was not well interconnected across the country. Indeed, it did not even consist of multiple interconnected grids like those of Europe and the United States. Rather, largely because of the corporate, bureaucratic, and political interests of the EPCOs and their regulators and allied politicians, as well as because of previous equipment installation decisions, Japan had ten separate grids that operated essentially as separate independent transmission networks. Each EPCO's regional grid was an island with limited ability to supply or receive power from other adjacent EPCOs. Adding to the fragmentation was a fundamental east-west split, under which three of the regional grids in eastern Japan operated on 50 hertz, while the seven in western Japan operated on 60 hertz. This divide, which arose from a long-ago decision to use different kinds of European and American equipment, proved disastrous.

Contrast Japan's fragmented grid to that of France, which was not only integrated internally but also externally with the rest of Europe, and moved power easily from regions of deficit to regions of surplus demand. In conjunction with this, a sophisticated wholesale energy market allocated energy around Western Europe, using electricity transfers booked more than twenty-four hours in advance based on weather and other conditions throughout the service zone. Congestion pricing operated so that demand was automatically allocated to be met by regions with excess capacity, thereby optimizing total system utility. Information about conditions on the grid was readily available to the public, rather than being limited to the incumbent energy generators or major industrial generators. The United States had had considerable experience with such wholesale markets as well, and the reforms in both Europe and the US had transformed their power grids into interstate highways for electricity transmission.

In contrast, each of Japan's EPCOs maintained only sufficient capacity to guarantee reliability in its own region. The Fukushima disaster had demonstrated dramatically the high cost of this narrow strategy to the overall national welfare. Just after the earthquake and tsunami, roughly 27 gigawatts of generating capacity had been lost. Isolated in its eastern Japan electric-power island, TEPCO could not call upon any of the western EPCOs for any serious help to relieve its sudden shortfall. Only three small installations from the unaffected Western regions could move a total of about 1.2 gigawatts to help TEPCO, and that was not nearly enough.

As part of its Fourth Energy Plan put forward in the spring of 2014, the Abe administration had addressed the grid problem, planning to establish an Organization for Cross-regional Coordination of Transmission Operations (OCCTO) sometime around 2015. This organization was intended to become a monopoly operator of the grid which, like EDF in France, would develop supply-demand projections, coordinate grid operations under normal conditions, and balance supply and demand in tight situations. Following up on this in February, 2015, the Abe cabinet issued a decision to create separate generation and transmission companies that would be entirely independent from each other. The feasibility of this plan was not clear, and whether the grids would be fully integrated, who would actually own them, how new technology would be incorporated, and how new energy generation sources would be connected was still to be determined. This lack of explanation was very troubling, because the existing structures militated against investment and innovation that could give Japan a more flexible, more diversified, more reliable, and ultimately less expensive set of energy sources.

"Smart grids" were going to be the wave of the future. These incorporated energy storage and balancing capabilities in the grid itself, and would allow the fluctuating power generated by solar, wind, and other renewable power sources—as well as alternating streams of power from different nuclear and fossil fuel sources— to be smoothly incorporated into the system and transmitted upon demand to users around the entire country. Japan was generally acknowledged to be one of the world leaders in smart-grid technology—including, very importantly, storage technology. But its continued leadership would be endangered unless the grid became truly integrated and not just "coordinated."

Likewise, any concept of developing renewable alternative energy sources would also be slowed or halted altogether if the grid did not become highly integrated. Solar, wind, geothermal, and tidal energy must be generated in locations where the sun shines, the wind blows, the hot springs flow, and the tides rise and fall. These places are not necessarily located right next to major centers of energy demand. Development of these energy sources therefore requires that they have entry into the grid, and that the grid be capable of moving them over long distances and, to the maximum extent possible, be able to store them in order to even out their natural fluctuations.

Another, even more ambitious project being delayed by the electric industry's structural barriers, which was not even mentioned in the Abe plan, was the Asian Super Grid. Designed to interconnect Asia in the same way as Western Europe was interconnected, this Super Grid would tap large wind farms in Mongolia, nuclear-power plants in China and Korea, solar farms in Japan, and possibly other sources in Russia to provide Japan and the rest of Asia the ability to import and export competitive electric power. This type of grid would also address the variability problems of renewable energy simply by its vast reach. For instance, the sun may not always be shining or the wind blowing in Japan. But the sun is always shining and the wind is always blowing somewhere. If the grid is big enough and has sufficiently low transmission costs, the fluctuations of renewable energy generation disappear. Of course, in the absence of an integrated national grid, solar power from Hokkaido couldn't even get to neighboring Aomori, let alone Mongolian wind power getting to Tokyo.

OPTIONS AND ROADBLOCKS

After the 2011 Fukushima disaster, the reaction of the ruling Democratic Party of Japan had been to shut down all the nuclear stations and to aim for minimal (ideally zero) nuclear power generation in the future. But with the advent of the Abe administration and the adoption of the previously noted Fourth Energy Plan, nuclear was again targeted as a major source of future power generation. Not only did the new policy call for restarting the existing nuclear plants as soon as safety inspections would allow, but also to consider extending the forty-year working life of many existing plants and to build a number of new plants. To be sure, the policy also called for development of a range of renewable energy sources, but set no targets or timetables and provided no increased funding. It seemed clear to most analysts that Japan was still going to bet heavily on nuclear for the future.

In the light of information collected by its traveling delegations, as well as events and technology developments subsequent to the publication of the Fourth Energy Plan, the Commission undertook a full review of the potential feasibility, costs, and benefits of all the energy options open to Japan. Conventional analyses showed coal and natural gas to be the most economical sources immediately available, followed by nuclear power, and then by wind, solar, and tidal power. But it had already been demonstrated that the real costs of coal and LNG were much higher than listed costs because of their greenhouse gas emissions; and while nuclear created no emissions, it had the potential for resulting in costly meltdowns and pollution by radiation. Furthermore, the costs of renewables were projected to fall as a result of economies of scale and rapid technological advances. In the immediate future, the argument for restarting the nuclear reactors was strong, because both the negative impact of the loss of nuclear energy on Japan's competitiveness and the costs of mothballing the nuclear plants would be enormous. But should they be maintained for their full rated life spans? Should their number even, perhaps, be increased if new and safer nuclear technologies with no radioactive waste proved commercially viable? Those were the two major questions, and the answers depended on the availability and costs of the alternatives. In view of the long-term risks and environmental costs associated with nuclear and fossil-fuel-based power, it was obvious that renewable energy sources would be preferred if their operating costs could eventually be brought reasonably close to those of the traditional sources. Of course, each source had its own prospects and pluses and minuses.

In November of 2009, Japan had introduced an FIT that required utilities to purchase excess solar power sent to the grid by homes and businesses at twice the standard rate for that power. Over the previous fifteen years, solar generation costs had fallen by nearly 70 percent; the FIT dramatically accelerated solar installation. By the end of 2012, capacity had more than tripled. It nearly doubled again in 2013, in the wake of changes in the FIT aimed at increasing solar power capacity in response to the Fukushima crisis. This pushed Japan ahead of Germany to become the top solar energy market in the world. It also created a land rush in Hokkaido, where about 25 percent of the major solar projects were being located. Here, however, the problem of the grid became a huge obstacle. Hokkaido was attractive because of its relatively large expanses of land available for solar farms. But the Hokkaido Electric Power Company, which produced only 3 percent of Japan's electric power, announced in mid-2013 that it could accept applications for only an additional 400 megawatts of capacity, despite having applications for more than 3000 megawatts. There would have been no problem if the Hokkaido grid had been integrated with the other Japanese grids. But, of course, it was not.

Hydroelectric power was not a new phenomenon, but it accounted for only 4 to 5 percent of total generation. While it was the cheapest, cleanest power available, and METI had plans to expand it, the potential was limited by the natural environment and climate. However, other types of water-based power showed great promise. Surrounded by the sea, Japan had an Exclusive Economic Zone (EEZ) of nearly 5 million square kilometers—the world's sixth largest—flowing with powerful ocean currents at a depth of 50 to 100 meters. This gave it enormous potential for development of energy powered by ocean tides and currents, which flow constantly and can thus provide uninterrupted power, giving them the same advantage that nuclear and fossil fuel power plants have over solar and wind energy. In 2012, a group including the IHI Corporation (Ishikawajima-Harima Heavy Industries), Toshiba, the University of Tokyo, and Mitsui Global Strategic Studies Institute produced a successful prototype model of a system that could be anchored to the ocean floor and produce 2 megawatts of constant power suitable for providing the base load electric supply at competitive costs. The consortium noted that a 5-knot ocean current produces more energy than a 350-kilometer-per-hour wind. Meanwhile, Nova Energy Development Company (NEDO) presented information noting that setting 800 ocean current turbines would produce 1,600,000 kilowatts—more energy than one large nuclear plant producing 1,350,000 kilowatts—at only one-third the cost of building a nuclear-energy facility. Turbines could be placed anywhere in the 100-kilometer width of the Kuroshio Current, a strong north-flowing current similar to the Gulf Stream. NEDO estimated that the cost would be in the same range as solar and wind power by 2030, with the advantage of providing continuous power. Of course, here again, to be usable, such energy would need a way to be stored or fed into the grid.

Like hydropower, geothermal power had always held significant potential because of Japan's abundant geothermal resources—the world's third largest. But tapping these resources was difficult because most potential sites were within environmentally sensitive national parks. In the late 1990s, Japan ceased research and development on these sites in order to focus on nuclear power. On several occasions in late 2012 and early 2013, Icelandic Ambassador Stefan Stefansson had urged Japan to take a lesson from Iceland, which generated most of its electric power geothermally. He estimated that Japan's geothermal resources could replace as many as twenty-five of its nuclear plants. Until the Fukushima disaster, no new geothermal plants had been constructed in Japan in over fifteen years, and installed capacity had remained tiny, consisting of just seventeen facilities. In April of 2013, however, in the wake of the application of the FIT to all renewable energies, METI announced that twenty-one additional new geothermal plants would be built. While this would more than double the existing capacity, it would leave geothermal energy as a relatively small source of Japan's total power.

Water-based power was not the only alternative. Biomass (fuel derived from wood, switchgrass, bagasse, etc.) had always been part of Japan's energy supply, but didn't grow much until 2003, when Tokyo began requiring certain levels of renewable energy use. By 2016, use of biomass sources had doubled, but Japan's geography and natural resource base intrinsically limited the future potential. The bulk of Japan's biomass energy came from industrial waste. This might have been changed by reduction of the tariff on imported rice, thus forcing Japanese farmers to shift away from rice growing to cultivation of switchgrass and other plants specifically for biomass energy-generation purposes, or by undertaking serious development of algae and sea-based biomass. But in 2016, there were no such plans.

Wind farm capacity tripled between 2003 and 2012 to a still relatively small 2.5 gigawatts (Japan's total electric generation capacity was about 280 gigawatts at that point), with plans for production of another 2 gigawatts by 2020. This was mainly a result of the 2003 government requirement for increased use of renewable energy sources. After 2012, the application of the FIT further spurred development, with long-term plans for a total wind capacity of 7 to 10 gigawatts. However, the potential for wind power in Japan remained unknown. For onshore projects, there were simply too few large, windy areas outside of Hokkaido and Tohoku. Offshore wind offered large potential of up to eight times the capacity of all the Japanese power companies. But the steep fall of the Japanese shore to very deep ocean made construction extremely expensive. A possible solution was floating offshore wind plants. Three pilot plants had been established by 2015, but much more experience and development was needed to address the frequent typhoons, heavy seas, and other natural risks to offshore wind stations. And there was again the question of connection to the grid.

One of the most promising energy alternatives was methane hydrate. This offered the same game-changing potential for Japan as the fracking of shale gas and oil had offered the United States in the ten years between 2005 and 2015. In March of 2013, METI had announced that a consortium of Japanese companies had successfully extracted methane gas from methane hydrate drawn from the deep waters of the Nankai Trough off the coast of Aichi prefecture. Known as "burnable ice," methane hydrate is a crystalline solid that stores gas molecules within a cage of frozen water molecules. For a long time, the key question had been whether the frozen ice-like structure could be made to release the methane gas in a way that could eventually become commercially viable. The METI announcement answered that question. The Japan Oil, Gas, and Metals Company estimated that the Nankai Trough alone contained enough methane hydrate to supply all of Japan's gas needs for eleven years. Separately, the Japan National Institute of Advanced Science and Technology estimated that in all the waters around Japan there was enough methane hydrate to supply the country's gas needs for about a hundred years. Flow tests in the Nankai Trough resulted in greater volume of gas extraction than expected. This led METI officials to state that the results could be sufficient to lead to commercialization at costs competitive with LNG, of which Japan was the world's largest importer. Consequently, a target was established for large-scale commercial production by 2028.

A final promising alternative was a variation on the old nuclear theme. Between 1984 and 1994, America's Argonne National Laboratory had developed the Integral Fast Reactor (IFR), which could operate by burning nuclear waste from traditional reactors, and would reprocess its own fuel until the final waste contained no dangerous elements and could essentially be thrown into a normal garbage can. Moreover, dangerous weapons-grade materials like plutonium could not be extracted from the IFR process, and there was no danger of meltdowns arising from internal accidents or external events such as earthquakes and tsunamis. This was because in the IFR reactor, any stoppage of the coolant flow simply stopped the nuclear reaction, and there was no buildup of heat or danger of meltdown. Despite its virtues, however, the IFR project at Argonne had been discontinued by the US Congress, three years short of completion, in 1994.

MOVING TO ENERGY INDEPENDENCE AT LOW COST

As noted earlier, the nuclear power plants that existed in 2015–2016 had a permitted lifespan of forty years, after which they would either have to be relicensed or decommissioned and mothballed. In considering its recommendations, the Commission observed that if no more nuclear plants were built and none of the existing plants were relicensed, all Japan's nuclear reactors would be shut down by between 2036 and 2040. The Commission concluded that the costs and security risks of decommissioning the nuclear plants immediately were too high. With the right policies, however, energy derived from methane hydrate, solar, tides and currents, wind, other renewable sources, and IFR nuclear generation would be cost-effective and fully capable of fully replacing conventional nuclear energy by 2030. In addition, the Commission highlighted another important energy option: conservation. If Japan could achieve the same level of per-capita electricity consumption as Germany, that alone would allow it to close half its nuclear reactors. If it could drop its energy consumption to that of Denmark, it could close nearly all the reactors. Thus the Commission decided that Japan should aim to close all the existing reactors by 2030, building no new ones unless they were of the IFR type. It further recommended that over the next fifteen years all efforts be made to develop renewable and IFR nuclear energy sources to their maximum extent, while also creating a truly interconnected, responsive grid.

One of the Commission's recommendations appeared a bit contradictory—the idea of actually increasing the number of coal-fired plants in the immediate future. This was to provide a transition period during which energy from a source that was unlikely to be interrupted would provide low-cost electricity and a secure base load for the grid while renewable energy sources were developed. Of course, these coal plants were to be clean coal facilities with carbon-capture capability, and they would later be converted to gas from methane hydrate. The Commission foresaw that ultimately 35 to 50 percent of Japan's electricity would come from renewable sources, while the rest would come from methane hydrate and IFR nuclear.

To achieve these goals, the Commission recommended five steps. First was the formation of a special government entity called the Nuclear Corporation, which would issue special purpose bonds and use the proceeds to take over all fifty-four existing nuclear facilities. The Nuclear Corporation would then license the nine EPCOs that owned reactors to operate twenty-five of the safest, most modern reactors. The rest would be decommissioned; those left operating were to be given a time frame for eventual shutdown. The EPCOs wanting to operate the active reactors were to submit bids specifying not only the economic terms of their proposed arrangement, but also outlining in detail the safety measures they would enforce during the remaining years of operation. All reactors not restarted were to begin the decommissioning process, which the Nuclear Corporation would be responsible for funding.

Second, the transmission power grids of the ten EPCOs would be nationalized into a new government-owned and operated Grid Corporation, in which no former EPCO managers or board members would be allowed to participate, in order to avoid any undue influence by the EPCOs. Grid Corporation would then be split into three entities—north, west, and middle—and shares in each entity would be sold to private investors. These three new companies would be regulated by a newly established independent Grid Oversight Agency, which would have no connection to METI. The middle power-grid territory was to include portions of the grids on both sides of the frequency divide to force investment in greater east-west interconnection. The northern grid would be specifically incentivized under the licensing process to allow the Asian Super Grid to connect to the national grid. Capacity upgrades were to be funded through special tariffs, much as privatized auto routes in some countries fund capital improvements through tolls.

The third step was a large increase in taxes on residential and commercial electricity and a smaller tax increase on electricity for industrial use by medium and large corporations. The objective was to encourage energy conservation and to use the tax receipts to subsidize renewable energy, clean nuclear, and conservation investments. In addition, residential energy storage was to be deregulated, and flexible FIT systems were to be introduced. The Commission hoped that this would encourage residents and small businesses to come up with creative and effective means of energy conservation using plug-in electric vehicles, solar generation, and energy storage.

The fourth step was to invest heavily in development of solar, tidal, methane hydrate, and IFR nuclear-based power. While not technically a renewable energy source, methane hydrate had vast potential that offered Japan perhaps its best chance of gaining full energy independence, particularly if it could be combined with IFR nuclear, which had all the advantages of conventional nuclear power without any of its disadvantages. Development of methane hydrate power, of course, would involve not only establishing the extraction and processing technology, but also developing carbon-capture capability and constructing a national pipeline for distribution to power plants and users around the entire country.

The final step would be to use regulatory and tax measures to force conversion of most of the nation's auto and truck fleet to electric or super-hybrid (diesel plus electric) propulsion.

THE DREAM COME TRUE

As we see now in 2050, Japan's longtime dream of low-cost energy independence has finally come true. The Commission's five-step program worked better than anyone could have imagined. The old nuclear plants were all closed down by 2030, and replaced by fifteen IFR plants. The national grid is now highly interconnected, with great capability for transferring energy from areas of surplus to areas of demand. The new competition between the EPCOs has led to reductions in power costs, even as new energy sources have been introduced. Renewable energy sources and gas from methane hydrate have been developed and commercialized more rapidly and cheaply than initially forecast. A big surprise was the development of energy from the ocean currents, which has become nearly as important as methane hydrate. The Asian Super Grid has brought unexpected amounts of wind power from the plains of Mongolia, and Japan has surpassed Denmark in terms of conserving its electricity consumption. After an initial slowdown and even a slight increase in greenhouse gas emissions due to increased coal and gas usage, Japan has now surpassed its long-term reduction targets. Aside from power coming over the Asian Super Grid, the nation imports virtually no energy while enjoying low costs similar to those in the United States. In short, Japan has indeed reached energy nirvana.

CHAPTER 8

From Japan, Inc. to Germany with Japanese Characteristics

You're a bit disappointed at the decline in the number of bars and late-night drinking establishments since your last visit—the kinds of places where pretty hostesses would serve high-priced drinks and sit on the laps of executives sipping with their bosses late into the night. You've noticed that the lights don't burn as late as they used to in the offices and that the bars of yore have been replaced by family restaurants, or food retailers selling to couples hurrying home to dinner with their children.

No doubt the peculiar manners of the old Japan, Inc. had their rhyme, reason, and charm. But over the quarter-century from 1990 to 2015, the fabled Japanese corporations—the ones that had conquered world markets after the Second World War and turned "made in Japan" into a symbol of quality, style, service, innovation, and value—faltered. Nissan was only able to save itself by establishing a partnership with Renault of France. In 2012, once-mighty Panasonic recorded the biggest losses of any Japanese company in history. Hitachi exited hundreds of businesses and had to slash employment by nearly 100,000 employees to save itself. Former semiconductor giants Elpida and Renesas came close to bankruptcy. Even the great juggernaut Toyota suffered some decline of market share.

Most significant, however, was the late 2016 announcement by Sony that it had accepted an offer to become part of South Korea's Samsung, forming a new company that would be called Samsung-Sony. This was truly stunning. Founded in the wake of World War II by Japanese entrepreneurs Akio Morita and Masaru Ibuka, Sony had come to epitomize all the globally perceived virtues of Japanese industry. Starting with a license on unused US transistor technology, the company had led the Japanese conquest of American and European consumer-electronics giants like RCA, GE, and Philips with its Trinitron televisions and Walkman music players. Morita had transplanted himself to the United States and learned English to become one of the first truly global CEOs.

But with the passing of its founding generation, Sony seemed increasingly to lose its way. It started making "me-too" products and insisted on developing virtually all of its technology in house, often figuratively reinventing the wheel rather than adopting and adapting already-existing technology from outside. It developed powerful internal silos, each of which was primarily focused on preserving its own existence and none of which spoke with any of the others. Coordination tended to take place only at the highest level, and by the time issues became apparent, it was already too late effectively to address them. The company became unwieldy, unfocused, bureaucratic, and increasingly afraid to take risks and to make critical investments. Although it possessed world-class flat-panel display technology, it hesitated to invest in this area, even as its South Korean rivals Samsung Electronics and LG Electronics forged ahead with massive new capital spending programs. Similarly, in television, while Sony dithered, Samsung invested.

In the smartphone business, Sony's joint venture with Sweden's Ericsson lacked the vision and responsiveness to face challenges from competitors, first from Apple and its iPhone and then from Samsung with its Galaxy series of Android phones. Despite its reputation for being global, Sony found it difficult to bring foreign experts into the home offices to provide cross-fertilization for its own teams. Indeed, because of the silos within the company, even collaborative work between internal groups was limited.

Ironically, by 2013 Sony was looking and acting a lot like failing American companies such as Kodak and Motorola. It sold the building where its headquarters were housed and began investing in new fields such as medical technology. It lost money in its traditional digital electronics, game, video, and mobile phone businesses while making money on its secondary businesses in financial services and music. Founded as a company that might have been called Japan's Apple, and once taking great pride in regularly introducing innovative products that created whole new industries, Sony hadn't had a hit in eighteen years. Indeed, it had all the technology to be first to introduce things like the Apple iPhone and iPad—those products should have been the Sony iPhone and the Sony iPad. But Sony hesitated, and Apple seized the opportunity. By doing so Apple became the world's most valuable corporation, while Sony's value declined dramatically.

As it turned out, mobile phones proved to be the decisive turning point for Sony. Once a pioneer in the business, in 2001 Sony had embarked on a joint venture with Sweden's Ericsson in a bid to maintain its global competitiveness. In 2007, its global market share had been more than 10 percent. By the end of 2012, however, that had fallen to 1.7 percent, putting Sony far behind Samsung's 22.7 percent. Sony's leadership resolved to make a major effort to regain significance in this market, which was of such great importance to a wide range of electronic technologies.

The company put everything it had into development of the new Experia Z model, introduced early in 2013. It was a superb product, and initially sold extremely well; for a short time, there was a sense of euphoria at Sony headquarters in Shinagawa. But then Samsung introduced the new Galaxy S5. Not only was this phone technologically a step beyond all other phones, including Sony's, but Samsung executed a massive global marketing campaign that overwhelmed its competitors, with the single exception of Apple—and even Apple's market share fell by 25 percent.

Not only was Sony unable to compete in the phone business, but its other divisions—including television, gaming, and electronics components—were all facing the same kind of onslaught from the agile, super-aggressive Korean giants. Rather than continuing to try to fight them, Sony decided to join them.

THE ORIGINS AND EVOLUTION OF JAPAN, INC.

The decline of so many leading companies raised serious questions about the efficacy and viability of the long and widely imitated Japanese management system. Was it really an effective system for running businesses, or had it succeeded only because it existed within particular circumstances at a particular time?

The key elements of this system were lifetime employment; boards of directors consisting exclusively of a company's top managers; company membership in a powerful corporate group that maintained cross-shareholdings; primary funding from banks with cross-shareholdings in the group rather than by outside investors; emphasis on market share rather than profit; absence of a market for corporate control; relatively small differences between worker and manager compensation; and seniority-based promotion and pay schedules. Not all of these had been longstanding features of Japanese corporate management.

From the late nineteenth century into the 1930s, Japanese capitalism and Japanese management closely resembled systems in Europe and the United States. Up to and during World War II, Japanese corporations were typically owned and controlled by their shareholders. Corporations financed themselves by means of internal cash flow and issues of shares. Banks did not play any major monitoring role. By the 1930s, the large family-controlled conglomerates known as *zaibatsu* had emerged as a major part of the Japanese business scene—just as "trusts" had done in early twentieth-century America before antitrust laws had broken up many of them. The *zaibatsu* families used holding-company structures and teams of professional managers to run their enterprises.

An ongoing management problem in this period was that of finding and retaining skilled workers and managers. Frustrated by the fact that they would often invest a lot of time and money in training employees only to see them take their new skills to another company, some of the larger corporations introduced the idea of lifetime employment contracts. Managers and some skilled workers were guaranteed lifetime employment and continuing training, along with pensions and other benefits, if they promised not to leave the corporation. By the end of the 1930s, a number of the larger groups and companies were offering lifetime employment, although the majority of the business community was not.

Attempts to organize labor unions at this time were stymied by parliamentary opposition to union-authorizing legislation, as well as by the organization of factory councils by corporate management. During the Second World War, the few unions that did exist were absorbed into the Industrial Organization, the government body directing industrial wartime production, which effectively abolished them.

Of course, the wartime economy greatly increased the role of the government, and especially that of the Ministry of Munitions, in regulating and directing the production and supply activities of the corporations. But the management system that came to be known as Japan, Inc. was really birthed by the American Occupation, which had dissolved the *zaibatsu* by having the government buy their shares, imposing capital levies on the wealthy owners, and nullifying wartime guarantees of corporate borrowing. These steps inevitably greatly enhanced the importance of government officials and professional managers (as opposed to shareholders) in running the major corporations.

With very little private capital available, investment had to be done on the basis of bank lending backed by the government. The banks thus essentially became arms of the Bank of Japan and the Ministry of Finance, which imposed capital controls and directed the banks to lend to designated priority projects. The corporations came under the strong influence of the Ministry of International Trade and Industry (MITI), which controlled access to foreign exchange and largely determined the priority of investment projects.

High growth was achieved on the basis of lending backed by the Bank of Japan and by the flow of funds from the government's Finance Investment Loan Program. Indeed, the banks were kept in an over-loan situation, with lending to corporations being as much as eight or nine times the amount of invested capital. Thus, the interest that companies paid to the banks was far more important than the dividends it might pay on its shares. Consequently, the shareholders of the corporations became far less influential and powerful than their managers and bankers. Indeed, management propagated the notion that it should not only be in control, but that there should never be a change of control from outside its ranks. Corporate managers also adopted the lifetime employment concept, but broadened it into a corporate family framework that provided an equalizing element between management and employees. In other words, management and "regular" (permanent) employees were all identified as part of the same lifetime-employed family, with strong ties and obligations to each other, but with no need for outside unions and no obligations to outside shareholders. In this way, management, in partnership with the powerful government bureaucracy and docile lifetime-employed labor, became the driving force of the corporation. Regular shareholders were left in limbo.

Actually, labor was not initially cooperative. One of the first actions Occupation authorities had taken was to adopt a trade union law that for the first time allowed workers to organize, strike, and bargain collectively. This resulted in a rush of labor organization; by the end of 1949 nearly 60 percent of all workers were in a trade union.

The advent of the Cold War changed everything, however. Instead of continuing to push democratization and unionization, Occupation authorities aligned themselves with the conservative forces in Japan, opposing liberal labor and socialist elements. The old *zaibatsu* were reassembled, but in a new form known as *keiretsu*, which were no longer controlled by a family or large shareholder, but by a council of CEOs of companies with cross-held shares and with the same main bank. The *keiretsu* were subject to government influence known as "administrative guidance." Under this new alliance, Occupation authorities broke strikes and worked with corporate management and conservative government and Diet leaders to break the power of trade and industry-wide unions and transform them into individual company unions (heirs of the factory councils) that also could form federations of company unions. The essence of the arrangement was that management would assure lifetime employment, at least for regular employees, and that management pay would not be vastly greater than wages. For their part, workers would avoid strikes and disruptions, and both management and labor would share in the successes and failures of the corporation, with top managers taking responsibility when things went wrong. To avoid excessive internal conflict and rivalry, as well as to keep employment costs low, manager compensation and promotion would be largely based on seniority.

Thus, the Japan, Inc. system of strongly rooted managerial autonomy and cooperative labor under strong government guidance was established. In this framework, Japanese management had two fundamental goals: to maintain management autonomy and to maintain the company as an independent and eternally living body. Profit maximization was never a primary objective, and for many was not even an accepted value. The measures of success were company size and relative ranking, revenue growth, market share, reputation, and ability to fund investment either from internal cash flow or from bank lending.

With this structure and method of operation, the companies focused on achieving high quality, ensuring continuous improvement, reducing costs and raising productivity through just-in-time delivery, boosting exports to achieve world-class economies of scale, and increasing investment to maintain growth and increased market share. These characteristics became the hallmarks of the Japanese management system.

This all fit perfectly with the Japanese business environment at the time and also helped to shape it. From the 1950s to the 1970s, Japan had a baby boom that poured young people into the job market. It was efficient for companies to hire them as they left school and to train them over time in the corporate philosophy and discipline. At the time, as there were few seniors in the companies, the seniority system of compensation kept personnel costs low. Because all members of a class moved up together, the system also diminished internal conflicts and rivalries. The government's financial and industrial policies assured funding and reduced risk for companies in favored industries. The quasi-resurrection of the old *zaibatsu* in the form of the new *keiretsu* meant that a number of companies would have cross-holdings in each other, and a main bank, which held shares in each of them, would be their primary lender. There was usually a related insurance company that was a substantial shareholder as well. The bank and the insurance company, along with the cross-shareholders, were considered stable shareholders who would not sell their holdings and who could be counted on in difficult times to lend to and help restructure the companies in the group. This all reduced investment risk and assured stability and safety in the sense that there were no hostile corporate takeovers, mergers, or acquisitions; no activist shareholders; no legal action by disgruntled shareholders; and that share price movements were relatively modest, because most of the shares were never sold. The *keiretsu* structure also reduced domestic competition: entry by newcomer companies was extremely difficult and distribution *keiretsu* operated to diminish retail price competition. Furthermore, the government's anti-monopoly office was given a minimal staff and budget and was strongly opposed by the other powerful ministries like MITI. As a result, a significant portion of Japanese industry consisted of cartels.

Several other factors were integral to this Japanese management system and to the broader national economic strategy. The government minimized foreign investment in Japan, and—initially, at least—the domestic market was protected from imports by high tariffs and a variety of non-tariff barriers. Thus, there was no competitive threat from outside, and as a result of the domestic cartels, prices for consumers were kept high, thereby underpinning the financial health of the producers. At the same time, the yen was kept undervalued, at first by capital controls and then by government intervention in the currency markets. The government also strongly supported exports with a variety of subsidies and tax deductions.

A final important point about this system is that at the time it was put into place, Japanese companies were largely shooting at known targets. Textiles, steel, autos, television sets, and even semiconductors were existing products and industries for which the technology was widely known and available. Japanese companies didn't have to invent dramatically new products or industries; rather, their main task, and that of their workers, was to make existing products better and more cheaply than their foreign competitors did.

In the heyday of the Japanese company and Japanese management techniques, they accomplished this goal with breathtaking speed and efficiency. First in textiles, then in steel, consumer electronics, autos, machine tools, semiconductors, and many other industries, Japanese companies like Toray, Nippon Steel, Sony, Hitachi, Matsushita, Toshiba, Toyota, Nissan, Fujitsu, and NEC used their own skills and management techniques in the context of the structure of their economy and their government's policies to outstrip US and European competitors such as General Motors, Motorola, Philips, British Motors, Milliken & Company, Cincinnati Milacron, and many others. The great Japanese corporations seemed invincible, and books about them filled library shelves as executives all over the world attended seminars to learn the secrets of Japanese-style management and the magic of the Japanese corporation.

BIG CHANGE

The great Japanese asset bubble burst in 1992, and it suddenly seemed that Japanese management could do nothing right. Not only did the Japanese economy slide into two decades of stagnation and deflation, but, as noted earlier, many of the biggest and most important corporations suffered dramatic reversals and sustained poor performance. Had all the hype about Japanese management been merely propaganda? Had the success of Japanese companies been mainly due to an undervalued yen, protected domestic markets, and direct and indirect government subsidies? What had happened to make the world-champion managers suddenly look like clowns?

The Japanese economic system had become characterized by networks of strong relationships among suppliers and manufacturers, sellers and buyers, banks and borrowers, executives and enterprise union leaders, bureaucrats and business executives, and schoolmates and classmates. In a fast-growing economy, such relationships reduce transaction costs by establishing trust, thereby facilitating speedy decisions and conflict resolution. Over time, these relationships displace the legal system (which is used mainly by outsiders whose lack of close personal ties inhibits their ability to enter the markets). Despite their advantages, such relationships also lock participants into what effectively are moral commitments. It becomes very difficult to break relationships without serious loss of reputation. For Japanese companies at this time, terminating supplier relationships and laying off workers was virtually impossible. In a rapidly growing, highly regulated, and easily predictable economic environment, the system worked like magic: all the participants in the system were getting what they wanted, mistakes were easily obscured and forgotten, and the relatively few serious problems were swiftly handled by the main banks and the government. Although not at all transparent, the system worked and was widely trusted and accepted.

It must be remembered, however, that the system had been built in order to "catch up" economically to the United States and Europe. By the late 1970s, and certainly by the end of the 1980s, Japan had caught up. Moreover, it had caught up at a moment of rapid globalization and of increasing economic integration, complexity, and sophistication in world business, which brought with it a number of fundamental changes. The 1985 Plaza Accord, a global currency agreement between Japan, the United States, the United Kingdom, France, and West Germany, resulted in a substantial revaluation of the yen. Global markets became more competitive with the rise of South Korea, Taiwan, Singapore, China, and others. To offset the impact of the newly strong yen, the government dramatically increased the money supply, which made credit easier, but also fed an immense asset bubble.

Although the profits of many Japanese companies had been falling in the 1980s, these declines had been more than offset by the capital gains created by the bubble. Thus, the bursting of the bubble in 1992 left in its wake enormous debt problems that put excruciating financial pressure on corporations and banks throughout the economy. Investment and growth came almost to a halt. For too long, both business and government did little, hoping that a rebound of growth would come along to fix all the problems. But it didn't, and in this new environment characterized by low growth and more global competition, many of the perceived advantages of the Japanese management system increasingly began to look like disadvantages.

Of course, many actual management practices such as *kaizen* continuous improvement, *kanban* just-in-time delivery, six-sigma quality, and emphasis on customer satisfaction remained valid and powerful. But these practices could be—and were—copied by global competitors, and there was an erosion of this Japanese advantage. At the same time, the cozy personal and corporate relationships, opaque reports and procedures, and seniority-based promotion and reward practices that had been seen as accelerators and facilitators of fast growth were now understood to be selfish vested interests that were choking Japan's recovery. Last but not least, the lifetime employment and seniority reward systems increasingly looked like millstones around the necks of the companies. It had become clear that companies had to make at least some reasonable profit; lifetime employment for too many workers could mean no profits and thus no employment for any workers. Decisions by old-line companies like Hitachi to begin laying off thousands of workers signaled that the system of lifetime employment was coming to an end—or at least to a major reform.

But it wasn't just lifetime employment that was at stake. The appointment in 2001 of French-Lebanese-Brazilian Carlos Ghosn as the CEO of number two Japanese automaker Nissan demonstrated dramatically that the whole much-praised Japanese system of corporate governance and management was on the line. Here was a foreigner being parachuted in by the traditional board of one of Japan's most important and most favored companies not only to take over its leadership, but to carry out a management revolution by doing what a top Japanese manager could never do—changing not just the company's structure and practices, but also its culture. Ghosn laid off 21,000 workers, closed five domestic plants, auctioned off prized assets such as the company's aerospace unit, and, most important of all, ended Nissan's reliance on its *keiretsu* network of suppliers with cross-shareholdings in Nissan. For this he became known as the "*keiretsu* killer." He also became known for changing the company language from Japanese to English and for including key executives from North America and Europe in the company's major global strategy sessions. Within a year, Ghosn had Nissan in the black; within three years it was one of the global industry's most profitable companies.

It gradually became clear that the situation had changed, and that the old management doctrines and practices weren't going to be very effective in the future. By 2003, it had become fairly widely accepted that good management and performance ultimately had to be founded on open disclosure and competitive markets, and that the cozy relationships of the past weren't going to continue. Rising global competition, the distress of the banks in the wake of the bursting of the bubble, the need for dramatic debt reduction, and erosion of the stable shareholding system all led to deregulation, de-cartelization, and a shift of power from management to shareholders, who were becoming increasingly distressed that the companies, having paid down their debt, were now sitting on big piles of cash with which they were doing nothing.

Three other phenomena indicated significant changes afoot in the Japanese business world. The first was the increasing pressure on Japanese companies to maintain high earnings in order to achieve the high share prices necessary to obtain financing in global markets and to engage in merger and acquisition activity abroad. Firms like Komatsu, Tokyo Electron, Nidec, and others, finding themselves in competition with the likes of Caterpillar and Applied Materials, needed to be able to make acquisitions in the US and other foreign markets. These kinds of globally enmeshed firms also needed sources of financing other than the Japanese banks that had been badly wounded in the aftermath of the bubble.

The second phenomenon was the rise of some truly Silicon Valley–like start-up enterprises in Japan. For example, Softbank, which was founded as a kind of software bank in 1981 by Masayoshi Son, had evolved into a huge global telecom-munications, Internet, gaming, and publishing company with large ownership shares in Yahoo, E-Trade, and other high-tech services corporations. By April of 2013, it had a market capi-talization of US$53 billion, greater than that of the venerable NTT telecommunications firm. Similarly, Rakuten, the online retailing and e-commerce company founded in 1997 by Hiroshi Mikitani, quickly became the largest e-commerce site in Japan, with a market capitalization over US$13 billion and about 10,000 employees worldwide. As with Softbank, market capitalization and profits were extremely important to Rakuten, because it could not rely on some *keiretsu* main bank, and its global strategy drove it to make acquisitions in the United States, France, Germany, Spain, the UK, and Brazil. Also important to both companies was the use of English as the lingua franca. Rakuten made English its official company language for internal as well as external com-munication in 2012. Meanwhile, Softbank, aiming to improve the English ability of its staff, offered its employees a million-yen (roughly US$8 thousand) bonus for scoring over 900 on the TOEIC (Test of English for International Communication).

The third important indicator of change was employment practices. Instead of taking on "regular" employees who, once hired, could never be fired, Japanese companies increasingly hired temporary or "irregular" workers who could be dismissed once the task for which they were hired had been completed. In 1984 about 15 percent of the workforce consisted of irregular workers; this number had climbed to 25 percent by 1999 and to 34 percent by 2013. This widespread use of contract workers was a strong indication of the possible end of the lifetime employ-ment policy of the Japan, Inc. system—but it was dying hard. Companies like Canon, Toyota, Mitsubishi, and others clung persistently to the old ways.

The merger of Sony with Samsung in 2016 finally triggered the strong move to complete the reform and restructuring of Japanese business. The demise of an independent Sony had particular significance, because it had once been seen as an outsider and maverick company in the Japanese system. Moreover, it had made many of the changes that reformers were always calling for, such as putting company outsiders, foreigners, and women on its board of directors. Like Nissan, it had brought in a foreigner as chairman and CEO. Yet so ingrained were the dysfunctional habits of Japanese corporations that none of those measures had been enough to save the company.

There were many reasons for this. Sony had thrived in an era of standalone electronics, and was late in adjusting to the Internet. Born as an entrepreneurial start-up company, it had become an enormous bureaucracy. Unlike Nissan and Rakuten, it did not adopt English as the company language, and, as noted earlier, its various divisions failed to speak to each other even in Japanese. Its habit of Japanese consensus building was too slow in the face of the rapid, aggressive style of decision making utilized by the South Koreans. When it tried to reduce staff it ran into Japanese employment laws that restricted employee layoffs; this was compounded by its own lingering culture of lifetime employment. As Howard Stringer, Sony CEO from 2005–2012, said, "If we were actually able to take advantage of the combination of our assets we would be a very powerful company." But why, exactly, couldn't Sony get its act together? In an interview, Stringer explained: "I didn't know I wasn't in control. It was a natural part of Japanese companies to be consensus driven, and I had to spend a lot of time trying to achieve consensus." Sony and the Japanese management system had just run out of time.

A NEW JAPANESE MANAGEMENT MODEL

To the Extraordinary National Revitalization Commission, the Japanese business community seemed like a frog that had been sitting in warm water when the heat was turned up. In such a situation, frogs do not jump out of the pot. Rather, they stay in and gradually boil to death. Now the pot was boiling, and the Commission decided it was imperative to throw the frogs out. Japan faced an existential need for greatly improved productivity. In light of the inevitable short-term decline of the population, it was clear that meeting the costs of the national debt, health care, and pensions, along with rising national security spending, would require at least a doubling and perhaps a tripling of productivity growth rates. For example, Morgan Stanley had charted the combinations of labor-force participation and productivity growth rates that would achieve the cabinet's targeted real GDP for 2020 while allowing pension funds and health-care systems to meet all their obligations. At the 2014 labor-force participation rate of 82 percent, the productivity growth rate would have to rise from its current 1 percent to 2.8 percent. Or, if productivity growth remained the same, labor-force participation would have to rise to 95 percent in order to meet the target. Clearly, a rise in productivity was imperative. To achieve it, the Commission focused on five key elements: innovation; economic structure; corporate governance; taxes and finance; and labor relations and workforce training.

INNOVATION

Everyone on the Commission agreed that Japan had to find a way to unleash the inherent inventiveness and creativity of the Japanese people. One member noted that even as thousands of good ideas were bottled up in corporations like Sony, the number of new start-up companies in Japan was declining. While there were many specific reasons for this, the major problem seemed to be fear of failure. In countries like the United States, which had many start-ups and a very active new venture sector, there was much talk of risk taking. But actually, the risk was quite low in America, where an enterprising person could leave a present job to establish a start-up, and return to the old job or find a new one if it failed. Employers would actually view the entrepreneur in a positive light for having tried something. Indeed, it sometimes happened that the former employer would invest in the start-up and even lend it resources.

In Japan, this was all much more difficult. If someone left a company to establish a start-up, not only would he not be able to return to that company, but he probably would have trouble getting hired at any other company. Moreover, there were no bank lenders, venture capital investors, or angel financiers for those looking to establish start-ups. Nor was there an infrastructure with lawyers, accountants, marketing consultants, public relations consultants, and others willing to take part-time assignments or partial compensation in the form of equity options, as there was in the United States. In short, the mindset and practices inherent in the prevailing Japanese system were hostile to the innovation Japan so desperately needed.

To remedy this, the Commission proposed several measures. One, a kind of venture failure insurance scheme, would make payouts to founders and employees of failed new ventures to help pay their expenses while they searched for new employment or new venture funding. Initially, the fund would be financed with donations from the government and from interested private sources. But its continuous funding would come from payments by successful ventures that had registered for the insurance support during their start-up period. The fund would also receive a certain portion of shares in any new venture it insured, and the eventual sale of these shares would also finance the long-term operations of the fund. Finally, the fund would undertake to establish the infrastructure of lawyers, accountants, and consultants necessary to get new ventures off the ground.

In this context, the Commission also noted that Japan had quite a strong and often neglected entrepreneurial capacity among its specialized medium-sized and small enterprises. Somewhat like what the Germans called their "Mittelstand," these companies, which included Anritsu, Nidec, Omron, Fanuc, and many others, were offering highly advanced products and technologies, and held strong global positions in their market segments. In the first fifteen years of the twenty-first century, however, these companies were facing several problems. In the semiconductor industry, for example, Japan's materials, chemical, and equipment companies were all very strong, but the Japanese semiconductor device makers were losing market share and leaving the business. The supplier companies were becoming stranded, meaning that their domestic market was shrinking and their major customers were increasingly in other countries—many of which, such as South Korea and Taiwan, had supply industries of their own that they were trying to promote. With the decline in the number of engineers and scientists graduating from Japanese universities, Japanese suppliers were also finding it more and more difficult to recruit the talent they needed. Moreover, as technology development became ever more costly, the ability of the small and medium-sized companies to continue spending on research and development was increasingly strained. Furthermore, in many of these companies, the owner-operator was aging, and lacked a suitable family member or senior executive to take over.

The Commission responded to these problems by proposing that Japan's Shoko Chukin Bank, a specialist in dealing with small and medium-sized businesses, extend long-term, low-interest credit to support the global marketing efforts of these "Mittelstand" companies. It also suggested that overseas talent recruiting efforts by the Japanese government be particularly focused on recruiting engineers and scientists for these companies. The Commission called for the establishment of a German-style apprenticeship program under which high-school graduates could be trained in technical skills that did not require a full engineering or science degree. This program would be completed in classrooms and on the job in the companies, and would be jointly funded by the government and the companies. Another idea from Germany was that of the Fraunhofer Society, which carried out cooperative technology development with small to medium-sized companies. For example, the Fraunhofer Society had developed the key algorithms for MP3 coding and essential components for solar energy systems. A similar organization would be established in Japan, with national and local governments providing 30 percent of the funding; the other 70 percent would be earned by the institute's work on engineering and R&D projects for private companies. In this way, small and medium-sized companies could continue to stay at the frontier of technology. Yet another idea taken from Germany was that the government would pay 20 to 30 percent of a company's wages during an economic recession. This "Short-Time Work Assistance," as it was called in Germany, would be temporary, lasting only until the recession was over. By keeping workers on the job who otherwise might have to be laid off, valuable teams and skills would be conserved. The Commission saw this as a measure that fit very well with traditional Japanese concepts.

ECONOMIC STRUCTURE

In the wake of World War II, the Japanese economic system had been structured to deter foreign investment. As a result, even in the first decade of the twenty-first century, Japan had one of the lowest rates of foreign direct investment, and also had less price competition than other developed economies. To stimulate more dynamism through competition, the Commission proposed two measures: greater foreign direct investment and stronger anti-monopoly regulation.

For the first measure, the Commission proposed that Japan adopt the Singapore system of identifying and attracting desirable foreign investment. Indeed, after initial inquiries, the Economic Development Board of Singapore actually worked with METI, the Ministry of Finance, and other Japanese agencies to establish a sophisticated system of attracting investment to Japan. This led to the incorporation of the Japan Investment Attraction Agency (JIAA), which has staff members both in Japan and in most of Japan's overseas embassies, as well as in the venture-failure insurance fund's administrative arm, local governments, and private entities. These representatives, some of whom have been independently dispatched from the private sector, identify industries, companies, and capabilities that Japan would like to have in its economy.

Having identified candidates for transplantation to Japan, JIAA contacts and woos them with a variety of incentives such as tax abatement, favorable financing, assistance with the recruiting and training of workers and executives, and assistance obtaining necessary infrastructure. JIAA, in partnership with regional and local authorities, has also established several technology industrial parks similar to those in Singapore and Taiwan. In addition to providing facilities for foreign investors, these industrial parks also act as incubators for new Japanese ventures.

Japan had long functioned with a lack of full competition, supported by collusive activity in a number of industries. Agriculture was perhaps the best example. Here a vast network of arrangements and special deals governed an industry into which full competition never intruded. The medical field was another in which allocation of resources was left mostly up to doctors and bureaucracies rather than to market forces. For example, inexpensive generic drugs were as not widely available in Japan as they were in other major economies. A further example was the bid-rigging clubs known as *dango* in the construction industry, where collusion and price-fixing were notorious. To stimulate competition, the Commission proposed doubling the staff and budget of the anti-monopoly office, which now in 2050 aggressively undertakes much more active investigations of anti-competitive relationships to ensure that buyers are getting fair prices.

CORPORATE GOVERNANCE

In considering the slow decision making of major Japanese companies, the Commission concluded that the major problem was the inability of mostly insider boards to resolve the differences between their own cliques, or even to compel the cliques to communicate with one another. As solutions, it proposed two alternatives; corporations would have to choose one or the other. The first was to alter the composition of the board so that instead of consisting entirely or mostly of insiders, it would have a majority of outsiders, of whom at least two would be non-Japanese. The second alternative was to adopt the German-style two-board system. Under this arrangement, the management board, consisting of all the key company executives, would be in charge of continuing operations. Over this board, however, would be a supervisory board consisting entirely of outsiders except for the chief executive of the company, who would serve on both boards. This supervisory board would be responsible for choosing and evaluating the top company executives and for making decisions regarding long-term strategy and government and community relations. It would also be mandatory that at least two members of this board be non-Japanese, and that the board members be from a variety of backgrounds, such as science, community leadership, and so forth.

Whereas in many countries shareholders are very powerful and can force changes on management, in Japan the opposite was the case. In fact, the Japanese company had been less a company than a management protection society. To overcome this imbalance among the company's stakeholders, the Commission proposed the creation of a Shareholder Ombudsman Agency. This would be an independent agency with the power to impose fines, challenge administrative rulings, and halt bankruptcy, merger, and acquisition activity on behalf of shareholder interests. It would continually monitor corporate activity and would also respond to anonymous complaints by shareholders and issue warnings or fine corporations where appropriate.

TAXES AND FINANCE

When the Revitalization Commission was created, Japan's fiscal, investment, and monetary situation was dire. The ship of Abenomics had been sinking and was taking the yen, government bonds, investment, and national consumption down with it. With the "third arrow" of structural reform producing little increase in investment, employment, or GDP growth, the Bank of Japan's aggressive quantitative easing policies had been fueling a rapid rise in inflation. While the inflation had helped reduce the burden of the national debt, it also had begun to raise interest rates to prohibitive levels, soaking up government revenue and inhibiting any new investment. To alleviate this situation, the Commission called for an emergency levy on the cash balances of all corporations with more than US$1 billion in sales revenue, which would be used for purposes of paying down the national debt to manageable levels. In return, the corporations were granted equity stakes in national assets such as bridges, roads, and national parks, and were to be paid an annual return of at least 5 percent on the amount of the national levy, beginning after five years. Of course, the state also had the alternative of returning the cash to the corporations with interest paid out of the intended national budget surpluses.

By thus stabilizing the government's finances as well as the yen, the Commission's recommendations, in conjunction with the other fundamental structural reforms already in place, created an extremely attractive environment for new investment by both Japanese and global investors. To make the environment even more inviting, the Commission had added tax reforms that cut the country's corporate marginal income tax rate to 15 percent (similar to Singapore and Ireland), reduced the consumption tax to 6 percent, and introduced a steeply graduated personal income tax that levied low taxes on the poor and middle classes but that dramatically closed loopholes for privately held companies and imposed marginal rates of 75 percent or more on high personal incomes. High rates had also been imposed on some kinds of capital gains (those arising from generally rising real-estate prices, for example), but not on gains achieved as a matter of true innovation and productivity.

LABOR RELATIONS AND WORKFORCE TRAINING

The Commission concluded that, while the lifetime employment system may have been an asset during Japan's high growth period, it had now become more of a burden than a benefit.

Under the conditions created by a shrinking, aging population, the problem was how to achieve maximum labor efficiency. The danger of unemployment or of corporations not properly caring for their employees was quite small. On the other hand, the risk of workers being stuck in one place and not being used in way that would benefit the whole economy was quite large. Consequently, the Commission proposed abolishing the artificial separation between regular (permanent) and irregular (temporary) employees. Salaries, wages, promotions, and other forms of compensation would no longer be based on seniority or regular and irregular status. Positions would have clear job descriptions spelling out required skills, knowledge, experience, duties, goals, and expectations. Hiring would be done on the basis of these requirements, and not, for example, on the basis of having attended a particular university. Employees would receive formal job-performance evaluations based on how well they had fulfilled the requirements of the job description. Annual promotions would not be guaranteed, but would be based on the work the employee had actually done at the company, and not on special relationships or seniority. Good performers would receive large bonus payments and poor performers would receive small ones— or none. Particularly for young technology personnel, this would open opportunities while also benefiting the companies. Even though research has shown that people tend to have their best and most creative ideas around the age of twenty-seven, the seniority and lifetime employment system of Japan was smothering these people and their brilliant ideas. Other forms of discrimination would also be abolished, such as job postings specifying age and gender, and job application procedures that required a photograph of the applicant and information about his or her family situation. No more, said the Commission.

Finally, compensation for part-time work would be proportional to pay for full-time work. There would be no more lump-sum retirement payouts—they would instead be incorporated into the normal retirement and pension system. Companies would make contributions to the national health and pension systems, but an employee's health and pension benefits would not be dependent on employment by a particular company. Rather, these benefits would be portable, meaning that the employee would have the right to them even if they moved to another company.

A major issue concerned the possible layoff of employees. Of course, this discussion mainly pertained to so-called regular (permanent) employees. Although widely perceived as applying to all Japanese workers, in fact, lifetime employment, or "regular" status had never applied to the large number of Japanese workers who were employees of small and medium-sized companies, or to those who worked part time. The term "layoffs" inevitably brought to mind an image of raw American-style capitalism from which the Japanese recoiled. However, under the law prevailing in the first two decades of this century, a Japanese company had to demonstrate that it was in immediate danger of bankruptcy before it could lay off any regular employees. It further had to demonstrate that it had taken all possible alternative steps, such as cutting executive salaries, offering early retirement, reallocating workers, and so forth, before resorting to layoffs. Finally, it had to demonstrate that it had a rational basis for choosing those who would lose their jobs. This kept layoffs to a minimum, but ironically, being forced to keep excess employees only weakened companies and made them more likely to fail and to lay off everyone in the long run. Moreover, the knowledge that they had little labor flexibility caused companies to avoid hiring if at all possible.

To rectify the situation, the Commission called for new labor laws that would justify workforce reductions for purposes of gaining productivity and profitability whenever a company's performance fell below the industry average.

RENAISSANCE

The combination of all these measures sparked the long and strong business renaissance that Japan is still enjoying today. Almost as soon as the reforms were introduced in 2017–2018, Google, which had previously stayed out of Japan, established one of its computer farms near Kyoto. This decision was also based on the progress Japanese researchers were showing in developing inexpensive and reliable forms of alternative energy. Shortly thereafter, Taiwan Semiconductor Manufacturing Company established a new foundry in Japan, and a steady stream of investments from other non-Japanese companies followed.

One of the most interesting developments was the entry into the Japanese auto market of General Motors and Hyundai. Taking advantage of the new anti-monopoly regulations, they were able to find Toyota, Honda, Nissan, and Mitsubishi dealers who were willing to establish dealerships for Buicks made in China and Hyundais made in South Korea. In other sectors the number of start-up companies exploded: instead of ten or twenty new start-up companies annually, by 2025 there were hundreds of such ventures, and the number continues to grow each year. There have also been many, many spinoffs of divisions of old companies that have been reborn as independent firms.

The takeover of Boeing in 2025 by Mitsubishi Aircraft Corporation was greatly facilitated not only by the failing fortunes of Boeing, but also by the soaring stock price of Mitsubishi Aircraft, which did the deal entirely in exchange for its shares. And by the 2020s the Japanese "Mittelstand" was better known than the German one. Indeed, many people now think Mittelstand is a Japanese word.

Most gratifying has been the performance of Samsung-Sony. The company's headquarters is now in Tokyo; its Walk'n'Talk technology has become ubiquitous, while its God Cloud stores about 75 percent of the world's corporate data. It long ago displaced Apple, Google, Huawei, and Microsoft, and is now by far the world's most valuable corporation.

In short, it has all worked out fine.

CHAPTER 9

Overthrow of the Insiders

T he corporations you've been visiting on this business trip have a different feel from the ones you remember from your last visit here in 2015. Gone are the old guys who would spend their days sitting by the window reading the newspaper—the so-called *madogiwazoku* (beside-the-window tribe), a term used to refer to unproductive workers who couldn't be fired because of the lifetime employment system, and who were instead literally pushed to the side, with no expectations made of them, although they continued to receive a salary. The lifetime employment system, you learn, has been abolished. The offices where your meetings have been held have struck you as vibrant places staffed by motivated, busy, and apparently contented personnel; you've noticed in particular the number of training courses for new employees that have been in progress as you tour the premises of your Japanese host companies. There must have been some fundamental shifts in government attitudes to the corporate system during the last thirty-five years, you realize, and you wonder how these came about.

To understand what happened, we need first to take a step back for a broader historical view of the Japanese economy and employment practices. Let's start with the period of US-Japan trade frictions in the 1980s, when American businessmen and officials continually complained that the Japanese market was closed to imports and foreign investment, while Japanese leaders insisted the market was open to foreigners and Japanese alike without discrimination. The founder of ceramics maker Kyocera, Kazuo Inamori, who went on to become a member of the Extraordinary National Revitalization Commission, threw some light on this situation in an interview in 1983 by telling the Kyocera story.

Inamori's family had not been well-placed or well-off, and he had graduated from the relatively unknown Kagoshima University in provincial Kyushu, rather than from a prestigious school like Tokyo University. Upon graduation, he had not joined an established corporation, but had decided to pursue his interest in ceramics by founding his own company in 1959. This turned out to be quite difficult. Banks would not lend to a new company headed by a young, unknown president with no special connections, no customers, and no workers. Workers did not want jobs with such a company, and worst of all, customers would not order from such a company. Nor were there any venture capitalists who were willing to invest in high-potential, high-risk new companies. Inamori explained that he had managed to scrape up some small loans from friends and family, and had produced a few prototype products, including some ceramic packaging for semiconductors. Japan's semiconductor makers, however, showed no interest. Without contacts, speaking no English, but desperate, Inamori traveled to America in the hope of meeting some US semiconductor makers. He was amazed when engineers at Texas Instruments accepted his request for a meeting. He was even more amazed when they gave him some orders for test quantities. The products tested well, bigger orders followed, and Kyocera became a major supplier of semiconductor packaging materials to US semiconductor makers.

Then, Inamori explained, some of the Japanese semiconductor companies finally began to place small orders, and gradually Kyocera gained a large share of the Japanese market as well. In conclusion, Inamori explained the moral of the story: "The Japanese market is not just closed to foreigners. It's closed to Japanese!"

That was a sentiment that Commission member Carlos Ghosn could well understand. He explained that after being invited to rescue Nissan, he had found it necessary to revolutionize a company of "insiders"—lifetime employees dealing with lifetime suppliers and all doing business in the same, unchanging "Nissan way."

From another perspective, Commission member and Softbank founder Masayoshi Son could also understand the concept of Japan being closed to Japanese. He had been an unknown Japanese-Korean entrepreneur who succeeded by using his wits and his daring investments in new cell-phone and Internet technology to surmount enormous obstacles and rise to the top of the Japanese business world. Commissioner and former Yokohama mayor Fumiko Hayashi, one of Japan's few female political leaders, had yet another perspective on the same issue. As a woman in the boys' club of Japanese politics, she knew how closed Japan could be to Japanese.

For the unfavored, the whole Japanese economy prior to the beginning of the twenty-first century sometimes appeared to be an ascending series of insiders' mutual protection societies. Agriculture was highly protected and subsidized. Large construction projects often involved collusion by *dango* bid-rigging clubs. As noted in chapter 7, the electric power companies monopolized Japan's electric industry and sometimes colluded with the regulatory authorities. Manufacturers had their exclusive supplier and

2012 OECD LABOR PRODUCTIVITY LEVELS

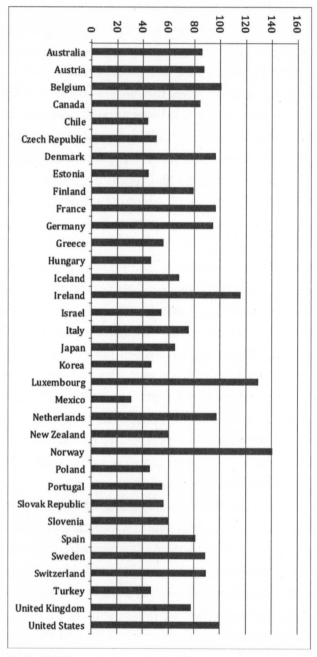

Source: OECD Statistics, Labor Productivity Levels

dealership networks. For example, auto dealers were exclusively tied to only one producer, and would not sell imports from other makers, as was common practice in America. In industries such as paper, flat glass, fertilizer, and cement, the market shares of the main producers had not varied substantially for more than half a century. In 2013, Japanese auto-parts makers were found to have been colluding on prices for auto parts sold to all global auto producers over the past decade. This was just a repeat of the behavior of the consumer-electronics producers of the 1970s and '80s. Indeed, it was a manifestation of the fact that the whole postwar *keiretsu* system, with its cross-shareholdings, managerial dominance, and strong ties to elite bureaucrats, had been constructed to favor insiders. And while the cross-shareholdings had gradually diminished, the resistance to outsiders remained strong and was sustained by associations such as the Keidanren business association, the Rengo trade-union confederation, the Japan Agricultural Cooperative (JA) group, the Japan Medical Association, and others.

While in the short term this no doubt benefited the producers and associations involved, it seemed to harm long-term national productivity—the ultimate determinant of a nation's welfare. In the OECD productivity index of 2012 shown opposite, the US rate was set at 100. Norway, Luxembourg, Belgium, and Ireland were a bit above that. All others were below, with the Netherlands at 97.7, France at 96.6, Germany at 94.6, Sweden at 88.9, Spain at 81.2., the UK at 77.6, and Italy at 75.8. Japan finally appeared further down, at 65.1 percent of US productivity. Why was Japan doing so poorly? Could it be that the Japanese system was only good for those who ran it?

In the long run, high productivity makes a country rich, while low productivity leaves it in poverty. Especially for countries with aging and declining populations, like Japan in 2015, national welfare could only be increased by productivity growth high enough to overcome the negative effect of population decline. Japan's low ranking meant that it was steadily heading into poverty.

Of course, many factors underpin productivity, but the 2012 OECD report found that 40 percent of the gain in any country's total productivity arose from the displacement of older companies by younger ones. Moreover, another 13 percent of total productivity arose from the process by which efficient companies took market share from less effective producers in the same industry. This was because the new firms brought new technology and ideas into effect more quickly. Older companies with lots of existing capital and workers in more rigid systems hesitated to make bold moves or were unable to become more flexible due to social and political factors. Thus, the OECD emphasized that constant entry of new firms into the marketplace was necessary for healthy national productivity growth.

Perhaps even more important was that inefficient companies should be allowed to die, thus liberating the valuable resources of trapped capital and talented people. This had also been shown in studies of Japan in the 1990s, which demonstrated that resistance to the exit of old corporations in the face of competitive new ones had kept the "zombies" alive while the new firms died. Yet, as *Oriental Economist* editor Richard Katz noted in 2013, the productivity of the new firms that died was much higher than that of the zombies who barely managed to stay alive by feeding on direct and indirect subsidies. Economist Kyoji Fukao confirmed this with a series of studies around the turn of the twenty-first century showing that, in a variety of industries, the total-factor productivity (TFP) of the exiting firms was higher than that of the survivors. Thus, a kind of reverse Darwinism had evolved in which "survival of the un-fittest" was the rule. The effect of

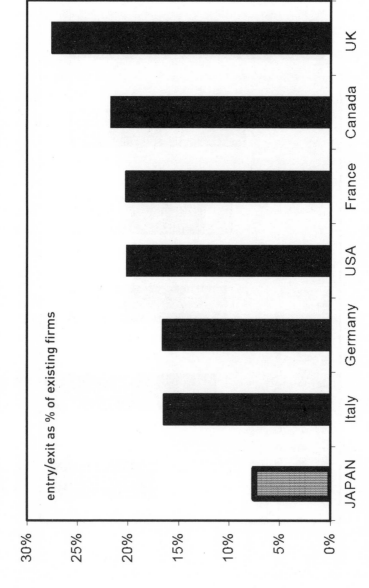

TURNOVER OF FIRMS IN JAPAN VS. THOSE IN OTHER G7 COUNTRIES

entry/exit as % of existing firms

JAPAN   Italy   Germany   USA   France   Canada   UK

30%   25%   20%   15%   10%   5%   0%

Source: OECD (2001) and Management and Coordination Agency

TFP GROWTH RESULTING FROM COMPETITION AND CORPORATE MOBILITY

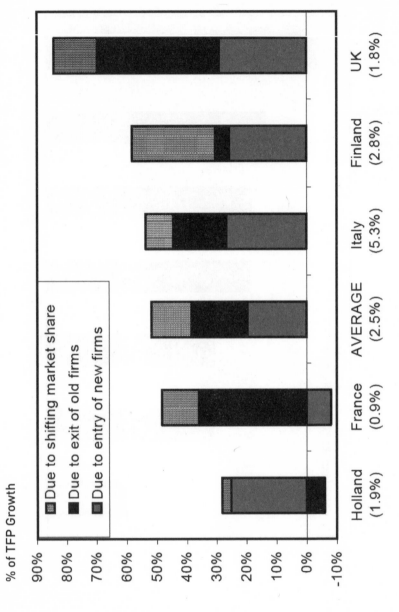

% of TFP Growth

Source: OECD (2001). Note: Numbers in parentheses are annual average TFP growth in manufacturing

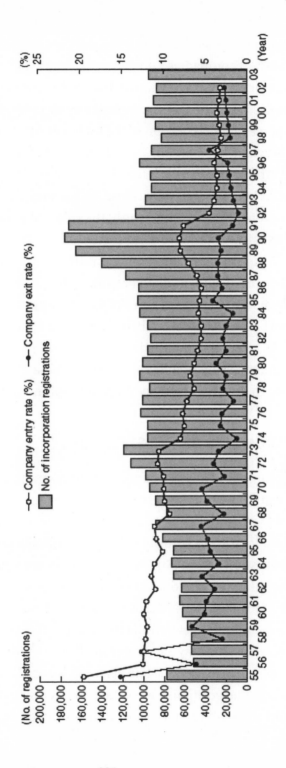

TRENDS IN NUMBER OF INCORPORATION REGISTRATIONS
AND COMPANY ENTRY AND EXIT RATES

—○— Company entry rate (%)   —●— Company exit rate (%)

■ No. of incorporation registrations

(No. of registrations)

200,000
180,000
160,000
140,000
120,000
100,000
80,000
60,000
40,000
20,000
0

(%)
25
20
15
10
5
0   (Year)

55 56 57 58 59 60 61 62 63 64 65 66 67 68 69 70 71 72 73 74 75 76 77 78 79 80 81 82 83 84 85 86 87 88 89 90 91 92 93 94 95 96 97 98 99 00 01 02 03

this dynamic could be seen in country comparisons of the entry and exit of companies into and out of markets. OECD data over a number of years in the late twentieth and early twenty-first centuries showed that the annual rate of entry of new firms in Japan was about 4 percent of the total corporate base (see graphs on previous pages). This was half the rate of Sweden, which itself had among the lowest rates of new company formation in the OECD. At the same time, Japan had among the lowest rates of corporate death. In other words, the Japanese pattern was to keep the existing order alive at all costs.

This was particularly evident from comparison of export and domestically oriented sectors. While there was significant change in market share, ranking, and entry of new firms in the export sector, there was virtually none in the domestic sector—which, after all, accounted for most of the economy. It was as if the domestically oriented companies had agreed among themselves to do anything to avoid competition.

IMPLICATIONS OF THE STATUS QUO

In a rapidly growing economy with a young population and a steady flow of relatively low-wage younger workers into the workforce, a stable corporate system that provides for training as well as long-term security has a lot of advantages. But what the Commission saw in 2015–2016 was a low-growth economy and a declining population, while a huge gap widened between old and young in society. Because the seniority system was so strong, older—and often less productive—workers were favored. To be sure, as the economy had stagnated, those workers had been subjected to changing hours, transfers, and reduced bonuses, but their fundamental positions were secure. Court rulings had made mass layoffs impossible, and, in any case—as noted in chapter 8—the government often subsidized firms to prevent layoffs. In addition, unemployment payments and pensions were linked to a worker's job and corporation. Thus, the older, core workers were protected by all of Japan's standard social safeguards.

But they were far from the entire labor force. By 2015, approximately a third of the workforce was composed of part-time and temporary workers without adequate safety nets. Nor was the trade-union confederation Rengo very helpful in this regard. By definition, union members were insiders, and because Rengo headed the federations of enterprise unions, it was a powerful opponent to a more flexible workforce. Rengo was naturally more concerned for the existing core workers than for underemployed and unemployed younger workers.

In 2014, the unemployment rate for Japanese under thirty-five was 8 to 10 percent, or twice the overall national average. The total number of officially unemployed was around 1.5 million. However, so-called freeters—casual part-time workers with unstable jobs—comprised about 4 million people, according to government estimates. Furthermore, as professor and Chiba University of Commerce president Haruo Shimada noted in a series of articles and books over the period from 2010 to 2015, the total of those with "non-regular" work status amounted to about 18.81 million, all of whom were working under low-wage, insecure conditions. Of these, about half were young people, meaning that at least 10 million young workers had low incomes, no prospect of training, and no hope of being able to support families or eventually receive pensions. In 2015, there had been eight workers to pay for one retiree of age seventy. But when the twenty-year-olds of 2015 reached retirement age, it seemed likely there would be only 0.7 workers available to support one retiree. Thus a young worker could not expect to receive in pension payments even as much as he or she had contributed. To make matters worse, it was estimated that about 40 percent of registered pensioners were not making their required contributions to the pension system. The very existence of any future pension system was in question. The medical insurance system was also close to bankruptcy, with very dim future prospects.

What Kyocera's Inamori had said in 1983 was even truer in 2015. The Japanese economy was "closed to Japanese." The established companies and institutions—in other words, the insiders—were scorching the earth in order to stop anything new from arising. The old were giving birth to very few young, and were then proceeding to overburden the few children they had. The irony was that enormous future insecurity was being created in the name of maintaining, at all costs, the present stability and security.

Of course, the Abe administration had not been totally blind to this. Its "third arrow" of economic reform, launched in 2013–2014, had been aimed at achieving major structural shifts to resolve many of these issues. As noted earlier, it had called for increasing the role of women in the corporate world and had established a fund to help stimulate development of "crazy" ideas and start-up companies. In addition, it had created six special economic zones in which taxes had been reduced, regulatory measures eased, layoff rules liberalized, and personnel evaluations based on productivity rather than seniority or hours worked. It had tried to reduce the political power of industry and agricultural associations such as the JA. The problem was that while all of these were good and necessary steps, they were insufficient, and had in any case been diluted in their implementation by being applied only in parts of the country or only in certain narrowly specified instances, or by slow rollouts.

The Commission thus called for full and fundamental reform in five areas: social security and safety-net systems, job training, agriculture, medicine, and competitive practices.

THE SAFETY NET

Ironically, in the early twenty-first century, Japan's social security and safety net systems actually exacerbated insecurity, because they were tightly linked to employment in an established organization. If a worker could not get a regular job or lost the job for any reason, there was little public support either for living expenses or for retraining. This created public pressure on government and industry to keep organizations alive in order to assure continued employment for as many as possible for as long as possible. In effect, Japan's unemployment insurance system was zombie organizations.

While it looked like Japan had relatively low unemployment, underemployment was very high. The Commission found a solution in Scandinavia. Like Japan, the Nordic countries valued a high degree of income equality and social harmony. Like Japan, they had experienced rapid economic growth from 1950 to 1975. Then, also like Japan, these nations had begun accumulating structural problems that resulted in banking crises, stagnation, and recession beginning in the early 1980s and continuing until the late 1990s. In Denmark, unemployment had gone over 9 percent in 1993, and for nearly a decade thereafter, GDP annual growth had been far below 1 percent. In Sweden, GDP had fallen by 6 percent between 1991 and 1993, unemployment had risen to over 9 percent in 1994, and the government budget deficit had climbed to 13 percent of GDP; meanwhile, in an attempt to maintain the strength of the kroner, the central bank had raised interest rates to as high as 500 percent in 1992. The collapse of the Soviet Union at the end of 1991 had deprived Finland of its main market, and Finnish GDP had fallen 13 percent in 1992–1993, while unemployment had risen to 17 percent. Commentators around the world had begun to speak of the death of the "welfare state."

But the Scandinavians restructured their economies by continuing to emphasize the fundamental equality and security of the Nordic model while removing unproductive policies, organizations, and practices. Rather than abandoning the welfare state, they restructured it. Over the twenty years from 1992 to 2012, they achieved some of the highest rates of GDP and productivity growth of the OECD countries while reducing unemployment to 5 percent or less. In the aftermath of the global economic crisis of 2007–2009, unemployment had risen somewhat, but not as much as in the rest of Europe or the United States, and while growth had slowed, there was no Japan-style deflation. In 2013, the World Economic Forum ranked Finland number three and Sweden number six among the world's most competitive countries. In the 2006 Lisbon ranking of which countries were best fulfilling Europe's agenda for growth and competitiveness, Denmark and Sweden were ranked first and second. Most important, though, as demonstrated in the chart opposite, was the fact that the Nordic reform and recovery did not come at the expense of workers and ordinary people. The citizens of the Scandinavian countries enjoyed among the highest wages, lowest unemployment rates, and highest levels of income equality in the world over the two decades of 1995 to 2015.

They had achieved this by devising a system called "flexicurity," by which they meant a flexible system that responded to market signals while at the same time providing security and a high degree of equality for its people. The key element was a switch from emphasis on "job security" to emphasis on "income and employment security." Rather than trying to maintain a person in a particular job at a particular organization, the flexicurity system focused on providing generous and easily accessible unemployment compensation, payment for and assistance in developing new skills, active help in finding a new job, and full

SHARE OF NATIONAL INCOME AFTER TAXES
AND GOVERNMENT SPENDING

	Poorest 30%	Middle 40%	Richest 30%	Ratio*
Norway	16.4%	36.6%	47.0%	2.9
Denmark	16.0%	42.9%	41.1%	2.6
Sweden	15.5%	42.1%	42.4%	2.7
Finland	14.8%	41.5%	43.8%	3.0
Japan	11.7%	41.3%	47.0%	4.0
United States	10.9%	39.2%	49.9%	4.6
Average	13.7%	39.8%	46.6%	3.4

Source: OECD 2005 and 2007. Data on 19 countries from 2000.

health-care and pension coverage unlinked to a particular firm or job. In other words, security and the means for maintaining a high degree of equality were provided directly to the citizen rather than indirectly through an employer.

As a result, Scandinavians welcomed change, even if it destroyed their existing organizations and jobs, because such changes actually improved their living conditions. Companies and jobs might come and go, but citizens continually got new and better jobs at new, more innovative companies, and were better off because of economic and productivity growth. This growth was in turn spurred by the fact that the flexicurity payments gradually diminished over a couple of years so that citizens couldn't just take a vacation when they lost employment. Rather, there was pressure on them to get retrained as fast as possible.

The impact on the structure of society was interesting. As illustrated in the graph on the previous page, OECD studies of the world's richest countries carried out between 1995 and 2010 showed that, based purely on market dynamics, the least well-paid third of Japan's population had a higher share of national income than the same third in the other countries. However, after taxes and transfer payments, it was the least well-paid in Norway and Denmark that had the highest share of disposable income. Japan ranked in the middle, and the United States was at the bottom. And while Denmark and Sweden did the most to shift income from rich to poor, the United States and Japan actually did the least, instead shifting a far larger percentage of income from the rich to the middle class. Indeed, almost all of Japan's redistribution appeared to be to the middle class. In an OECD study in 2000, Japan ranked third in social equality before government measures, tenth in equality after government interventions, and last in terms of the impact of government measures.

One factor in the Scandinavian system was that it ensured equality not just across income classes, but over an entire life cycle. Thus, loss of a job or a health crisis was not a prelude to loss of the home and impoverishment. In the Japanese system, equality appeared to be a natural market outcome, but was actually achieved through manipulation of the whole economic structure. Now, however, the combination of market-oriented reforms, the shift to irregular workers, declining competitiveness, and globalization was eroding the apparent market-based Japanese income equality, effectively remaking Japan in the American mold.

FITTING WORKERS TO JOBS, NOT JOBS TO WORKERS

The Commission, wanting very much to avoid this remaking of Japan, called for implementation of a flexicurity model tailored to the Japanese environment. It would be a tripartite system consisting of good macroeconomic fundamentals: a globalized, market-oriented business and labor structure, and a high degree of income security and equality. Low inflation policies would make it unnecessary for workers to obtain giant wage increases that would make the country's production uncompetitive. High growth and productivity would raise employment and government income. This in turn would provide the means to finance social benefits, including adequate unemployment compensation, public child care, health care, and education and retraining programs. All of this would lead workers to embrace the changes necessary to reinvigorate the national economy by giving them what the Scandinavians called "employment security" rather than "job security."

To make this work, it was absolutely essential that high-quality, widespread retraining and up-skilling programs be available to workers and acceptable to companies and other hiring organizations. In the Nordic countries, as well as in the Netherlands, the governments were spending 1.5 percent or more of GDP on these kinds of programs in the early years of the century. As a result, at any given time, as many as 30 percent of Danish and Swedish adults were involved in adult education and training programs. In this way, one could think of flexicurity as a kind of *kaizen* (continuous improvement) for people. For the system to work, a balanced labor-management structure was necessary. Fortunately, Japan's existing system of enterprise unions operating in federations under the trade union confederation Rengo already functioned on a broad basis, with an annual wage campaign and emphasis on economy-wide issues. Thus, it seemed to the Commission that flexicurity, perhaps with its own Japanese characteristics, should be easy for Japan to adopt. But the Commission was careful to emphasize that adoption of flexicurity would mean the end of preferences for zombies, the end of strict limitations on corporate workforce reductions, and the end of the seniority system. Rengo would have to shift its focus to facilitating training and retraining, to stimulating the start-up of new companies—perhaps even with venture investment—and to supporting the restructuring of zombie corporations.

THE END OF THE JAPAN AGRICULTURAL COOPERATIVES GROUP

The economic sector most resistant to change—and the one that provided the best example of the old killing the young and of the inefficient killing the efficient—was agriculture.

Japan's roughly 2 million farmers in 2015 were anything but free-market capitalists. The land they cultivated was strictly defined and regulated. Land designated as farmland could not be leased or sold for use for other purposes, and could not even be leased by a small farmer to a larger farmer for purposes of greater efficiency. Indeed, a large part of agricultural policy revolved around limiting the amount of land to be used for rice-growing and even taking rice land entirely out of production. Aside from government regulation, the life of the farmer was controlled by the JA, the government-authorized body directing the management of the country's seven hundred local farm cooperatives through which agricultural policy and much else in the farmer's life was administered. Formed in 1942 as part of the effort to increase wartime production, the JA included virtually all farmers, as they had to go through this entity to obtain equipment and credit and to sell their crops. Unlike other cooperative organizations, the JA was allowed to establish its own financial organizations. Thus, it received subsidies from the government on behalf of member farmers and wired the funds to members' accounts after deducting the cost of fertilizer and other items it supplied. This money was placed in accounts at the JA Bank. The JA also provided all necessary insurance through the National Mutual Insurance Federation of Agricultural Cooperatives (total assets of ¥50 trillion [roughly US$400 billion]) and, of course, took a commission for distributing and selling through its cartel the rice grown on the controlled lands. The power of the JA to do all this was based on the votes of small and hobbyist farmers who comprised 1.3 million of Japan's 2 million farmers, and who, under a one-farm, one-vote rule, constituted a large majority. Large, efficient farms with no need of the JA were forced to operate under its monopoly rules by the inefficient majority. On top of that, the JA was exempted from the anti-monopoly laws.

While farming itself was largely unprofitable, the JA made money from the majority of its activities and had a nicely profitable business overall. But the business was based on three increasingly uncertain pillars. One was the continuation of farming within a structure that maintained a lot of small farmers. The second (which followed naturally from the first) was continuation of cultivation on numerous small plots with high growing costs. The third essential pillar was a high government-managed price for rice. Indeed, the OECD estimated in 2009 that the Japanese government's spending on agriculture (¥5 trillion [US$4.2 billion] annually) was roughly equal to the total of its agricultural GDP. This system was being maintained only because the political system was distorted to enable it to do so. Gerrymandered districting meant that rural districts were allocated up to 2.4 votes for each vote in a metropolitan area. Because the JA's businesses constituted the core of the entire rural economy, and not just farming, support for its policy agenda was far wider than would be suggested by the 0.9 percent of Japanese GDP and 3.8 percent of total employment generated by farming. Indeed, the JA had a strong hand in the selection of 45 percent of Lower House members of parliament and as many as 60 percent of Upper House members because of the overweighting of the rural votes. Political leaders were deeply afraid to oppose the JA, and a major result was that agriculture prices in Japan were horribly distorted. For instance, Japanese consumers paid about seven times the global average price for rice.

In 2013–2014, the Abe administration had moved to abolish restrictions on land use, and had called for the JA to reform itself voluntarily. Not surprisingly, the JA had not done so. Rather, it had lobbied hard and successfully to water down and obstruct the Abe program. But Abe had fought back, realizing that he had to somehow reduce the power of the JA or lose everything. In 2015, he managed to push through decisions to separate some of the parts of the JA. Thus, Zenno, the organization's trading company, was to be made independent and subject to the anti-monopoly law from which it had previously been exempt. Also, the financial branches of the JA were to be supervised by the government's financial oversight bodies rather than by the Ministry of Agriculture, Forestry and Fisheries (MAFF) as had traditionally been the case.

While this had seemed like enormous progress at the time, the Commission decided it was not enough. It called for the immediate breakup of the JA and its banks, insurance companies, and distribution rights, along with suspension of all of its monopoly privileges. It further called for the dissolution and complete restructuring of the MAFF. Finally, it called for immediate removal of all restrictions on the leasing and sale of farmland and complete removal of agricultural import tariffs. This effectively abolished the price maintenance system for rice and agricultural land. In order to quickly gain competitiveness in new areas of agricultural production, the Commission recommended a system of one-time payments to older farmers who would retire early and sell their land to larger, more efficient producers or to agricultural innovators who aimed at producing high value-added crops.

GOOD HEALTH AT LOW COST

After agriculture, the medical care system in early twenty-first century Japan epitomized the essential problem of inefficiency overcoming efficiency, and of the old living well at the expense of the young. Ironically, the country had excellent medical technology and amazingly good health as a nation, with the world's greatest average life expectancy of 84.6 years. It had more MRI and computed tomography capability per capita than any other country, and was at the cutting edge of advanced medical technology. For example, in mid-2013, Sony, despite all its corporate troubles and reverses, had introduced a head-mounted scanner that would allow a surgeon to see internal organs in three dimensions with both eyes while operating. It was developments like this that had prompted Prime Minister Abe, in his "three arrows" program of 2012–2015, to establish medical technology as a new target industry for Japan's future. Yet the success of Japanese medical technology and the health of the Japanese people was more despite the medical care system than because of it. Indeed, ironically, the system was increasingly putting their health at risk.

After its establishment in the early 1960s, the Japanese national health insurance program had operated what appeared to be an ideal model for the entire population. All citizens were covered, the cost as a percent of GDP in a rapidly growing economy with a young population was relatively small, and life expectancy was long and increasing. Citizens were required to make only a small co-payment, could visit any hospital or clinic for any ailment, and were free to visit several doctors, hospitals, and clinics for the same problem within the same time period. These visits could result in multiple tests and other treatments by multiple doctors for the same ailment. Indeed, there were cases of patients checking in with the excuse of some problem who really simply wanted to chat with their friends. All was paid for by the insurance; furthermore, as payment was for each procedure, doctors tended to do a lot of procedures.

But this fairyland became less ideal in the late 1980s and early 1990s, when economic growth slowed and the population began to age rapidly. Added to those two factors was also the rapid advance in sophisticated but increasingly expensive medical technology. Gradually, the costs grew and the system became increasingly at risk of bankruptcy. The government responded with policies aimed at controlling the numbers of procedures and the pegging of prices. As Chiba University's Professor Haruo Shimada said, Japan's medical system in 2015 resembled, in many ways, the planned economy of the old Soviet Union. The use of private insurance was severely limited; for example, it could not be used in combination with national insurance to cover a part of a procedure not covered by the national insurance. The Japan Medical Association (JMA) opposed revision of this prohibition. Moreover, telemedicine and remote diagnosis was prohibited.

Medical records were often not kept electronically, and were not made available to others in the system. Thus patients would have multiple sets of records, and new sets would be created at any visit to a new institution or doctor. Nor could patients fully gain access to their own records. There were no ratings or benchmarking studies of clinics, hospitals or services—largely because doctors mostly preferred not to be subject to oversight and comparison, so the JMA balked at providing the necessary information. This was made worse by the growing custom of "tipping" doctors, which came about when the government began strictly regulating fees and prices in an effort to control costs, and patients tried to gain preferential admittance and treatment by offering doctors extra money.

These problems were further exacerbated by restrictions on the participation of licensed foreign doctors and nurses in the Japanese medical system despite chronic shortages, especially of nurses. Because doctors tended to prefer practicing in cities, a shortage of doctors in rural areas was a particularly serious problem. In some areas of Japan, the shortage of doctors was such that the residents actually paid for the medical education of Vietnamese students who would promise to practice in those areas upon graduation. As in the case of agriculture and the JA, the insiders were profiting at the expense of everyone else on the outside, and this was gradually causing the entire system to collapse.

The solution was found in the United States and Europe. The Commission called for something similar to the system instituted by US company Kaiser Permanente, under which patient records were fully digitized and available online to anyone at the direction of the patient and doctor. The Commission particularly emphasized that the prime minister should push for the development of e-infrastructure and e-health. It also called for a system in which regional hub hospitals would serve as highly advanced, fully equipped centers for emergencies and surgeries, while local clinics would handle diagnosis and routine patient treatment. Of course, the hub hospitals and clinics would be linked by computer, and patient records and other data would be fully available to doctors anywhere. This kind of system was seen as particularly appropriate for Japan, because its unparalleled public transportation network made it easy for patients to get to the best locations for their individual treatment.

The Commission further called for a mixed insurance system like those prevailing in Europe, under which the public insurance provided a base level of coverage that could be freely supplemented by the citizen with whatever private insurance they desire. Under this arrangement, fees and prices were to be decontrolled, but insurance reimbursements were to be placed on a "pay-for-performance" basis in place of the traditional "fee-for-service" method. In this context, the government insurance would extend only to services provided by hospitals and clinics that provided data for and participated in benchmarking programs to establish and improve quality and efficiency of performance. Finally, the Commission called for revising the internal rules of the Japan Medical Association in order to establish transparent and competition-friendly standards and procedures for the organization.

TOO MUCH PROTECTION, TOO LITTLE COMPETITION

As noted earlier, Japan suffered from relatively low productivity compared to other advanced countries largely because of the poor performance of Japanese companies operating primarily in the domestic markets. In 2000, the consultancy McKinsey & Company had analyzed productivity on an industry-by-industry basis and found that low productivity was highly related to lack of competition. For instance, Japan's retailing sector had especially low productivity because large-scale, efficient retailers had not been able to overcome government protections offered to small, traditional retailers. Located in town centers, these retailers employed only two or three family members each, yet, in total, accounted for 55 percent of retail employment, while larger, more efficient retailers were responsible for only 12 percent of retail employment. Because the smaller retailers had little buying power or knowledge of marketing, prices were high while product availability and overall services were poor. Their small shops were kept alive by zoning regulations that limited the entry of larger retailers and by subsidies and loans amounting to well over ¥6 trillion (US$50 billion) annually.

Similarly, the food-processing industry suffered from very low productivity (about 35 percent of French and US levels) because of lack of large-scale production. Japan had six times as many food processors as the United States, and yet produced far less. Most processors produced only for local markets and faced little national competition, largely as a result of the predominance of many small, protected retailers. As a result of this structure, the processors tended to produce small amounts of a wide variety of localized products, which prevented them from achieving economies of scale in their production operations. For example, one local milk producer received milk for processing from farms in seven areas around his facility. Rather than mixing all the milk together and processing it efficiently in one large batch for sale in all the surrounding areas, the producer processed the milk from each area in small, separate batches that were sold only in the areas from which the milk in each batch had come. The producer did this without any indication of consumer preference, simply assuming that consumers in each area would prefer locally produced milk. Of course, as a result of this low-productivity approach, all the milk was quite expensive. But because of the absence of competition, consumers had no choice but to pay up.

A further example was the residential construction industry, in which productivity was only about 30 percent of the US rate. The industry was dominated by small, self-employed carpenters who used hand tools and traditional methods of construction.

Because these builders had little project management experience and few large projects on which to work, Japanese home buyers paid higher prices for fewer varieties of housing than could easily have been available. Competition was severely limited by zoning rules, tax incentives for small builders, regulatory building standards, builder associations, and lack of information transparency in the real-estate sector (for example, the prices at which houses were sold were not published).

In the case of the large, domestically oriented industrial sectors, competition also frequently seemed weak or nonexistent. Prices in industries such as glass, cement, plastics, fertilizer, chemicals, and paper were relatively high, and the market shares of the main producers had remained virtually unchanged over many years. One reason was that the anti-monopoly law and the Fair Trade Commission that administered it were very weak. Another reason was that the Keidanren business federation, which was very strong, lobbied against any effective use of the law.

A case decided by the Tokyo High Court in early November, 2013, was a good example of how things worked. The Japan Society for Rights of Authors, Composers, and Publishers (JASRAC) had been founded by the Cultural Affairs Agency as a monopoly in order to collect copyright fees on behalf of artists. It collected 1.5 percent of broadcasters' revenue, regardless of how often a tune under its copyright management was broadcast. The music under JASRAC management accounted for 99 percent of total broadcast music royalties of about 26 billion (US$200 million) annually. To use music not managed by JASRAC, broadcasters had to pay more. Although new laws in 2001 had removed JASRAC's official monopoly status, it had continued its operations in the same old way, and had prevented independent artists from getting their music on the air. Also because of this monopoly, recorded music in Japan was much more expensive than in other developed countries. Yet the Fair Trade Commission (FTC) took no action to enforce the new law. Indeed, it had actually rejected complaints from artists and consumers. Only when the High Court ruled on a complaint in 2013—twelve years after the liberalization law was passed—did anything change.

This weakness of the competition policy was rooted in a long history. The Occupation authorities had introduced the first anti-monopoly law and the FTC as they disbanded the *zaibatsu* after World War II. However, as part of the 1952 San Francisco Peace Treaty negotiations, the Occupation agreed to relax application of the law and to legalize cartels in various circumstances. The law was strengthened in the 1970s as the result of pressure from US trade officials and foreign businessmen, and also as the result of price-fixing scandals discovered among the Japanese oil companies during the 1973 oil crisis. But this had little real impact. The Ministry of International Trade and Industry (MITI, which later became METI) ruled over the FTC and kept it on a short leash as anti-competitive practices proliferated. Courts lacked contempt powers to ensure compliance with FTC orders, and, in any case, penalties were relatively low, and were perceived as just another cost of doing business.

The response of the Revitalization Commission was to call for a new FTC modeled somewhat after the German Bundeskartellamt and the European Competition Authority. The Commission demanded that the new FTC be separated completely from METI and allocated a much larger budget and staff than in the past, so that it would be completely independent. Funding was to come directly from the Diet and not be part of the budget of some other organization. In addition to making investigations and imposing fines, the FTC was to have the power to make criminal charges and impose jail terms on corporate or other institutional leaders found in violation of fair-trade laws. Fines were to be increased to include triple damages both for the institution found guilty and for its directors. Most importantly, the Commission called for the new FTC to be concerned with maintaining an open and competitive business and institutional environment. Its brief was not only to look for and prosecute violations of the law, but to constantly study and evaluate the openness of all markets and make recommendations on removing outdated regulations, changing zoning laws, cutting subsidies, and overhauling any other rules and practices that might retard innovation, favor insiders, keep newcomers out, and undermine competition. In other words, the Commission called for the FTC to be the true guardian and defender of an open business model and society. The Commission also called for the courts to be empowered to use contempt orders to enforce FTC directives.

Finally, the Commission moved to prevent Keidanren and other powerful lobbying groups from distorting the political process. It called for rules similar to those of Canada, where only natural persons—not corporations or associations—could fund political actions.

NEW JAPAN MODEL

Of course, today, in 2050, we see the results of these bold steps all around us. There is no longer a two-tier economy in Japan. Not only are the global Japanese companies tops in productivity, but so are the retailers, banks, hospitals, clinics, and other small and medium-sized enterprises. Japan has experienced a second economic miracle. The bifurcation of society between those with lifelong, safe jobs on the one hand, and freeters and temporary workers on the other, is gone, as are the inefficient companies that needed subsidies to stay alive. Now, new training and skills are made readily available to those seeking work or needing to change jobs. Personal security is assured by unemployment payments and retraining stipends. The person, not the company, is protected and promoted. All workers operate under the same status; there is no longer a division between regular and irregular employees. All are paid on the same basis and receive the same benefits on the same prorated terms. It is easy for newcomers to join a company and for old-timers to leave when they so desire.

Furthermore, as a result of the introduction of private insurance and the surge in medical technology and innovation, Japanese medical treatment has become the best in the world, as have its agricultural products. Indeed, exports of Japanese food and agricultural products are flourishing in the wake of Japan's agricultural reform and its membership in the Trans-Pacific Partnership. Flexicurity, free trade and freedom of agricultural land use, a mix of private and public health insurance and e-health, and open markets in all sectors have returned Japan to its former glory.

CHAPTER 10

Up with the People, Down with the Bureaucrats

You thought Tokyo was impressive, but now, upon arriving in Osaka, you are wondering if instead of coming to a different city, you have come to a different country. The name Singapore keeps recurring in your thoughts. Everything here seems a bit newer, a bit better conceived and executed, and there is a human energy and dynamism that is particularly noticeable. Despite its obvious achievements, Tokyo seemed somewhat freighted with formality and other lingering elements of the bureaucracy and heaviness of the old centralized Japanese government, pervaded at times by the sense of loss that one often feels in the capitals of formerly great empires. Here in Osaka there is none of that. In fact, quite the reverse. Here you sense that bureaucracy and central power have been overturned and local people-power unleashed. This exciting and futuristic city has become a center of excellence in a plethora of fields ranging from medicine to engineering to cuisine, and is looking firmly forward to the future. You inevitably wonder how the old, centralized Japan you knew and loved came to adopt such a dramatically new form of governance.

THE FUKUSHIMA EXAMPLE

Despite its destructiveness, one aspect of the Fukushima catastrophe was very positive. That was the behavior of the Japanese people, especially those who lived in the immediate area of the earthquake, tsunami, and nuclear meltdown. In stark contrast to the looting and rioting that regularly occurred in other countries like the United States and the Philippines under similar circumstances, there had been no such scenes in Japan. Indeed, the world was amazed by the example of patience, good order, brave suffering, and quick organization of relief demonstrated by the ordinary people. This was Japan at its best. Those who knew Japan often remarked that the country's greatest strength was the stoic, long suffering nature and sound common sense of its citizens. Left to their own resources, they seemed automatically to organize and achieve their objectives in the most efficient, rapid, and equitable manner possible—without a lot of shouting and contention.

But, of course, Japan was also a country with a Confucian ethic that paid great respect to elders, superiors, and officials. Some of these attitudes and thinking were well captured in the old phrase *kanson minpi* ("revere the official—despise the people") that was used by historians and writers in pre–World War II Japan to express the relationship between the governors and the governed in Confucian societies. In this system, which had originated in China and been imported to Japan, a highly educated mandinarate or bureaucracy exercised more or less absolute power in the name of the emperor. Officials were highly honored and rewarded, and families wanted at least one of their sons to become a highly placed official. Of course, one reason why the officials were so powerful was that ordinary people had no rights and could thus be despised by the bureaucracy without fear of retribution.

In the course of its late nineteenth and early twentieth century period of modernization, Japan had adopted a system of governance that concentrated power in the hands of central officials in Tokyo, somewhat similar to the French model in which control was exercised mostly from Paris. Far from loosening this system, the postwar Allied Occupation of Japan had actually tightened it. The American occupiers that took nominal control of the Japanese government in 1945 had, of course, very little knowledge of Japan and how to make it run. They actually administered Japan largely through its existing bureaucracy. With the Japanese military defeated and being disbanded, the prewar *zaibatsu* in the course of being dissolved, and the American overlords knowing nothing about what they were doing, this bureaucracy immensely expanded its power. With strong American backing, the Liberal Democratic Party became the dominant political party, and the elite bureaucracy formed close ties with the party as well as with the big businesses that fell under bureaucratic regulation. These firms typically provided a second career for bureaucrats, who, upon reaching the mandatory retirement age of fifty-five, were granted what was called *amakudari*, a descent from bureaucratic heaven into the less rarefied but more lucrative atmosphere of corporate money-making. Indeed, just establishing the vast network of special counselor and business association positions into which retiring bureaucrats typically descended was a big business by itself. Large parts of ministries were engaged in planning the parachuting of their members into new positions after retirement. This situation changed a bit in the 1990s in the wake of scandals and with the rise of new political parties. Nevertheless, the structure of governance remained highly centralized, bureaucratic, paternalistic, and stultifying for regional and local governments as well as for ordinary private enterprises.

LOCALIZED REFORM

In response to this oppressive situation, some local leaders launched their own regional reform and restructuring efforts. In chapter 4, there is an outline of the actions of local government in Yokohama with regard to child care. In the early 2000s, the mayor of Tokyo's Suginami Ward, Hiroshi Yamada, went much further with his vision of "Smart Suginami," which aimed to achieve small local government with efficient services using fewer resources. For starters, he privatized a part of the school lunch program. Despite strong opposition from public labor unions and their related political organizations, the move ultimately proved successful, resulting not only in huge savings for the municipality, but in an improved service that even allowed children to pre-order their favorite dishes. In addition Yamada closed some municipal offices, introduced the use of machines to issue resident certificates, and subcontracted various municipal chores to nonprofit organizations. Through these and other measures he was able to reduce the number of the city's employees by more than 600 and to gain savings of ¥25.4 billion (roughly US$200 million). In doing so, he cut the municipal debt nearly in half and more than doubled the municipal savings fund. Yamada also introduced tax deductions for nonprofit organizations that supported child care, elder care, and a variety of other municipal services. In addition, he established a local bus service that provided convenient transportation for Suginami Ward residents while also earning a profit by collecting a small fare. This Suginami example demonstrated that if a leader has a clear vision and is able to communicate well with his people, local reform can be achieved without begging from or praying to the central bureaucracy god.

This trend was reflected elsewhere in the country. At around the same time, the governor of Japan's provincial Tottori

Prefecture, Yoshihiro Katayama, was carrying out something of a democratic revolution. He insisted on transparency in every public activity. He made all meetings and official documents open to all citizens at all times. Indeed, the media and public were encouraged to personally visit the government offices and observe the work whenever they wished. Katayama did away with the traditional, private *nemawashi* (extensive pre-selling) procedure for developing legislation and regulatory rulings and insisted on open debate by all concerned. Thus, working committees that had usually been closed were opened to the public. This meant that working-commitee members could not just sit and say nothing. The traditional Press Club of media representatives was closed down and the issuance of press releases was halted. As Katayama pointed out, since the press was able always to be present when discussions and decisions were taking place, there was no need for press releases or special arrangements for journalists. The prohibition on decision by *nemawashi* led to the cancellation of several public works projects that had been agreed to behind closed doors but that were certain to be money losers and thus a drain on the prefectural budget. As Katayama pointed out, the local assembly was accustomed to automatically passing things that had already been secretly agreed to through *nemawashi*. This kind of deal making inevitably meant that some of the people involved in the decision owed something to others who had also been involved in the decision. This led to corruption. When the actual power of decision making shifted to the speakers on the floor of the assembly, policies and projects were adopted only on the basis of their potential contribution to the public good, he argued.

There were occasions on which Katayama's proposals were rejected by the assembly, something that had never occurred in the case of previous governors. His view was that this was good, because it demonstrated that even a governor could be over-ruled by the representatives of the people. Too often in the past, he said, the assembly discussion had been simply a Kabuki play. The end of *nemawashi* resulted in more young members of the assembly becoming active in debate and in many new and good suggestions. Similarly, after Katayama's establishment of the rule that there be a mandatory report of any assembly member's intervention with the local government asking for a *kuchikiki* (special consideration), the number of such actions dropped dramatically, as members were forced to consider whether such a request could survive open debate of a bill in the assembly.

Other cities and regions followed this lead toward more local initiative. In the south of Japan, beginning around 2009, Mayor Kenji Kitahashi began promoting Kitakyushu City as an "eco-town" with low carbon emissions, aiming to establish the city as a hub of Asian eco-collaboration. He and his team also promoted establishment of new connections to Nagoya and other regional cities by local start-up Fuji Dream Airlines. At around the same time, Toyama City's mayor, Mori Masashi, focused on developing his municipality as a "compact city" that could deal well with an aging society. This entailed designing the city so that hospitals, shops, administrative services, and other important centers were easily reached by public transportation. To take advantage of these services, the city also encouraged elders to move into the city center by providing low-cost residential space. Meanwhile, Yuji Kuroiwa, the governor of Kanagawa Prefecture, promoted Kanagawa as a center for "new frontier health care." He even went so far as to sign Memoranda of Understanding with overseas cities and regional governments. The agreement with the state of Massachusetts in the United States is a good example. Signed in May, 2014, it covers shared development of medical devices, life sciences, and health-care industries. Thus

Kanagawa and Massachusetts exchange experts and research reports, and each benefits from the advances of the other. The agreement also established a collaboration between Kanagawa Prefecture and the Massachusetts Life Sciences Center and the Massachusetts Clean Energy Initiative.

The most important center of local and regional governmental reform activity was, of course, Osaka, where, beginning in 2011, Mayor Toru Hashimoto set out to achieve much greater regional autonomy and smaller, more efficient government for the whole of Osaka Prefecture, including the city of Osaka itself and the neighboring city of Sakai. Some of his more controversial reforms included privatization of the metropolitan subway, cutting the city's payroll of 38,000 in half, reducing the power of the teachers' union, cutting support for the Osaka Philharmonic Orchestra and artists guilds, and withdrawing long-sacrosanct subsidies to the traditional puppet theater companies. He also provided for free tuition at both public and private high schools, privatized the government audit, and revitalized the Osaka airports. More broadly, he emphasized the necessity of greater regional unification and autonomy. As one official noted, "We used to have to get four or five different permits from Tokyo just to move a stop sign." Or, take the situation of land use. The city of Osaka owned about 26 percent of its own land area, but as one of the city's consultants explained, it was very difficult for the city to use the land in the best way because of regulations and control from Tokyo. In one case, the city of Osaka purchased a museum owned by the central government with the intent of making it into a hospital, but had difficulty in doing so because of objections from MEXT. Nor could the city do as it wished in terms of infrastructure development because of the way the tax and urban financing system were structured. Only about 33 percent of the taxes sent by Osaka to the national government came back to the region. The rest stayed in Tokyo or were sent in the form of subsidies to support other regions, particularly agricultural ones. This resulted from the fact that there was no system of self-funding for local governments. Indeed, because of the opposition of the central Ministry of Finance, municipalities could not even issue bonds without the permission of the central government. Of course, their taxing power and ability to use taxes and other financial incentives to attract investment, foster innovation, or fund and develop top-notch regional universities and schools was also severely limited. Osaka had been the center of the booming textile industry in the years after World War II, but that business had long ago left Japan for developing countries like China, Vietnam, and Bangladesh. The city and region desperately needed to develop and attract new industry, but, like other regions outside of Tokyo, was hampered in doing so by the oppressive regulation of the central government.

What Osaka really needed, according to several of the Commission members studying the situation, was not deregulation, but complete decentralization. This view was eventually adopted by the full Commission, and Osaka, along with most other Japanese cities and prefectures, was mostly freed from its Tokyo overlords with the exception of matters relating to defense and foreign affairs, which continued to be handled centrally. The result has been that Osaka is now often compared to Singapore as a kind of oasis of excellence where everything is well planned, well operated, and functional. As a result of the privatization of its health-care industry, it is now a global medical center with patients visiting from all over the world to benefit from its advanced treatments and world-class doctors. By reducing corporate taxes from nearly 40 percent to 10 percent for all companies located and operating within its jurisdiction, the city is now experiencing a rush of new investment, production, and innovation from companies that can spend much more on R&D. Osaka students have become well known for their fluency in English. This is the result of the privatization of the municipal elementary and middle schools, which has allowed the replacement of non-English speaking English teachers with professionals who are fluent in the language. In this environment, innovation, new business, and new culture are blossoming and flourishing. Moreover, with Osaka as the guide, decentralization has been spreading all over the country, making Japan once again an example among nations.

FULL DECENTRALIZATION

Having thoroughly reviewed Japan's economic structure and system, carefully studied other economies around the world, considered the positive results of the local reform efforts, and analyzed how revitalization in Japan had occurred in the past, the Commission came to a fundamental conclusion. It was that the problem in Japan was not essentially economic; rather it was political. The most important issue facing the country was governance. When left to govern themselves, the people of Japan did amazing, innovative, productive things. But when highly controlled by a central governing elite, they were unable to operate at their full capacity and to fulfill their great potential. For Japan to realize that potential in the future would require a dramatic change from the prevailing centralized political structure to a decentralized system.

Thus, the Commission's final recommendations in 2016 led to a dramatic restructuring of the map of Japan. In place of the long-existing forty-seven prefectures, there are now fifteen large regional cantons organized similarly to the states of the United States or the Lander of Germany. Like the former prefectures, each canton has a legislature and a governor. But the greatly expanded powers of these bodies make them almost entirely self-governing except for defense, foreign affairs, and central banking. Perhaps most important is the fact that the new cantons are self-financing. They have the power to borrow and issue bonds, but also the possibility of accumulating too much debt and falling into bankruptcy. The central government shares its powers and can only intervene in the cantons under very limited circumstances. Thus, for example, MEXT might develop general guidelines for school curriculums, but it would be up to each new canton to decide its own specific curriculum and to determine which books would be used for instruction. Each new canton decides whether its teachers should have civil service status and can privatize schools and universities, use voucher systems, or keep the schools as government institutions, depending on the wishes of its citizens. The new cantons of course have inherited the bulk of the nation's taxing power including income tax and corporate tax. One result of this has been a dramatic reduction of corporate taxes as the cantons attempt to attract new corporate investment. The old national system for the recruitment of civil servants has been abolished, and each new prefecture has its own civil service exam, and decides itself what the terms of employment of civil servants will be in its region. The new cantons compete with each other on economic policies and processes and have the authority to open and expand free-trade areas as they see fit. In this way the power of the regions has been dramatically increased and the potential of their citizens unleashed, while the power of the central government and of Tokyo to monopolize talent and crush new ideas and new people has been reduced, although the areas of national security and foreign policy remain the monopoly of the center.

The Commission members debated long and intensely among themselves before adopting the decentralization policies that have led to this dramatic evolution. Those who first proposed doing so had several strong reasons for their view. First, they noted that competition increases innovation, efficiency, and productivity. Centralization and concentration of government, business, or anything else tends to produce uniformity, waste, inefficiency, and stagnation. Combating this tendency in business was the rationale for the existence of the Fair Trade Commission just as it was for the existence of the American antitrust laws and the European Union's Competition Commission. In the same way, and for the same reasons, there needed to be competition in governance. Such competition would increase innovative trials, attract investments and more residents, and raise competitiveness both in the regions and in the nation. It would make Japan wealthier and stronger by fully materializing its potential power and ideas, and would increase the welfare of its citizens while raising the ability of the nation to meet economic and political challenges from abroad such as those then being posed by China.

The proponents further argued that concentration of power and activity in Tokyo was not only a major cause of economic stagnation, but also a national security danger. The United States had several major power centers such as Washington, New York, Chicago, and others. China had Beijing, Shanghai, and Guangzhou. But if Tokyo were to be incapacitated by a nuclear calamity like the meltdown at Fukushima, a major earthquake or typhoon, or a missile attack, the whole country would be put out of action.

A third point was that if Tokyo continued to absorb most of the talent and wealth in the nation, the rest of the country would be left as an aged, indigent ward of the government living a miserable life on subsidies. This led to the final argument in favor of the proposal, which was that change in Japan has always come from outside the center. The modernizing changes of the Meiji period at the end of the nineteenth century came about because of outside pressure from the United States and from Japan's own provinces of Satsuma and Choshu, which were located far from Tokyo and had long managed to maintain a high degree of independence from the central authorities. Japan's defeat in World War II and the Allied Occupation that followed had again provided outside pressure that opened society to change and structural reform, resulting in the economic miracle of the 1960s. Innovation in Japan had usually been sparked by outsiders, by people not born or educated in Tokyo. Thus, there was much potential dynamism in the regions, and it was a great loss to have this stymied and smothered by central government. Moreover, because of Japan's outstanding communications and transportation infrastructure, there was really no need to have most of the country's talent and virtually all government bureaus and corporate headquarters in Tokyo. Everyone could easily get to Tokyo if that was necessary, but there was no reason to stay there all the time. Thus, the supporters of decentralization concluded that allowing the continued death of the regions would eventually cause the death of Japan.

Those who were initially undecided about decentralization raised several concerns. They feared that this kind of strong regional governance could result in some regions becoming very wealthy while others became more impoverished. The gap between rich and poor could become greater, and they feared this would be dangerous for a country that had long idealized the economic equality of its citizens. Their greatest concern, however, was more a matter of timing and conditions than of principle. They strongly felt the challenge being posed by China and the need for Japan to have a strong economy in order to respond to this challenge. At that moment, the country was still suffering from lagging competitiveness and other economic illnesses. It needed to recover strong economic momentum before making such a fundamental change in the structure of its governance, the undecided ones suggested. Perhaps, they argued, in ten or fifteen years, conditions would be more favorable.

But that was just the problem, the proponents replied. The country was always waiting for better conditions in order to change. But better conditions never seemed to arrive, and, thus, change never occurred. Everything continued as it had always been, getting sometimes better and sometimes worse, but trending always downward. Could the reason that better conditions had not arrived be that no change had occurred? Could the lack of change in governance be the primary reason for the continued absence of better conditions? Yes, the supporters said; it was precisely the lack of change that was the main cause of continued economic weakness. Japan, they argued, had to change its governance in order to become strong and capable of responding to challenges from China or anywhere else.

Eventually, that way of thinking came to be accepted by a large majority of the Commission. Thus, its final and most important recommendation was for the country to proceed with decentralization immediately. As we now know, that recommendation was also adopted by the Diet. The result, of course, was the restructuring of governance and a huge wave of new competition, innovation, and rising productivity that has resulted in the third Japanese economic miracle. By allowing the Japanese people more fully to organize their own work and lives and by not insisting on directing everything from the center, Japan's leaders have achieved far more than they had ever hoped. It turned out that less leadership was actually more.

Thus, it has truly been the Japanese people who have brought about the third reinvention of Japan in the course of the first half of the twenty-first century and who, by 2050, have made Japan number one again in terms of its living standard, quality of life, and peaceful relations with neighbors.

Why Japan Matters to America and the World

I f, as a non-Japanese reader, you have gotten this far, you may well be silently mouthing the words—*so what*? Yes, you say, this is all very interesting and one can see that Japan is facing some major—even existential— issues and of course one wishes the Japanese well. But really, outside of Japan, aside from sympathizing with the plight of the poor Japanese, why should anyone really care?

Let me count the reasons. For starters, there is the fact that we live in a global economy of which Japan forms the third largest part after the United States and China. Much has been made of the BRIC (Brazil, Russian, India, China) countries, their rapid economic growth, and their contribution to the lifting of hundreds of millions of people out of poverty. But we must not forget that Japan's economy is roughly equivalent to those of Brazil, Russia, and India combined. We must also keep in mind that Japan is an enormous exporter of capital, with more than US\$1 trillion of direct investment overseas. This investment directly supports about 4 million workers, and indirectly supports two to three times that many in a variety of countries around the world.

In the United States alone, Japanese investment comes to more than US$300 billion and directly supports about 700,000 jobs, each paying around US$78,000 annually, according to a 2011 *Select USA* report on foreign direct investment. Indirectly, this investment supports hundreds of thousands of additional jobs. In addition, Japan is the second largest investor in US Treasury debt, with holdings of US$1.24 trillion, just behind China's US$1.25 trillion. Thus, the erosion of Japan as a gigantic economic power would have immense negative consequences for the global economy and for the United States particularly.

But the numbers don't begin to tell the full story. Consider for a moment what is commonly called the "global supply chain." This refers to the system of global production of things like the Apple iPhone in which various parts of the product are manufactured in several different countries, delivered to be assembled in another country, and then delivered to be sold in all the countries of the world. Under this system, all the parts must be produced precisely at the right time to be picked up by a logistics company such as FedEx, in order to be delivered at precisely the right time to an assembler halfway across the globe, in order to be assembled at precisely the right time again to be picked up by FedEx and delivered on schedule to your local Apple store. Where did this concept of "just-in-time delivery" originate?—In Japan, of course. Prior to Japan's 1960s economic miracle, manufacturers around the world maintained large lots and warehouses to store materials and components while waiting put them onto the production line. This required extra space to be bought or rented, as well as extra bank financing for the materials sitting around waiting to be used. It was the Japanese who came up with a solution to this problem—perhaps because of their traditionally small living spaces, or perhaps because of some special gene, or perhaps because the Japanese people, more than any other in the world, hate clutter and waste—what they call *muda*. In trying to achieve ever-lower costs, the Japanese manufacturers of the 1950s and 1960s realized that if components could be delivered on a precise schedule by the suppliers there would be no need for the warehouses and holding spaces. Thus was developed the concept of just-in-time delivery, a process that underlies today's global supply chain.

But an even more important concept was essential to the realization of just-in-time delivery. This was high quality and continuous quality improvement, or what the Japanese call *kaizen*. What good was it to deliver a component just in time if the component was faulty? In fact, that was worse than maintaining the warehouses and holding lots. At least if you had the parts in storage, you could readily find a replacement for a faulty part. But without a parts inventory, a faulty part delivered just in time would, in fact, be just in time to shut down your whole production line. So, unless a producer had a strong degree of confidence that a supply of very high quality parts would be available without interruption more or less eternally, there was no sense in producing on a just-in-time basis. But Japanese makers did have this confidence because throughout the country's entire industry the insistence on ever-higher quality and ever-greater perfection was unrelenting. It was from Japan that the emphasis on high quality spread throughout the world. If you appreciate the quality of your Ford or Volkswagen or Hyundai today, you can thank Japan. And the same is true for virtually any other manufactured product you buy or use.

In short, Japan has been the source of some of the most fundamental concepts and processes underpinning the modern world economy. These have been copied by the most advanced countries like the United States and Germany as well as by the Asian Tigers and China's emerging Dragon. The loss to the world of such unique concepts and processes emerging from the soul of Japan would be incalculable.

But now let's look at some things that may be more important than production and supply chains. When my wife and I first lived in Japan in the early 1960s, we encountered raw fish in the form of sushi, a dish virtually unknown outside of Japan and Korea. After all, who would eat something weird like that? But we loved it. Indeed, my wife suggested that upon returning to the United States we should look into opening a sushi restaurant or even a chain of such restaurants. Said I: "No way. Americans will never swap burgers and dogs for something like raw fish. Forget it!"

"Okay, maybe you're right," said my wife. "But I have another idea. You know those rice crackers wrapped in seaweed? I'll bet they'd be a big hit in the US if we exported them from Japan." Again, my reply was negative: "Dream on. You think Americans are going to eat seaweed or some kind of cracker made out of rice? No way. Forget it!"

Of course, I'd be a very rich man if I had only listened to my wife. My only consolation is that there are a lot of other men who could say the same thing. But fortunately, others saw and acted upon the instincts my wife had. Now, it's not at all surprising to find excellent sushi and other Japanese cuisine in Paris, Dallas, Tel Aviv, Beijing, and everywhere else around the globe.

Or consider the concept of *shibusa*—the Japanese ideal of unobtrusive beauty. Beautiful objects in Japan (a tea house, a Zen garden, a ceramic bowl) appear at first to be simple and spare with an economy of form and effort. Yet, upon further observation, they reveal textures or subtle imperfections that create a balance of simplicity and complexity inspiring a sense of timeless quality, tranquility, and endless new discoveries, all of which makes for ever-enhanced value. In the realm of the theatre, Japanese Kabuki and its occasional contrast of the notions of *tatemae* (the formal face of persons or things or situations) and *honne* (the actuality of persons, things, and situations) is perhaps the most perfect articulation of the large and small hypocrisies that people all over the world indulge in for the sake of social harmony.

Or take manners and personal relationships. Japanese are sometimes seen by outsiders as excessively formal, stylized, and inhibited. On the other hand, the manners of Japan reflect a general sense of deep respect for others. How many times have I purposely left a memento behind in a Japanese hotel room because I didn't want to carry it on the trip home only to have a hotel employee track me down before departure—or even at the airport—to return it to me? And you'll never be kept waiting if you have an appointment with someone in Japan, no matter his or her rank. By the same token, any Japanese person visiting you will be exactly on time. Indeed, they will probably have done a dry run the day before to ensure their punctuality.

Are all these rich Japanese streams of cuisine, art, culture, and manners to be lost to the world as the giant increasingly falters? If so, the we all will be greatly the poorer for it.

Of course, these are the concerns of the long term. More immediately, the world is experiencing a transformation of epic proportions. For most of recorded history until about 1850, China and India were the world's two largest economies, and Asia as a whole had a far bigger economy and was far wealthier than Europe and the Americas combined. By 1950, these two great Asian nations had become mere shadows of their former selves, as Western Europe and then the United States emerged as superpowers dominating the global economy and global politics. We are now experiencing a reversal toward the old norm. It will likely not be a complete reversal, but at market prices, China's economy is already about three-fourths the size of that of the

United States (it is actually larger if one uses purchasing power parity measures that are adjusted to take into account the tendency of developing economies to have abnormally low prices for household commodities), and India's is now rising almost as rapidly as China's (more rapidly by some measures). Almost certainly, the world will be turned upside down once more by the year 2050. That is to say that Asia will be back on top—at least in terms of total GDP.

This transformation began in 1992, when the states of the former Soviet Union, India, and China all abandoned communist and socialist economic policies and turned to some form of capitalism. Western observers at the time, such as Francis Fukuyama, hailed this "globalization" as the "end of history" and the beginning of a final liberal and democratic age of humanity. Some American political leaders claimed that globalization was just Americanization by another name. The notion, espoused by such figures as former president Bill Clinton and *New York Times* columnist Tom Friedman that "globalization will make all countries rich, and, as they become rich they will become democratic, and, being democratic, they will not go to war because we know that democracies don't fight each other" became a frequently repeated mantra. The best and the brightest of America and the West became convinced that the globalization of capitalism would bring democracy and peace to revive the suffering world.

Of course, it hasn't worked out that way. Indeed, the reverse seems increasingly possible. Far from becoming a more politically liberal, free-market state, China appears to be developing a kind of state-guided capitalism under a more authoritarian political direction. The success of this model has great attraction for other countries, especially Russia. Indeed, the state-capitalist concept is being increasingly extended into the open market. Keep in mind that the world's major corporations are global, which means they don't really have a nationality. It is a mistake to think of Apple, for example, as an American company, or to imagine that Shell Oil is either a Dutch or a UK company. They are global companies, with most of their operations outside the country of their incorporation or headquarters. The great irony is that globalization has made them less subject to the power of the liberal free-market democracies and more subject to that of the authoritarian countries pursuing varying degrees of state capitalism. In Washington or Brussels or London, a company like Apple or Google or Mercedes-Benz or Barclays is a major political player. Its CEO can see the president of the United States or the head of the EU with ease. He has legions of lawyers and lobbyists at his beck and call to influence, promote, or stop legislation. He can sue the US government and win in court. He has hundreds of millions of dollars available for political donations.

In Beijing, however, this same CEO is not a player at all. He is a supplicant for permission of one type or another from the Chinese government and its ruling Communist Party. To be sure, the surroundings are plush and tea is politely served. But make no mistake. The CEO is on his knees. He may well be found promoting the Beijing line in Washington.

Japan has been a successful non-Western democracy and thus a powerful model for developing countries in the rest of Asia and around the world. At this time of shifting balances of power, with increasing uncertainty about the extension of the rule of law around the globe, the slow death of Japan would be a terrible blow to the hopes of those who believe in democracy and a rule of law.

Even more importantly, Japan's continued demise would be tremendously destabilizing, especially in the Asia-Pacific region, but also globally. As things stand while I write in February of 2015, much of Asia is becoming less stable and secure as the result of five key factors. One is the insistence of the United States on continuing to patrol the waters and skies around China as it did during the Cold War, despite the fact that the Cold War is long over, that China poses no threat to the United States, and that America has said it welcomes China as a global partner. Another is the rapid expansion of China's military forces and its sometimes aggressive claims to rights in disputed waters and territories. Yet another destabilizing factor is that World War II is still not really finished. Then there is the erosion of Japan's vitality that we have been discussing. Finally, there is the increasing divergence between the interests of the United States and those of its Asia-Pacific allies.

A complex logic is at work here. Because the Allied Occupation authorities retained the emperor and the vast bulk of Japan's wartime bureaucracy at the end of World War II, and also because of the rapid follow-on of turmoil caused by the communist revolution in China and the outbreak of the Korean War, neither Japan nor the countries it had invaded and occupied ever experienced the kind of postwar catharsis that occurred in Germany and Western Europe. Japan's new no-war constitution served as a kind of surrogate for such a catharsis, but, of course, it was only viable in combination with the US-Japan Security Treaty of 1951, under which the United States took unilateral responsibility for Japan's defense. This was essentially an agreement by Japan to outsource its foreign policy to Washington in return for a guarantee of security and support for what would become the Japanese economic miracle. Indeed, the then Prime Minister Shigeru Yoshida explicitly emphasized that Japan should focus on economic recovery while leaving the rest to the United States for a time. Underlying this arrangement was the implicit assumption that the interests of the United States and Japan would be more or less exactly the same indefinitely.

During the Korean War and most of the Cold War period, this was a pretty good assumption. It began to fray a bit in the 1980s, when Japan's mercantilist economic development and trade policies began to undercut important US industries. But the priority of Washington's Asia-Pacific geopolitical objectives, and the need for forward bases in Japan to fulfill them led the US, while complaining loudly, to maintain a steady course.

Now, however, the end of the Cold War, the rise of China to great power status, the increasing alignment of South Korea with China, the continued bitterness between South Korea and Japan, and the relative decline of American power have greatly altered not only the economic calculus, but—far more importantly— the geopolitical calculus as well. The interests of the United States and Japan are no longer completely congruent. It is not in America's interest to be drawn into a confrontation that could lead to war with China over who owns what in the East China or South China Seas, or anywhere else for that matter. The continued ambiguity of Japan with regard to many of the incidents of World War II—for example the "comfort women" issue or the Rape of Nanking—makes it increasingly difficult for Washington to rationalize the old security arrangements. All present forces are pushing toward some greater degree of separation between Japan and the United States.

And yet. And yet. It is greatly in the interest of the United States to have a robust, democratic, militarily strong Japan that has made its peace with World War II, that conducts its own peace-oriented foreign policy, and that is willing to contract mutual security arrangements both with some of its key immediate neighbors and with the United States, as well as others such as Australia and India. Such a Japan would greatly lessen the geopolitical burden of the United States while also strengthening democratic forces globally and contributing to worldwide economic growth.

The rest of the world, and especially the United States, has a huge stake in having this kind of a Japan restored.

Acknowledgments

Special thanks to Hiromi Murakami and William (Bill) Finan. Indeed, the book was originally Bill's idea, which quickly generated strong support from Hiromi. Both of them assisted greatly with the conceptualization, research, fact checking, and editing of the book. My long time friends Ayako Doi and Henry Marini contributed essential advice and encouragement. *Oriental Economist* editor Richard Katz kindly provided key statistics and ideas. Long time friend Kyoko Hattori was, as always enthusiastic and cheerful and generously provided her home and facilities for my use. I want to thank Professor Ed Lincoln, Sakie and Glen Fukushima, Arnie Nachmanoff, Ira Wolf, Richard Koo, Pat Mulloy, Dana Marshall, Jim Fallows, Karl van Wolferen, Steve Olson, and Mindy Kotler for their interest and help.

Last, but certainly far from least, I want to thank my long-suffering wife, Carol, who as always provided research and editorial support, patience, encouragement when needed, and discipline when absolutely necessary.

Index

The Tuttle Story
"Books to Span the East and West"

Many people are surprised to learn that the world's leading publisher of books on Asia had humble beginnings in the tiny American state of Vermont. The company's founder, Charles E. Tuttle, belonged to a New England family steeped in publishing.

Tuttle's father was a noted antiquarian book dealer in Rutland, Vermont. Young Charles honed his knowledge of the trade working in the family bookstore, and later in the rare books section of Columbia University Library. His passion for beautiful books—old and new—never wavered throughout his long career as a bookseller and publisher.

After graduating from Harvard, Tuttle enlisted in the military and in 1945 was sent to Tokyo to work on General Douglas MacArthur's staff. He was tasked with helping to revive the Japanese publishing industry, which had been utterly devastated by the war. After his tour of duty was completed, he left the military, married a talented and beautiful singer, Reiko Chiba, and in 1948 began several successful business ventures.

To his astonishment, Tuttle discovered that postwar Tokyo was actually a book-lover's paradise. He befriended dealers in the Kanda district and began supplying rare Japanese editions to American libraries. He also imported American books to sell to the thousands of GIs stationed in Japan. By 1949, Tuttle's business was thriving, and he opened Tokyo's very first English-language bookstore in the Takashimaya Department Store in Nihonbashi, to great success. Two years later, he began publishing books to fulfill the growing interest of foreigners in all things Asian.

Though a westerner, Tuttle was hugely instrumental in bringing a knowledge of Japan and Asia to a world hungry for information about the East. By the time of his death in 1993, he had published over 6,000 books on Asian culture, history and art—a legacy honored by Emperor Hirohito in 1983 with the "Order of the Sacred Treasure," the highest honor Japan can bestow upon a non-Japanese.

The Tuttle company today maintains an active backlist of some 1,500 titles, many of which have been continuously in print since the 1950s and 1960s—a great testament to Charles Tuttle's skill as a publisher. More than 60 years after its founding, Tuttle Publishing is more active today than at any time in its history, still inspired by Charles Tuttle's core mission—to publish fine books to span the East and West and provide a greater understanding of each.